Urban Sustainability

The Urban Sustainability Book Series is a valuable resource for sustainability and urban-related education and research. It offers an inter-disciplinary platform covering all four areas of practice, policy, education, research, and their nexus. The publications in this series are related to critical areas of sustainability, urban studies, planning, and urban geography.

This book series aims to put together cutting-edge research findings linked to the overarching field of urban sustainability. The scope and nature of the topic are broad and interdisciplinary and bring together various associated disciplines from sustainable development, environmental sciences, urbanism, etc. With many advanced research findings in the field, there is a need to put together various discussions and contributions on specific sustainability fields, covering a good range of topics on sustainable development, sustainable urbanism, and urban sustainability. Despite the broad range of issues, we note the importance of practical and policy-oriented directions, extending the literature and directions and pathways towards achieving urban sustainability.

The series will appeal to urbanists, geographers, planners, engineers, architects, governmental authorities, policymakers, researchers of all levels, and to all of those interested in a wide-ranging overview of urban sustainability and its associated fields. The series includes monographs and edited volumes, covering a range of topics under the urban sustainability topic, which can also be used for teaching materials.

Ali Cheshmehzangi

Generative AI-Powered Urban Digital Twins

Pioneering Environmental Solutions for Sustainable Intelligent Cities

Springer

Ali Cheshmehzangi
Architecture, Design and Planning
The University of Queensland
Brisbane, QLD, Australia

ISSN 2731-6483 ISSN 2731-6491 (electronic)
Urban Sustainability
ISBN 978-981-95-4765-4 ISBN 978-981-95-4766-1 (eBook)
https://doi.org/10.1007/978-981-95-4766-1

This Springer imprint is published by the registered company Springer Nature Singapore Pte Ltd.
The registered company address is: 152 Beach Road, #21-01/04 Gateway East, Singapore 189721, Singapore

A poster developed by *Amir Cheshmehzangi* of Warwick University with AI about AI (*Note* permission is sought from the original owner)

To the courageous women of my motherland whose heroism in the face of silence, whose resistance in the face of oppression, and whose unwavering dignity in the harshest of conditions continue to inspire generations. This book is a tribute to your strength, your wisdom, and the quiet insurrections you lead each day. May your voices shape the future of our society and communities, just as your spirit has shaped the soul of our past.

Preface

> Generative AI has unlocked exciting possibilities in the realms of images and videos. Its manipulation and transformative capabilities offer new avenues for artistic expression, content creation, and immersive storytelling. As this technology continues to evolve, it is essential to leverage its power responsibly and ensure its positive impact on society.
>
> —Mohith Agadi, an Author and Entrepreneur

When the city begins to feel, to learn, and to care, it becomes more than a machine. It is already a living entity. It then becomes a mirror of us, of what we choose to remember, protect, and become.

The question of what kind of cities we want to live in the future is buried deep within the silent tremors of today's crises: flooded streets, scorching pavements, broken infrastructure, and growing urban divides. So what kind of cities do we actually want to inhabit tomorrow?

This book, *Generative AI-Powered Urban Digital Twins*, is born from that question. Not from a place of technocratic fascination, but from the intersection of planetary survival, ethics, and imagination. It is not merely a book about digital modelling or artificial intelligence. Reclaiming intelligence as a collective, dynamic, and fundamentally human force—enhanced by technology, to be sure, but driven by morality, empathy, and bravery—is the goal.

Efficiency is no longer sufficient in this day and age. Our cities are too complex, too damaged, too rich in history, and too full of aspirations to be reduced to prediction engines and dashboards. Now is the moment to broaden the horizon. The urban environment needs to be revitalized, not just managed. And nothing less than a new city-making ideology is needed for it.

Let's start by acknowledging a reality that many people overlook: our urban systems are failing because we have forgotten to ask more profound questions, not because we lack data or computational capacity. If intelligence is unable to foresee suffering, address injustice, or restore the ecosystems it has contributed to destroying, what good is it? If a city's genius comes at the expense of people who are ignored, invisible, and uprooted by advancement, what good is it to be "smart"?

This is why I have written this book. Because I believe we can do better.

Because I think generative AI can provide more than just operational benefits when applied critically and intelligently. It can develop into a force for systemic imagination, community memory, urban narrative, and care. Cities may be able to model not only efficient but also moral futures thanks to it. Regenerative, and not simply resilient.

The urban digital twin, a notion that is all too frequently misinterpreted as a managerial tool or sterile imitation, is at the core of this idea. I advocate for a radical reinterpretation in this work. The urban digital twin is a companion rather than a mirror. It is a living dialogue between data, design, and desire rather than a map. This twin becomes a co-author of potential when combined with generative AI, allowing for the exploration of not only how cities work but also how they may feel, develop, and change in fair and creative ways.

I come to this work not only as a scholar and practitioner, but as someone deeply moved by cities. Cities that beat with memory and contradiction. I have marched through cities in protest and silence, throughout the day and during the monsoon. I have seen streets once teeming with life engulfed by floods. I have witnessed planning used as a means of exclusion and innovation abused as surveillance. However, I have also witnessed the emergence of community gardens from vacant lots. AI-generated models help build aspirations for safer, greener, more inclusive neighbourhoods, and I have witnessed data being utilized to magnify voices that have not been heard.

Thus, this book is a map through that tension.

From theory to prototype, from simulation to solidarity, each chapter explores the changing terrain of AI-urban twin integration. The science and art of architecture, the difficulties of implementation, and the strict adherence to ethics will all be covered along the way. Above all, though, I hope you discover the pulse. The human tale. In the city, intelligence transforms into empathy, and technology facilitates the most fundamental act of compassion: working together to envision a better world.

We live in an age where the word "smart" is flung like a badge of progress. I questioned this matter when I coined and introduced the new concept and model of 'Advanced City'. We have to wonder, though: smart for whom? For what purpose is it smart? Allow this book to present an alternative: intelligent, sentient cities that are sensitive to the demands of the planet, receptive to the aspirations of their citizens, and constructed not only to endure but also to change with honour. This is what 'advanced' is about, not based on technologies and gadgets, but based on data-informed and human-centered methods of advancing our civilization for good.

This is a call to lawmakers, mayors, and planners to focus on values rather than just instruments; to reinterpret governance as stewardship and data as conversation. To academics and learners: may these pages stimulate fresh approaches and thought-provoking ideas. Allow research to imagine as well as analyze. Create meaningful research with genuine impact on society, not just for the sake of showcasing what you are capable of, or what you can achieve on celebrated publications of various sorts.

I challenge urban futurists, technologists, and designers to construct with care, transparency, and beauty. Let us envision a world in which AI collaborates with communities to co-author decisions rather than dictating them. Additionally, I offer this book as a call to action and a gesture of optimism to everyone who lives in a city, navigates the everyday heroism of life, and perseveres in the face of heat, noise, traffic, and floods.

The road ahead is not an easy one. Though yet in its infancy, generative AI has the potential to replicate the very injustices we are trying to eradicate if left unchecked. However, that is where our responsibility lies. Given that every urban model is a decision with repercussions, we must design with humility and rigour.

Let this be the century where cities learn to breathe again. Let our infrastructures pulse not just with energy but with empathy. Let urban intelligence no longer be measured by sensors alone, but by the extent to which it includes, uplifts, and regenerates.

This is the city we must imagine. This is the advancement we need to strive for. This is the intelligence we must build. This is the future we need to visualize—with boldness, with balance, and always, with care.

July 2025

Ali Cheshmehzangi
Head of School of Architecture, Design and Planning, The University of Queensland, Brisbane, QLD, Australia

Acknowledgement I gratefully acknowledge the generous support provided by the Faculty of Engineering, Architecture and Information Technology (EAIT) and the School of Architecture, Design and Planning (ADP) at The University of Queensland. Their ongoing encouragement, resources, and commitment to fostering interdisciplinary research have been instrumental in the development of this work. I am particularly appreciative of the Faculty's vision in advancing thought leadership at the intersection of technology, design, and sustainability, an ethos that has shaped and strengthened the core themes of this book.

Competing Interests The author has no competing interests to declare that are relevant to the content of this manuscript.

About This Book

Generative AI-Powered Urban Digital Twins presents a bold reimagining of urban futures through the convergence of generative artificial intelligence and digital twin technologies. This book presents AI-powered digital twins as catalysts for systemic change, civic empowerment, and environmental regeneration rather than just as planning tools at a time when cities are dealing with growing climate stresses, infrastructure stress, and profound social inequality.

The book explores the development of urban digital twins from data-driven models to intelligent, adaptive systems that learn, simulate, and co-design with their urban settings. It does this via eleven technically sound and conceptually rich chapters. It investigates how generative AI may improve climate simulation, manage floods, lessen urban heat, lower emissions, and promote participatory planning, all while posing important ethical, equitable, and governance issues.

The book covers open data standards, AI-twin integration architectures, and the difficulties of implementing prototypes into citywide systems, moving from fundamental theory to state-of-the-art practice. It demonstrates how these technologies can be used to depict community-driven urban scenarios, model circular material flows, and build green roofs. Throughout, the book maintains that cities' ability to restore ecosystems, incorporate a variety of viewpoints, and envision resilient and just futures are what truly define intelligence, not efficiency alone.

The book promotes a new urban paradigm where ethics are ingrained, intelligence is dispersed, and regeneration becomes the design axiom. It does this while keeping a close eye on both potential and responsibility. The book provides scholars, planners, technologists, and policymakers with a visionary yet doable road map for creating cities that are not just intelligent—but profoundly alive—by drawing on real-world examples, speculative design theory, and systems thinking.

This is not a book about managing cities more efficiently. It is a book about reconsidering the basic concept of urban intelligence and co-creating the urban futures filled with care, courage, and collective imagination.

This book:

- Proposes a visionary framework for regenerative urban futures;
- Bridges the gap between cutting-edge AI-twin integration and real-world urban challenges;
- Reconsiders city with ethics, equity, and imagination at the core of its urban intelligence.

Contents

Part II Environmental Solutions and Urban Sustainability

About the Author

Ali Cheshmehzangi is a Professor and Head of the School of Architecture, Design and Planning (ADP) at The University of Queensland. He is also an Adjunct Professor at the School of Architecture and Urban Planning at Hunan University. He is the Brisbane Olympics Committee member for Games Legacy and Growth Sub-Committee as well as the Expert member of the 2032 Games led by UQ. He has been in the World's top 2 percent field leader since 2021, recognised by Stanford University. He is among the top 20 global scholars in the urban sustainability research area.

Ali has a wealth of experience, expertise, and a strong commitment to innovation and excellence in the fields of architecture, design, and planning, the three core disciplines of his School at UQ. With a career spanning over two decades, he has made significant contributions to the academic and professional communities, with a focus on sustainable and environmentally conscious design. Prior to joining UQ, Ali held several strategic leadership and senior managerial roles, such as Vice-President for International Engagement and Global Partnership, Founding Director and Head of the Center for Innovation in Education and Research, Head of the Department of Architecture and Built Environment, Founding Director of the Urban Innovation Lab, Director of a university-wide Teaching and Learning platform, Director of International Research Network for Rural and Urban Development, Founder and Head of Research Group for Sustainable Built Environment, co-director of university-wide research priority areas, Director of Center for Sustainable Energy Technologies, and Interim Director of Digital Design Lab. So far, Ali has published over 650 journal papers, articles, conference papers, book chapters, and reports. This is his 48th academic book, alongside his many poetry collections that he has written in Parsi/Persian and English. Some of his previous academic books have received awards at the national, provincial, and municipal levels. He also has received international awards and recognition for his research on urban resilience studies and sustainability research, as well as a 2018 Vice-Chancellor's award for his impactful contribution to higher education.

Chapter 1
The Rise of Generative AI and Urban Digital Twins

1.1 Introduction: A New Era for Urban Innovation

Cities are about to enter a pivotal period in their development, when digital creations will no longer only depict real-world urban settings but will also start to influence them, predict how they will change, and work alongside humans to co-create futures. The convergence of urban digital twin technologies and generative artificial intelligence (AI) lies at the heart of this change (Lifelo et al. 2024), opening up new possibilities for how we plan, manage, and revitalize our cities.

This is more than just a convergence of technology. It is a change in perspective. The potential to model different futures, suggest flexible designs, and find answers that are invisible to the human sight is being unlocked by generative AI. Once thought of as real-time reflections of physical systems, digital twins are increasingly growing into ecosystems of synthetic intelligence that are dynamically foresighted, creatively generative, and always changing. Together, they provide a hitherto unheard-of ability to address the social, climatic, and environmental issues that characterize the twenty-first century.

Urbanization and ecological collapse on a global scale necessitate more than incremental innovation or reactive governance. We cannot out-optimize structural inequality, resource depletion, or climate change using traditional methods. These are intricate, multifaceted realities that call for answers that are proactive, flexible, and profoundly regenerative. We can go beyond data gathering to knowledge synthesis, beyond simulation to generative imagination, and beyond intelligence to environmental consciousness thanks to the combination of generative AI and urban digital twins.

This chapter presents this convergence in terms of philosophy, history, and technology. It charts their possible merger, examines the development of generative AI, and describes the emergence of digital twins in the urban setting. It questions the popular narrative of "smart cities" and makes the case for a shift to urban intelligence that is climate-positive, morally guided, and in tune with nature (Cheshmehzangi and

A. Cheshmehzangi, *Generative AI-Powered Urban Digital Twins*, Urban Sustainability,
https://doi.org/10.1007/978-981-95-4766-1_1

Pourroostaei Ardakani 2024). This is not a story about doing extra calculations just to be in control. It is an appeal to use artificial foresight and collective intelligence to enhance urban stewardship.

We will examine how AI-powered or AI-driven digital twins can optimize energy-water systems, promote green infrastructure, include citizens in co-designing urban futures, and serve as sentinels for the health of the planet as the book progresses. We must first comprehend the paths that led us to this point, as well as the conceptual framework that we now need to rethink.

1.1.1 Digital Twins in the Urban Domain: From Static Models to Dynamic City Mirrors

In the manufacturing and aerospace sectors, the idea of a digital twin—a digital duplicate of a physical asset or system—was first introduced. This allowed engineers to model and track the behaviour of high-risk systems, such as production plants or jet engines. From static 3D models, these twins developed into data-driven, dynamic platforms that could forecast malfunctions, maximize efficiency, and direct maintenance. Their usefulness was demonstrated in confined, regulated systems. Applying this reasoning to cities—complex, open systems with layers of unpredictability and constant change—was the next big step.

Digital twins have evolved from their technical origins to become platforms for urban informatics. Cities are using them more and more to develop comprehensive, real-time models of water systems, building performance, energy consumption, mobility, and even human behaviour. City managers may now evaluate disaster resilience, test design interventions, run simulations, and track sustainability measures thanks to urban digital twins. Understanding and controlling the city's intricate metabolism is the goal, not just digitizing it. However, despite their sophistication, the current generation of digital twins still has significant drawbacks. They rely on predetermined parameters and deterministic logic and are mostly descriptive or predictive. They can provide us with information about what is occurring or is anticipated to occur, but they hardly ever come up with original theories or recommend surprising courses of action. The development of generative AI becomes revolutionary at this point.

Twins that mirror the city are giving way to twins that fantasize and imagine with it. Generative algorithms enable a digital twin to generate numerous possible futures, optimize designs in real time, and adjust its knowledge based on feedback. Digital twins as instruments for observation and optimization are giving way to generative digital twins as catalysts for creativity and imagination. This change may be compared as going from a static dashboard to a live, breathing collaborator in the creation of cities. It enables planners to investigate issues such as: What if this district were reconfigured to achieve zero-carbon performance? In what ways could green corridors help cool cities throughout the year? In places that are vulnerable to flooding, what is the ideal spatial arrangement for fair public access? These aren't only "what is" inquiries. These are "what could be" inquiries—possibilities, scenarios, and provocations.

Crucially, urban digital twins are political and epistemological endeavours rather than merely technological platforms. The priorities, data structures, and power dynamics present in the cities they imitate are reflected in them. As they develop, they must be made to not only mimic infrastructure but also to question preconceptions, magnify multiple knowledges, and produce responses that are as social as they are technical. Thus, we are seeing the emergence of a new epistemic interface, where cities start to learn, reason, and act proactively through synthetic cognition rather of waiting for problems to be solved after the fact. Once a passive replica, the digital twin is today an active collaborator in reshaping the social and environmental future of the city.

1.1.2 Understanding Generative AI: From Language to Living Systems

We must first comprehend the nature and capabilities of generative artificial intelligence in order to appreciate the transformational potential of urban digital twins in the era of artificial intelligence (Chaudhary and Gill 2024). Generative AI creates original content, such as text, images, sounds, spatial patterns, or systemic behaviours, in contrast to typical AI systems that categorize, detect, or forecast based on historical data. It does more than just interpret reality. It produces new iterations.

The most well-known forms of generative AI are based on Generative Adversarial Networks (GANs), Transformers, and Diffusion Models. With the help of these designs and architectures, the computer can identify patterns in large datasets and produce original, non-replicated results. Generative models are excellent at one thing, whether they are writing essays, creating architecture, creating music, or suggesting urban layouts: synthesis through creativity and probability.

Generative AI, which was once praised for creating deepfakes and chatbot dialogues, is now becoming a useful tool for systems innovation and design. For instance, when used in urban settings, it may produce thousands of different spatial arrangements that balance pedestrian access, wind flow, and lighting. It can replicate the long-term effects of vegetation on microclimates. On the basis of rainfall data and topography patterns, it can suggest decentralized water systems. These are alternatives, iterations, and provocations rather than simple automations.

Fundamentally, generative AI makes it possible to move from optimization to the exploration of possibilities. In conventional planning, outcomes are singular, and limitations are fixed. Generative AI allows for multi-dimensional outputs and customizable limitations. Urban shape is now the result of dynamic discussions between objectives, limitations, and new opportunities rather than set blueprints. Therefore, rather of working against complexity, generative AI encourages planners to work with it.

Furthermore, it transcends both the spatial and the visual. We now have generative systems that can reason, translate policies, synthesize stakeholder inputs, and even create governance models based on cultural values and institutional histories thanks to large language models (LLMs). Consider an urban twin that not only proposes new zoning regulations but also revises them using language that is culturally aware and interactive. Imagine artificial intelligence (AI) technologies that act as a mediator between native worldviews and technical logic. It is coming, but this is not science fiction. But the most profound potential of generative AI lies in its synthetic intelligence: its ability to combine different forms of knowledge—textual, visual, spatial, environmental, social—into cohesive, novel, and context-specific solutions. This feature, when combined with digital twins' dynamic modelling power, changes AI's function from servant to collaborator—from smart assistant to co-designer of cities.

Yet, critical awareness is required to moderate this potential. The ethical, sustainable, and inclusive nature of generative AI depends on the values and data it is based on. It could mimic current urban inequities, disregard non-digitized information, or result in aesthetically pleasing but socially meaningless outcomes if it is not carefully designed. The ability to create is also the ability to erase. We must therefore rethink what we want generative AI to produce and why, in addition to implementing it. Do we want healthier social structures or more efficient traffic flows? Better energy efficiency or fair access to green space? Ecologically based communities or data-rich cities? These are not questions of technology. These are issues of accountability, justice, and vision. And they are at the center of the current confluence.

1.2 The Convergence: Toward Generative Urban Digital Twins (GUDTs)

Digital twins and generative AI together represent a conceptual shift rather than merely a technical advancement. It opens a new chapter in the planning, experience, and governance of cities by combining dynamic representation with synthetic imagination. We refer to this new hybrid as the Generative Urban Digital Twin (GUDT). In contrast to conventional digital twins, which depict the current status of energy, mobility, or infrastructure systems, a GUDT is always learning, suggesting, and adapting (Chen and Shi 2024). It doesn't wait for human inquiries anymore. It expects them. Scenarios are no longer run in a straight line. It creates whole, varied, intricate, and imaginative futures.

This convergence can be illustrated across five core capabilities (See Fig. 1.1):

1. **Scenario Generation at Scale**: Based on socioeconomic patterns, land use changes, climatic data, and other factors, GUDTs can model thousands of possible future routes for a city or district. Cities are able to "think ahead" in real time since these scenarios are dynamic and change in response to fresh facts.

2. **Multimodal Design Propositions**: A GUDT can provide integrated designs that concurrently consider functional, aesthetic, environmental, and spatial objectives by using generative models. It may recommend housing typologies that optimize community engagement while reducing heat load, or green corridors that serve as flood barriers.
3. **Data-Language-Spatial Integration**: GUDTs are able to combine environmental and spatial modelling with language-based reasoning. Within the same platform, an AI model may, for instance, analyze a zoning ordinance, evaluate it against community input and climate goals, and recommend adaptive revisions.
4. **Learning from the City as a Living System**: GUDTs learn over time, in contrast to rule-based planning tools. They are able to evolve their reasoning, identify patterns, and deduce system fragilities. The city turns into a learning partner rather than a static entity to be controlled.
5. **Participatory Interfaces and Narrative Simulations**: GUDTs can become easily accessible tools for residents, planners, and politicians alike through visual storytelling, natural language prompts, and user-friendly dashboards, democratizing the imagination of the future.

Think of a sea level rise-affected coastal city. Terrain, hydrology, ecosystem resilience, and population vulnerability can all be examined by a GUDT. It can replicate nature-based defenses, produce alternate land reclamation plans, and illustrate how public life might change on elevated platforms or in amphibious zones. More significantly, it can do it interactively and iteratively, integrating real-time input from people, scientists, and decision-makers. However, this convergence also brings up more profound institutional and philosophical issues: The generative models are controlled by whom? In the simulations, whose futures are given priority? How can we make sure the digital twin serves as a portal to multiple visions rather than a gatekeeper?

We need to adopt a new ethic of urban synthesis that values humility, pluralism, and uncertainty if we are to use GUDTs in an ethical manner. Cities cannot be solved like puzzles. They are dynamic ecologies of connections, goals, and limitations. At its best, generative AI broadens the scope of what is conceivable and feasible rather than imposing a solution. This convergence will be further explored in the following sections of this chapter, which will place it within the global framework of the environmental crisis, critique the narrative around smart cities, and investigate how regenerative intelligence might direct our future.

1.3 Planetary Urbanism and Environmental Imperatives

Natural resources, landscapes, and larger ecological systems have all fuelled the creation of cities, which have always been environmental creations. However, ecological externalization—extraction, emission, and expansion with no consideration for

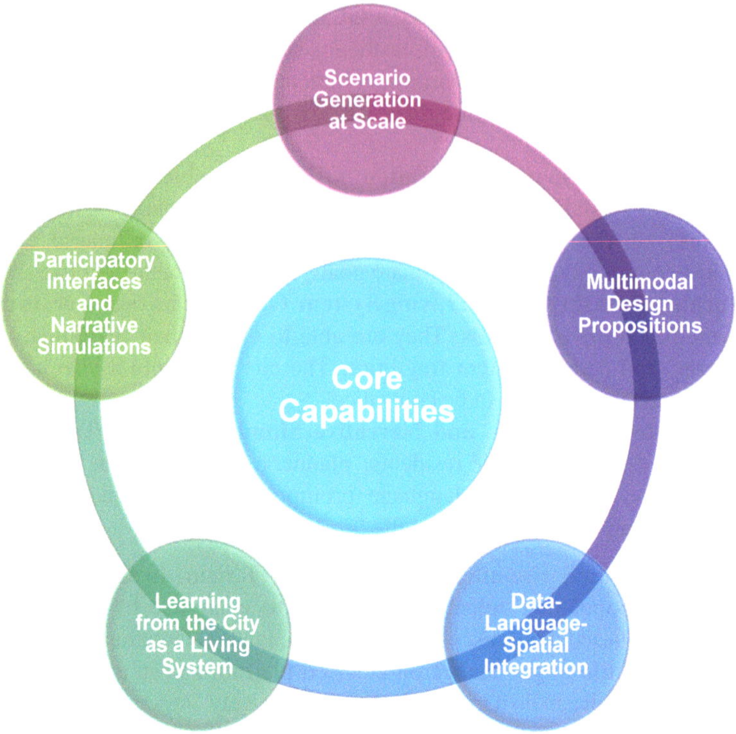

Fig. 1.1. The convergence toward generative urban digital twins (GUDTs) across five core capabilities

planetary limits—has been the main tenet of contemporary urbanization. Urbanization is becoming more than just a demographic trend or an economic driver as the climate crisis worsens; it is a biophysical threshold that will ultimately determine the fate of ecosystems and people alike.

The goal of digital twins is reframed by this existential truth. They are valuable because they enable us to comprehend, restore, and safeguard the fragile planetary systems that underpin all urban activity, not because they make cities more responsive or efficient in and of themselves. Convergence with generative AI becomes crucial in this situation. When combined, they can create place-based responses that are considerate of regional ecologies and global borders, model intricate feedback loops, and simulate planetary boundaries.

The need to protect the environment is no longer a theoretical concept. Cities deal with water scarcity, biodiversity loss, unbearable heat, and increasing sea levels. Decision intelligence, which includes tools that model non-linear outcomes, highlight interdependencies, and facilitate long-term thinking, is what urban planners and decision-makers need more than dashboards and data. GUDTs may be such instruments. They can assist cities in determining which urban form maximizes biodiversity and reduces flood susceptibility. What circular approaches lower emissions without sacrificing fairness? In what ways may unofficial settlements change without being displaced?

Generative AI has the ability to incorporate ecological intelligence into the design process itself, going beyond simulation. It can suggest solutions that mirror natural efficiencies, such as decentralized energy networks based on mycelial logic, distributed water cycles modelled on forest hydrology, and fractal designs for urban ventilation, all of which are motivated by biomimicry and systems thinking. This goes beyond AI for infrastructure alone. AI is being used to restore planets.

Additionally, GUDTs can facilitate the resuscitation of lost environmental information, such as traditional hydrological flows and indigenous land care techniques. Generative twins can promote epistemic equity in environmental planning by combining various knowledge systems, not just modern datasets. For example, community customs and traditional knowledge can influence a flood management plan just as much as satellite information and LiDAR scans. In addition to being smarter, the city also becomes more regenerative, courteous, and rooted.

A shift in measures is also implied by this planetary perspective. GDP per hectare and terabytes processed are no longer used to quantify success. Soil health, canopy cover, water retention, cultural survival, and climatic justice are all metrics used to measure it. If we choose to value these planetary indications, GUDTs are ideally suited to track, correlate, and forecast them. Accordingly, the combination of digital twins with generative AI is a civilizational endeavour rather than a technological one. It provides a way to transform urbanism into a restorative effort rather than an accumulation process. From extraction to reciprocity. From dominion to kinship.

1.4 Conceptual Shifts: From Smart Cities to 'Intelligent Cities' and then to 'Advanced Cities'

For these recent two decades, the phrase "smart city" has dominated urban discourse. It offers data-driven governance, real-time service optimization, and sensor-enabled efficiency. Although the smart city agenda has sped up digital infrastructure and created new opportunities for urban innovation, it has also come under fire for advocating a limited, techno-managerial vision that frequently puts profit before purpose, control above caring, and surveillance over solidarity. We must fight the urge to merely digitally improve the current situation as we stand on the precipice of AI-driven urbanism. Instead, we need to ask: What kind of city do we really want to construct? The potential to see beyond the smart city story and envision a new urban paradigm—what we may refer to as the intelligent city, is presented by the combination of generative AI and urban digital twins.

Blockchains and bandwidth do not define the intelligent city. Its ability to adapt, include, and regenerate is what defines it. It is a city that learns profoundly rather than reacting hastily. Its goal is to increase the collective intelligence of its citizens, not to automate decision-making. It is made for meaningful existence within the bounds of the planet, not just for optimization. The logic of control that supports a large portion of the infrastructure in smart cities is first called into question by this conceptual change. Why are sensors required for body surveys rather than tree protection? Why should AI prioritize parking over social trust? Instead of fostering civic imagination, why must platforms commodify human behaviour?

This reasoning is broken by generative urban digital twins. They encourage us to imagine futures for ethical and practical reasons, to create rather than to compute. They encourage communities to envision futures that are co-crafted via discussion, culture, and care rather than dictated by capital or the law. In this way, GUDTs are narrative engines that can tell multiple futures rather than just one, making them more than merely urban operating systems.

To operationalize this shift, several philosophical and practical reframing are required:

- **From Metrics to Meaning**: Moving beyond KPIs and toward indicators of cultural vitality, environmental reciprocity, and lived experience.
- **From Optimization to Plurality**: Accepting uncertainty and generating multiple possible futures instead of seeking single-point solutions.
- **From Ownership to Stewardship**: Designing data governance models based on custodianship and commons rather than proprietary control.
- **From Passive Participation to Active Co-Creation**: Creating participatory design interfaces where communities don't just consult but generate.

More recently, I presented the idea of a "Advanced City," which was a novel concept, way of thinking, procedure, and model. The Advanced City promises to be wiser rather than smarter. More introspective, but not quicker. Potentially, a city that uses digital twins and generative AI to move forward toward a new sort of urban life that is in line with diversity, dignity, and profound concern for the environment rather than trying to fix its previous errors. This new conception is based on data-informed and people-oriented thinking, which is summarised in a recent book titled "Advanced City" (Cheshmehzangi 2025).

As the next sections will demonstrate, this is no longer speculative. Experiments are already setting the groundwork in places like Helsinki, Singapore, Barcelona, and Kigali. But they are just the start. The real difficulty is in scaling our use of technology, not the technology itself, but our mindset and creativity.

1.4.1 Early Experiments and Global Trends

Globally, innovative initiatives in the integration of generative AI and the deployment of urban digital twins are beginning to show early indications of a significant change in environmental modelling and urban governance. Even though a large number of these initiatives are still in pilot stages or district-scale demonstrations, they provide important information about what is both politically and technologically feasible.

They also demonstrate the variety of strategies being used, from bottom-up, citizen-led platforms to top-down infrastructure-driven initiatives.

With its Virtual Singapore platform, a city-wide digital twin that combines 3D spatial data, real-time environmental inputs, and predictive analytics, Singapore continues to be one of the most ambitious instances. The platform was first utilized for urban planning and traffic optimization, but it is now being investigated more and more for sustainability simulations including flood resilience modelling, energy demand estimates, and shadow analysis. Its architecture is progressively being adapted to support AI-enhanced forecasting and optimization modules, even though it isn't quite generative yet.

Helsinki, on the other hand, has prioritized transparency and public participation. Public-use interfaces in its urban digital twin enable locals to model urban changes, such as pedestrianizing streets or installing green roofs, and observe their immediate environmental effects. In order to develop neighbourhood-scale low-carbon living options that locals may evaluate, alter, and rank, researchers are integrating generative design techniques.

With its massive digital infrastructure and fast urban growth, Shenzhen is making significant investments in AI-powered urban modelling (Yue et al. 2025). Here, the emphasis is on smart governance and infrastructure coordination: coordinating utilities, transportation, and construction while providing real-time feedback. Large-scale zoning plans and energy usage trends have been predicted through the application of AI in this context. Centralization, monitoring, and a lack of citizen engagement are still issues, though.

In other places, smaller-scale applications are being tested in places including Barcelona, Vienna, and Kigali. Barcelona has experimented with AI-assisted neighbourhood design, rearranging public areas for equitable access and thermal comfort through the use of generative algorithms. In order to make sure that renovations meet tenant requirements and carbon targets, Vienna has concentrated on incorporating digital twins into its social housing policy. In a leapfrogging approach, Kigali is investigating lightweight digital twin technologies to manage infrastructure resilience and water stress (Joel 2023) in quickly growing peri-urban areas.

The emergence of domain-specific twins, or customized models centered on important systems like food distribution, flood response, heat mitigation, or mobility equity, is an especially interesting trend. These are increasingly driven by generative algorithms that experiment with different metropolitan layouts under various economic or climatic conditions. For example, generative climate models that mimic adaptable infrastructure over decades are starting to be incorporated into flood-risk digital twins in the Netherlands.

Another significant institutional development that we are seeing is the contribution of public-private partnerships, universities, and urban labs to the development of these instruments. AI-integrated twin systems for precinct planning, carbon-neutral campuses, and disaster simulations are being actively funded by projects including Australia's Digital Built Environment Alliance, Canada's Future Cities Centre, and the UK's Connected Places Catapult.

The majority of deployments, however, continue to be institutionally cautious and technically dispersed in spite of this innovative landscape. Without unified platforms or shared urban epistemologies, generative AI is frequently employed in silos by mobility planners, policy modelers, and architecture firms. Moreover, a lot of cities in the global south are still left out of these advancements because of inadequate finance, infrastructure, or data accessibility. Thus, the unevenness of experimentation is a geopolitical as well as a technical issue.

Nevertheless, the momentum is evident. Today's developments are early indications of an urban future in which machine intelligence actively shapes urban complexity rather than just reflecting it. These experiments investigate how AI and digital twins may work together to fulfill the needs of population expansion, climate urgency, and inclusive innovation. They are prototypes for collaborative learning rather than endpoints.

1.5 Challenges, Risks, and Blind Spots

The combination of generative AI and urban digital twins presents a number of difficulties, some of which are well-known and others of which are completely novel, as is the case with any revolutionary technological trend. We must critically analyze the blind spots that frequently elude the techno-optimistic narrative if we are to embrace their promise without falling victim to unintended harm.

1.5.1 Data Governance and Digital Sovereignty

Massive amounts of real-time urban data, including private data on behaviour, mobility, infrastructure, and resource usage, are essential to digital twins. Another layer is added by generative AI, which needs training data, which could include historical records, environmental parameters, private messages, and spatial patterns. Who is the owner of this data? Who controls it, makes money off of it, or curates it? There is a genuine and increasing risk of data extractivism, in which private organizations take control of urban knowledge infrastructures.

Furthermore, if cities' twin systems are developed on proprietary platforms run by multinational firms, they run the risk of becoming digitally colonized. Public control is weakened, interoperability is restricted, and biases that represent business interests rather than public principles may be ingrained. Therefore, the drive for open standards and local digital sovereignty is a democratic imperative rather than a technical luxury.

1.5.2 Algorithmic Bias and Model Transparency

The fairness and inclusivity of generative AI systems are determined by the data they are trained on. It is possible for training data to contain gendered spatial conventions, racially infrastructure choices, and historical zoning patterns, which are then replicated in "optimized" urban designs. These technologies could maintain spatial inequities under the pretense of efficiency if they lack algorithmic transparency and auditability.

A digital twin that eliminates informal housing from flood-prone areas without addressing displacement or promotes gentrification as the best way to reduce carbon emissions is not an impartial instrument. It is a destructive mechanism. Implementation must prioritize algorithmic pluralism, where generative outputs are shaped by a variety of data sources and value systems.

1.5.3 Technological Lock-in and Institutional Readiness

Systems of urban governance are frequently underfunded, legally disjointed, and bureaucratically inflexible. Deep institutional adaptation is necessary to integrate AI-driven digital twins into current procedures. Many cities lack the cross-sectoral frameworks and technical know-how required to properly use such technologies. Even worse, they can be forced to use platforms that were accepted too soon, which would limit their flexibility in the future. Cities must place a high priority on interdepartmental cooperation, capacity building, and iterative design procedures to prevent this kind of lock-in. These are fundamental prerequisites for adaptive governance in the AI era, not just support systems.

1.5.4 Environmental Costs and Rebound Effects

Paradoxically, the technologies that are intended to promote environmental resilience also have environmental drawbacks. Large amounts of processing power are needed for generative AI systems, which results in higher energy consumption and carbon emissions. For instance, training huge language models can produce more CO_2 than many automobiles' worth of emissions over their lifetime. Urban digital twins necessitate constant data flow and processing, especially when viewed at city-scale resolutions. We can experience a technological rebound if it is not handled carefully, whereby instruments used to solve environmental issues also generate new environmental stresses. This paradox necessitates the use of green AI concepts, such as renewable energy-powered infrastructure, ethical data curation, and energy-efficient models.

1.5.5 Social Legitimacy and Public Trust

Last, but not least, without social legitimacy, urban innovation fails, regardless of how sophisticated the model or perceptive the simulation. Decisions concerning public space, housing, mobility, and safety—areas that have a significant impact on residents' lives—will be shaped by GUDTs. These systems run the risk of turning into technocratic mandates rather than democratic instruments in the absence of inclusive participation, open communication, and contestation procedures. Gaining the trust of the public requires participation, responsibility, and cultural fit. The lived reality of a varied, changing city can never be captured by a digital counterpart that just represents the goals of engineers or developers. The foundation of GUDT governance should include ethical review boards for generative systems, community interpreters of AI outputs, and participatory design interfaces.

The risks are not reasons for abandonment. They are prerequisites for maturity. We can only develop a more resilient, just, and regenerative use of these potent instruments by directly addressing them. Our objective is to not only foresee the future but also to modify it in an ethical, inclusive, and creative manner, as the latter portions of this chapter will examine.

1.6 The Road Ahead: Toward Regenerative Urban Intelligence

Regenerative urban intelligence—a paradigm in which cities actively restore ecological systems, mend social divisions, and regenerate the urban commons—must define the upcoming decades if the rise of industrial urbanism and the pursuit of smart urbanism defined the 20th and early 21st centuries, respectively. Digital twins and generative AI present a singular opportunity to design this future, but only if the proper principles, frameworks, and cooperative methods are incorporated early on.

To build regenerative urban intelligence, several critical shifts are required (See Fig. 1.2):

1. From Problem-Solving to Possibility-Crafting.

The active creation of futures worth living in must be the goal of urban planning, moving beyond limited technocratic classifications of problems. Generative Urban Digital Twins (GUDTs) should provide drastically varied urban imaginaries that are co-created with multiple publics, rather than only responding to mobility or climatic problems. Designing for care, justice, and ecological reciprocity as standard urban ideals is the result of large-scale creativity.

2. From Data-Driven to Ethics-Driven Governance.

Ethical governance must be prioritized as a fundamental design element rather than as a regulatory afterthought. This entails safeguarding against algorithmic harm, establishing open monitoring organizations, fostering public ownership of digital

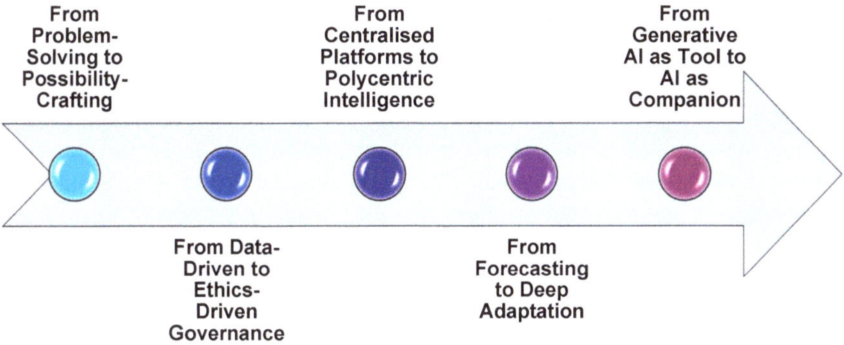

Fig. 1.2. Summary of five suggested critical shifts

infrastructure, and guaranteeing data equity. By facilitating accountable simulations, explainable models, and traceable decisions, GUDTs ought to aid in the operationalization of democratic government in the digital age.

3. From Centralised Platforms to Polycentric Intelligence.

Centralized command centers and single dashboards won't create regenerative cities. Polycentric systems—networks of intelligence dispersed throughout communities, organizations, and ecosystems—will give rise to them. GUDTs ought to be localizable, modular, and interoperable so that communities can create and modify their own urban twins using common technical and epistemic frameworks. Rather than erasing the diverse realities of urban life, these systems must represent them.

4. From Forecasting to Deep Adaptation.

We have to admit that no amount of foresight can stop every disturbance. Cities will experience shocks from systemic failures, migratory pressures, and the effects of climate change. GUDTs must encourage deep adaptation, which allows cities to change in a responsible and equitable manner rather of just recovering. This entails simulating not just infrastructure breakdown but also institutional transformation, cultural continuity, and community resilience.

5. From Generative AI as Tool to AI as Companion.

The most profound progress is relational rather than technological. We might start to think about AI as a companion intelligence—a learning partner that enables us to see, comprehend, and invent in new ways—instead of as a tool to be exploited or a risk to be controlled. In this context, generative AI is viewed as a component of our broader cognitive ecosystem, co-evolving with cities rather than existing independently of them.

Collaboration between sectors and disciplines is essential to achieving this goal. It is imperative that urban scientists, environmental planners, technologists, ethicists, artists, and activists collaborate in co-creative loops rather than sequential workflows. Academic institutions will play a crucial role in prototyping, mentoring, and scaffolding new urban epistemologies in addition to offering critique. Similarly, local governments need to provide the procurement methods, experimentation areas, and policy frameworks that support ethical innovation.

The next generation of urbanists, designers, and legislators must be taught to think about systems, ethics, and futures in addition to technical issues. Rather than teaching deterministic technologies, curricula should promote ecological reasoning, creative thinking, and digital fluency. The GUDT serves as a mirror to consider how we understand, envision, and maintain our cities in addition to being a platform to utilize. To put it briefly, the future lies in developing imagination rather than refining prediction. It's about realizing that urban futures should be created collaboratively, iteratively, and regeneratively rather than predicted.

1.6.1 Concluding Remarks: Planting Seeds for a New Urban Episteme

The remainder of the book, which is a call to reconsider what it means to envision, plan, and manage cities in the age of digital twins and generative AI, is built upon the framework established by this chapter. Its central thesis is straightforward yet impactful: technology is an invitation rather than a fate. An invitation to inquire: What level of intelligence do we want to see in our cities? Which futures are we hoping to create? And for whom?

We are experiencing a period of urban reinvention and global unravelling. The ecological crisis, societal disintegration, and political inertia are all causing old paradigms to crumble. However, new opportunities are arising in the fractures. One such possibility—a synthetic yet grounded type of urban intelligence that may assist cities in learning, adapting, and regenerating—is made possible by the combination of generative AI and urban digital twins. This pledge, however, is not assured. It demands that we be fearless in our design, exacting in our criticism, and modest in our intent. We must create healing systems as well as sensing systems. It asks us to think of cities as ecologies of care, conflict, and co-creation rather than as machines.

This book proceeds on that premise. Every chapter will examine the ways in which GUDTs might facilitate environmental change—not as commanding instruments, but as forums for discussion. Applications in energy systems, circularity, mobility, social infrastructure, and climate adaptation will all be examined. We will discuss worldwide exemplars, highlight the opportunities, and analyze the blind spots. Here, however, we start with a seed. A new urban episteme's seed. One that has the audacity to blend the poetics of place with the accuracy of AI. One that views technology as a reflection rather than a master. Additionally, it acknowledges that in order to revitalize our cities, we must first revitalize our imagination.

Two significant changes are occurring at the same time: the AI revolution is changing how we see, plan, and engage with the world, and the climate crisis is forcing us to rethink the logic of urban life itself. Beyond computing power, the combination of generative AI and urban digital twins offers a new episteme—a new approach to understanding, planning, and living in cities.

This is a future of possibility rather than prediction. It involves emergence, meaning, and memory in addition to efficiency. Making cities intelligent is more important than making them smart. We have examined the paths that have led us to this point in this chapter: from smart cities of surveillance to advanced cities of stewardship; from urbanism as management to urbanism as regenerative intelligence; and from digital twins as reactive models to generative systems of co-creation. We have witnessed both the shadows of risk woven into their design and the flashes of invention throughout international tests.

How we decide to move forward is what counts today. Insisting on ecological and human dignity while fending off the temptations of technological determinism requires bravery. We need to be creative in our approach, employing these tools not only to solve issues but also to pose more insightful queries that will open up rather than close off possibilities. We must move forward in humility, understanding that cities are living worlds that are complicated, contentious, and always evolving rather than being laboratories. Care must be taken as we move forward—care for people, places, and the planetary systems that support us.

This book will examine the ways in which this convergence occurs in the areas of public involvement, mobility justice, flood resilience, heat mitigation, carbon neutrality, and governance reform. However, let this chapter be a prelude—a conceptual call to reconsider not only what we do with AI and cities, but also what kind of urban life we think is worthwhile creating. Ultimately, it is not an issue of whether cities will develop intelligence. What sort of intellect will they exhibit is the question. The response has not yet been written. But we can still write it together if we have the correct resources, principles, and dedication.

References

Chaudhary A, Gill SK (2024) The AI-enhanced transformation: unveiling the synergy of digital twins and artificial intelligence. In: Ponnusamy S, Assaf MH, Antari J, Singh S, Kalyanaraman S (eds) Harnessing AI and digital twin technologies in businesses. IGI Global, Hershey, pp 400–410

Chen J, Shi Y (2024) Generative AI over mobile networks for human digital twin in human-centric applications: a comprehensive survey. Authorea Preprints

Cheshmehzangi A (2025) Advanced city: for the future of cities and opposing smart cities. Springer Nature, Singapore

Cheshmehzangi A, Pourroostaei Ardakani S (2024) Navigating the future with the nexus between digital twin computing and urban intelligence. In: Cheshmehzangi A (ed) Digital twin computing for urban intelligence. Springer Nature Singapore, Singapore, pp 245–256

Joel N (2023). Ecological sustainability in urban landscapes and smart cities, case study Kigali city, Rwanda. In: Proceedings of the 11th IALE world congress, Nairobi, Kenya, September 2023

Lifelo Z, Ding J, Ning H, Dhelim S (2024) Artificial intelligence-enabled metaverse for sustainable smart cities: technologies, applications, challenges, and future directions. Electronics 13(24):4874

Yue Y, Yan G, Lan T, Cao R, Gao Q, Gao W, Huang B, Huang G, Huang Z, Kan Z, Li X (2025) Shaping future sustainable cities with AI-powered urban informatics: toward human-AI symbiosis. Comput Urban Sci 5(1):31

Part I
Foundations and Frameworks of Urban Intelligence

Chapter 2
Digital Twins in the Urban Context: Evolution and Capabilities

2.1 Foundations of the Digital Twin Concept

In an era of cascading complexity and climate urgency, the need for cities to sense, understand, and adapt in real time has become existential. The digital twin is a technical advancement that goes beyond static city representations to create dynamic, data-rich simulations that change, adapt, and grow with us. Even while the phrase "digital twin" has only recently become widely used in urban discourse, its philosophical foundations go considerably further.

At its core, a digital twin is a virtual, real-time version of a physical system that is updated continuously via feedback loops, data flows, and behavioural modelling (Pourroostaei Ardakani and Cheshmehzangi 2024). From traffic and transportation to climate and community, from building operations to energy flows, from social patterns to infrastructure constraints, this refers to a virtual model that mimics and engages with physical urban processes in cities.

The idea of a digital twin originated in systems engineering and aerospace innovation, where precise digital models of intricate gear allowed for performance optimization, predictive maintenance, and ongoing monitoring. Its application to urban settings represented a substantial conceptual advance. Cities are living, breathing things that are shaped by millions of simultaneous interactions between people, systems, ecologies, and structures, in contrast to mechanical systems. Applying the digital twin to the city is therefore a socio-technical revolution rather than just a technical one.

The potential to bridge the gap between the digital and physical worlds is presented by digital twins. The physical layer (sensors, built infrastructure, urban activities), the digital layer (data streams, simulations, visualisations), and the cognitive layer (analytical models, predictive algorithms, decision-making frameworks) are the three fundamental layers they integrate to do this. Digital twins are positioned as more than just reflections of reality thanks to this third layer, or cognitive intelligence, which

A. Cheshmehzangi, *Generative AI-Powered Urban Digital Twins*, Urban Sustainability,
https://doi.org/10.1007/978-981-95-4766-1_2

is most in line with AI-driven methodologies. Instead, they develop into catalysts of understanding, flexibility, and vision.

Cities may transition from descriptive and diagnostic skills (what is happening and why) to predictive and prescriptive intelligence (what is likely to happen and what should be done) thanks to the convergence of artificial intelligence and digital twin technologies. In order to identify patterns, learn behaviours, and model outcomes, artificial intelligence (AI) systems analyze enormous and diverse datasets, including historical, real-time, and probabilistic data. AI opens up adaptive learning loops when integrated with urban digital twins, enabling cities to not only see how they operate but also take dynamic action. This has significant ramifications for areas including risk mitigation, mobility coordination, climate adaption, and energy optimization.

Moreover, the emergence of generative AI represents a turning point in the development of digital twins. Traditional twins concentrate on modelling known parameters and reacting to changes that are detected, while generative AI increases their capacity to make hypotheses, create scenarios, and suggest creative solutions that human planners would not have thought of. This enhances the twin's potential as a co-creative collaborator in urban innovation as well as a tool for governance. A generative twin, for instance, may model hundreds of adaption techniques in climate-responsive planning based on local vulnerabilities, socioeconomic objectives, and projected climate models. This would enable decision-makers to assess trade-offs and collaborate with communities to co-design future interventions.

Therefore, digital twins play a crucial—rather than incidental—role in creating intelligent cities. Previously, the phrase "smart city" frequently denoted disjointed arrays of sensors, dashboards, and data analytics that functioned in isolation and provided no systemic awareness (Mazzetto 2024). By acting as integrative, real-time platforms that integrate spatial, temporal, and operational dimensions, digital twins rectify this fragmentation. They make it possible for citizens, planners, and decision-makers to engage with the city as a cohesive whole rather than as a collection of disparate components. By doing this, they redefine intelligence as relational, situational, and purpose-driven rather than just computational.

In conclusion, the digital twin represents an advancement in urban thought rather than only the result of technological inventiveness. It represents a paradigm change in the way we view, model, and construct the city. The digital twin will become less of a novelty and more of an operating system for the city of the twenty-first century as artificial intelligence develops and becomes more integrated into urban governance and architecture. This conceptual underpinning, which is based on integrative urbanism, predictive intelligence, and real-time responsiveness, serves as the backdrop for the next sections of this chapter.

2.1.1 *From Aerospace to Urban Systems: A Cross-Sectoral Evolution*

Digital twin concept has its roots in aerospace engineering, where NASA created complex spaceship simulators to test manoeuvres, predict system faults, and continuously monitor mechanical conditions. The first real digital twins were these virtual representations, which could respond almost lifelike and provide dynamic input. They gave engineers access to a second pair of eyes, allowing them to watch, act, and model a physical object's future from a safe and manageable distance.

Slowly but surely, the aerospace industry gave way to cities, infrastructure, and architecture. Real-time data collection on movement, energy, temperature, air quality, and even human behaviour is now possible because to the widespread use of sensors, cloud computing, and Internet of Things (IoT) technology. As urban systems became increasingly complicated and interconnected, the importance of having a dynamic digital layer became clear. What started out as a jet engine management tool evolved into a platform for urban ecology management.

Digital twins are currently being investigated and used in a wide range of industries, including; energy, to model smart grid behaviour under various load conditions; mobility, to model congestion and coordinate traffic flows; climate adaptation, to predict flood risks, model heat island effects, and test cooling interventions; and construction, to test structural performance before ground is broken. In each instance, the digital twin serves as a mind and a mirror, reflecting the here and now while looking ahead to the future.

From sector-specific simulations to multi-scalar, multi-temporal urban mirrors, and from object-based replication to integrated system modelling, this chapter charts the development of digital twins in urban settings. It investigates their conceptual underpinnings, functional applications, and enabling technology. More significantly, it looks at how the city's ontology is changing because of digital twins, moving from a static location to a living, sensing, and changing entity.

The urban context stands out due to its exceptional degree of diversity and dynamism. Cities represent unpredictability in contrast to an airplane, which has controlled conditions and known trajectories. Environmental upheavals, behavioural changes, economic flows, and sociopolitical influences all influence them. Therefore, the use of digital twins in this field needs to embrace complexity, heterogeneity, and change rather than just technical modelling. As a result, hybrid digital twins—which include social data, behavioural patterns, environmental feedback, and physical parameters—have become more popular.

The evolution also reflects a deeper epistemological shift. Digital twins used to be about operational control and efficiency, but these days they are more about governance, resilience, and foresight. This shift is like the shift from linear systems thinking to systems-of-systems thinking, which is a crucial paradigm for modern cities with their intricate interdependencies in public health, housing, energy, transportation, and water.

Furthermore, the distinction between prediction and simulation keeps becoming more blurry as AI capabilities grow. These days, digital twins use machine learning to explore long-term policy scenarios, find anomalies, and offer insights that traditional planning models might otherwise obscure. An AI-augmented urban twin, for instance, may estimate the effects of a new zoning law on emissions, traffic congestion, and housing affordability over a ten-year period while accounting for past patterns, public opinion, and climate models.

In this sense, the cross-sectoral development of digital twins is a story of convergence rather than just technological spread. The everyday reality of streets, buildings, and neighbourhoods now serve as the foundation for what started in the void of space. The digital twin is not a borrowed idea, as the upcoming chapters will demonstrate; rather, it has been reinvented and transformed by the opportunities, complexities, and demands of urban living.

2.2 Functional Layers and Capabilities of Urban Digital Twins

One must look at both what digital twins can achieve and what they represent in order to fully grasp their power. Urban digital twins are functional systems that combine data streams, simulations, analytical models, and user interfaces to facilitate adaptive learning, decision-making, and intervention. They are more than just visual copies.

Their layered architecture, which consists of sensor technologies, data integration platforms, simulation engines, machine learning models, and user interaction tools, is what makes them operationally useful. Urban digital twins have an advantage because of this combination of hardware and software infrastructures, which allows them to not only replicate reality but also provide a framework for predicting and influencing it. The twin's power resides in its capacity to bring together temporalities—recording the present, predicting the future, and drawing lessons from the past—into a unified, intelligent framework.

At their most robust, urban digital twins possess five interrelated capabilities:

2.2.1 Real-Time Sensing and Monitoring

Data is what powers urban digital twins. This comprises social data (footfall, sentiment, health indicators), infrastructure data (traffic, energy use, building performance), and environmental data (temperature, wind, pollution). The digital twin can serve as a dashboard of urban metabolism by integrating such data in real-time, giving city managers the ability to spot stressors, inefficiencies, or emerging threats.

This fundamental ability turns urban environment into a sentient system where patterns and events are observable and measurable rather than unseen. This layer is improved by AI, which makes anomaly detection, trend prediction, and pattern recognition possible. An AI-enabled twin, for example, can automatically detect unusual temperature spikes in particular neighbourhoods and initiate heat mitigation or pre-programmed alert systems. Examples include energy grids that adjust according to consumption trends and the availability of renewable energy sources, or real-time dashboards for heatwave response that identify susceptible locations in connection to cooling facilities and demography. This sensory infrastructure serves as a municipal nervous system in addition to being a monitoring tool.

2.2.2 *Simulation and Forecasting*

Simulating "what if" scenarios is arguably a digital twin's most transformative feature. What happens if a district experiences a 30% increase in rainfall? What effects will pedestrianization have on traffic patterns? Which structures are at the highest risk of experiencing earthquake stress? These are not hypothetical questions since they can be examined in a safe online setting without running the danger of having real-world repercussions.

Proactive urbanism is made possible by these simulations. Cities may foresee, plan, and iterate through complicated scenarios instead of responding to inefficiency or calamities. AI-driven predictive models strengthen this capacity by incorporating machine learning algorithms that improve over time, using historic data to refine forecasting. These days, urban digital twins can incorporate population changes, land use change patterns, and weather models to more accurately anticipate long-term consequences. This promotes scenario-based planning and anticipatory governance, both of which are essential for sustainable development and climate resilience.

2.2.3 *Intervention Planning and Optimization*

Beyond simulation lies intervention. Digital twins make it possible to test and improve suggested tactics. A city can compare the cooling effects, costs, and community benefits of various infrastructure interventions, such as water retention parks, reflective surfaces, and green roofs. Planning is changed from linear projection to multi-scalar optimization using these capabilities.

Importantly, this optimization doesn't have to be only technical. It can combine objective measurements with subjective values by taking into account societal preferences like walkability, cultural identity, or public safety. AI-powered multi-criteria decision-making technologies can present decision-makers with optimal portfolios and balance conflicting objectives (such as social equality vs economic efficiency). This is especially helpful in settings with limited resources where trade-offs need to be clearly assessed. Digital experimentation prior to deployment lowers risk, enhances urban results, and improves design quality.

2.2.4 Stakeholder Engagement and Visual Communication

Digital twins have the ability to democratize information, which is a little-known but incredibly potent feature. A wide range of stakeholders, including legislators, students, engineers, and senior citizens, may now understand complicated urban systems through interactive dashboards, augmented reality overlays, or immersive 3D visualisations.

Deliberative planning, where several viewpoints can jointly examine the effects of choices, is made possible by this communication power, which promotes openness and confidence. Digital twins might act as visual interpreters in contentious development or public consultation environments, bridging the gap between technical know-how and general comprehension. Participatory governance and the legitimacy of urban decisions depend on this. This is further supported by AI, which ensures greater accessibility across linguistic, educational, and cognitive divides by providing automated translation, natural language explanations, and even summarization of complex model results.

2.2.5 Adaptive Learning and Feedback Integration

The most sophisticated digital twins facilitate adaptive learning by doing more than just monitoring and simulating. The twin adjusts its understanding, changes its models, and improves its suggestions when new information becomes available. In unstable metropolitan settings where things can change quickly, from climatic occurrences to behavioural patterns, this is essential.

Digital twins can develop into dynamic entities with ongoing calibration and learning capabilities through feedback loops, bringing cities closer to responsive, living systems. When combined with generative AI or reinforcement learning systems, which can assess the effects of earlier interventions and self-improve planning logic, this adaptive intelligence becomes even more powerful. Static models are no longer adequate in a world of rapid change; cities want instruments that develop, learn, and change with their citizens.

2.3 Scales of Deployment: From Site to City to Planet

Digital twins of cities or 'urban digital twins' function at different scales. Although they are frequently linked to citywide platforms, their use can extend from individual structures to whole urban ecosystems, each of which presents unique opportunities and difficulties. Instead of being distinct layers, these different sizes are a part of an ongoing spectrum of urban representation, each of which is nested within the others and connected by governance functions, data flows, and system dependencies. The ability of digital twins to synchronize across different dimensions and produce a cohesive model of urban life that seamlessly transitions from micro- to macro-levels is frequently what determines how effective they are.

2.3.1 Building and Precinct Scale

Digital twins are used to manage specific buildings or precincts on the smallest scale. These twins enhance energy use, air quality, occupancy comfort, and predictive maintenance by combining real-time sensor feedback with BIM (Building Information Modelling) data (Agostinelli 2024). With adaptive control of lighting, HVAC systems, and facade performance, high-efficiency buildings can help achieve net-zero operations.

Passive systems become intelligent environments when AI is integrated at this scale. For instance, machine learning-powered occupancy prediction models can dynamically modify lighting and ventilation, lowering operating expenses and energy consumption. Algorithms for predictive maintenance identify early indicators of equipment wear and tear, enabling preventative measures that reduce downtime. These models get more sophisticated over time, learning from usage patterns, environmental changes, and user behaviour to maximize performance without human intervention.

Precinct-scale twins, on the other hand, model integrated systems, including pedestrian patterns, waste cycles, microgrid coordination, and shared mobility flows. These are frequently utilized in innovation districts or eco-neighbourhoods as test sites for more extensive rollouts. Precincts are perfect places to test participatory governance tools, create AI-driven spatial optimization tactics, and pilot urban technology since they entail complex systems interaction while operating within a restricted boundary. This degree of digital twins can facilitate real-time co-creation platforms, which use shared data visualizations and scenario simulations to facilitate iterative design processes among planners, citizens, and stakeholders.

2.3.2 District and City Scale

At the city or urban district level, digital twins start to simulate intricate relationships between governance procedures, land use, infrastructure, socioeconomic demographics, and climate systems. The key here is integration: platforms must facilitate cross-agency collaboration, spatial resolution must be good enough to give meaningful insight, and various datasets must communicate with one another.

The interaction between political processes and technical systems is frequently found in city-scale twins. They make it possible for digital governance to be operationalized, allowing policy experiments to be tested virtually and their results to be replicated prior to actual implementation. Depending on the strategic priorities of the city, these twins may be layered with data on public health, carbon emissions modelling, disaster risk analytics, or mobility demand forecasting. It is important to note that they serve as platforms for both vertical and horizontal coordination: horizontal across departments (transport, environment, housing, etc.) and vertical across governmental tiers (from local councils to national agencies).

Singapore's city-wide twin, Helsinki's participatory interface, and Melbourne's Smart City twin—which is utilized for emergency response and floods simulation—are a few examples. These systems function as live policy tools and are frequently integrated into governance procedures. In order to provide policymakers with a portfolio of adaptable solutions under a range of future situations, advanced cities are increasingly incorporating AI-driven decision-support engines that synthesize policy outcomes across competing goals—economic, ecological, and social (Cheshmehzangi 2025). Anticipatory government, in which cities are not only governed but also directed toward desired futures, is made possible by such linkages.

2.3.3 *Regional and Global Scale*

Applying digital twin theory to urban-regional ecologies and even planetary infrastructure systems is one of the emerging frontiers. Consider integrating several city twins to model transboundary climate migration, water shortages, or carbon trade flows, or envision a networked twin of the entire Amazon basin. Despite their technical ambition, these initiatives demonstrate the growing necessity to recognize the interconnectedness of global urbanization and to twin across national boundaries.

Digital twins start to act as meta-systems at this size, gathering, integrating, and modelling data from many ecological zones and geopolitical borders. This makes it possible to make decisions at a larger scale on matters like biodiversity preservation, interregional water distribution, and decarbonization plans for cross-border energy corridors that cannot be handled in local or even national silos. From satellite imagery and climate models to socio-political indicators and economic measurements, artificial intelligence (AI) is essential to processing the vast amount and diversity of data at this scale.

The fusion of digital twin platforms with Earth systems models creates new opportunities for planetary stewardship. By combining metrics like poverty, energy availability, and environmental degradation into a unified monitoring and simulation environment, regional twins, for instance, might be in line with the Sustainable Development Goals (SDGs) of the UN. Since the collection and analysis of environmental and human data on such scales necessitates governance frameworks that are transparent, equitable, and just, the global scale also calls for new models of digital ethics and data sovereignty.

Digital twins start to blend with Earth systems modelling at these scales, contributing to larger discussions about ecological tipping points, planetary boundaries, and the coordination of regenerative policies (Saltelli et al. 2024). They represent a new generation of digital infrastructure that is integrated into planetary systems thinking rather than being limited to urban planning. By doing this, they expand urbanism's function beyond forming cities to include co-managing the planet's life-supporting infrastructure.

These interrelated scales—from the biospheric processes of the planet to the intimate systems of a building—allow urban digital twins to realize their full potential as integrative, adaptive frameworks that connect data intelligence, human experience, physical infrastructure, and planetary governance. Their success will not just depend on technological capacity, but on the imagination and values that inspire their deployment.

2.4 Interoperability and the Role of Standards

Interoperability is one of the biggest obstacles to—and facilitators of—urban digital twins. The value of a digital twin depends on the ecosystem it can access and impact. The coherence and usability of twin platforms are threatened by fragmented data systems, proprietary software, siloed governance, and incompatible ontologies.

As digital twins develop from standalone pilots to intricate, city-wide or transboundary platforms, this difficulty becomes even more apparent. For instance, a twin created for traffic simulation could need access to population distributions, carbon emission profiles, land use data, and real-time weather feeds. The twin's usefulness and potential are reduced if these datasets are incompatible, located in various institutional jurisdictions, or are part of proprietary, black-boxed systems.

Several initiatives are under progress to provide uniform standards for data formats, APIs, spatial schemas, and digital ethics in order to combat this. The industry is moving toward more modular, reusable, and scalable twin architectures with to initiatives like the Open Geospatial Consortium (OGC) (van Rees 2013), ISO standards on smart cities, and openBIM frameworks (Pal and Hsieh 2021). These programs seek to promote cross-vendor integration, enhance platform compatibility, and reduce entry barriers. To ensure that digital twins can interact across institutional and geographic borders and that the data they generate can be trusted, reused, and shared, open ontologies and reference data models (such as CityGML, IFC, and SensorThings API) must be developed.

Interoperability must be pursued across multiple, interlocking layers:

• Technical Layers.

This is interoperability's fundamental aspect. It entails making it possible for various software and hardware systems to interact and run simultaneously. Simulation engines must be able to ingest, process, and visualize data in both real-time and asynchronous modes; sensors must be able to transmit data to cloud infrastructures; and user interfaces must be responsive, accessible, and platform-neutral (Emeakaroha et al. 2015). Technical interoperability includes precision, compatibility, and smooth operation in addition to connectivity. To lessen reliance on proprietary tools and promote innovation throughout the ecosystem, modular software architectures, open-source protocols, and loosely coupled systems are becoming increasingly popular.

Furthermore, middleware platforms, data brokers, and edge computing nodes are examples of digital infrastructure intermediaries that play a crucial role in enabling scalable technical integration. One of the key challenges of the upcoming deployment phase will be making sure algorithms can function on decentralized, heterogeneous datasets while preserving security and performance, as AI and edge analytics become increasingly integrated into digital twins.

• Institutional Layers.

Interoperability is not merely a technological hurdle—it is an institutional one. With their own goals, priorities, and data regimes, agencies, departments, utilities, private actors, and community organizations make up the various levels of government that oversee cities. A digital twin must manage this complexity and provide cooperation across frequently disjointed governance frameworks in order to operate efficiently.

Establishing shared data governance frameworks, cooperative access protocols, and interoperable planning tools that can benefit many user groups is known as institutional interoperability. Political alignment is also necessary to make sure that digital twin projects are viewed as essential resources for urban equity, environmental governance, and economic growth rather than just as the purview of IT departments. Successful examples of institutional interoperability are evident in cities like Vienna and Amsterdam, where cross-departmental digital strategies enable planning, mobility, and climate teams to access shared simulation environments and co-develop interventions based on the same data foundations.

In this case, public-private collaborations are also crucial. Since many digital twin components—such as sensors, platforms, and data analytics—are supplied by outside companies or startups, it is crucial to draft contracts that guarantee data interoperability, ownership clarity, and ethical protections. The potential to extend twin capabilities across cities and regions will be defined more by the function of legal interoperability (i.e., harmonizing regulatory frameworks across countries) and public interest technology.

• Temporal Layers.

Urban digital twins must operate across multiple timescales: immediate sensor feedback, short- to medium-term forecasting, and long-range scenario modelling. Designing systems that can synchronize these periods without sacrificing accuracy or usability is necessary to ensure temporal interoperability. A five-year infrastructure investment plan, for instance, might be informed by a digital twin used to manage traffic congestion in real time. This would necessitate integrating live sensor feeds with historical mobility data and population projections for the future.

When AI is incorporated into digital twins, temporal interoperability becomes even more important. AI models need to be tested against future scenarios, validated against current conditions, and trained on historical data. This necessitates temporally rich datasets that are also consistent over time. Without this, data drift skews or renders AI predictions unreliable. Thus, to support the temporal robustness of urban digital twins, it is imperative to develop metadata standards, time-stamping procedures, and longitudinal data governance.

• Epistemic Layers.

Moreover, interoperability is epistemic as well as technical. Finding a common interface necessitates a variety of knowledge types, from technical data to cultural narratives. In this regard, digital twins are infrastructures of translation as well as control, rendering disparate types of intelligence comprehensible to one another.

Numerous epistemologies are involved in urban planning, including legal frameworks, community knowledge, qualitative insights, quantitative models, and sensory experiences. This pluralism must be respected and incorporated into an interoperable digital twin. This could entail incorporating Indigenous place-based knowledge into spatial models, combining environmental simulations with participatory storytelling, or overlaying statistical indicators with data reported by citizens. When properly implemented, epistemic interoperability improves the digital twin outputs' legitimacy, inclusivity, and relevance. Ignoring it runs the risk of minimizing the city to what can be quantified, leaving out what is most important.

As a result of this realization, a new field known as "ethical interoperability" has emerged, in which moral integration of values parallels technical integration of systems. Growing attempts to create civic-oriented digital twin concepts that are in line with democratic values, data fairness, and public benefit mandates are reflected in initiatives like Canada's Digital Twin Charter and the European Commission's "Living-in.EU" program.

All things considered, interoperability is the glue that keeps the ecosystem of digital twins together. It is a continuous, negotiated process that is technical, institutional, temporal, and epistemic rather than a singular accomplishment. The success of digital twins will depend more on the coherence of the whole than on the intelligence of its component parts as it grows in ambition and complexity. Standards are more than just administrative requirements; they foster creativity, teamwork, and change in the cities of the future.

2.5 Digital Twins as Civic Infrastructure: Rethinking Urban Futures

For the future of urban digital twins, some form of civic imagination is required. Digital twins, in their most ambitious form, are new municipal infrastructures rather than merely tools. Similar to parks, libraries, and public transportation, they are communal assets that support life, promote inclusivity, and help cities deal with uncertainty. They are powerful not just because of what they can control or model, but also because of what they make possible, visible, and controversial. If steel and concrete shaped cities in the 20th century, data and code are reshaping cities in the 21st. However, if digital twins are only considered technical artifacts, their deeper potential will be missed. They are also social artifacts, moulded by the standards, ideals, and beliefs we instil in them.

Digital twins must be created with public values in mind, not merely technical accuracy, in order to fulfill this civic duty. Both democratic legitimacy and algorithmic correctness must be supported by their architecture. Their interfaces must be comprehensible, their operations transparent, and their outputs responsible. Their value is determined by equity as well as efficiency, just like any other civic institution. Not just in terms of demographics, but also in terms of goals, history, fears, and dreams, they must represent the variety of the communities they serve.

This reinterpretation challenges us to pose audacious queries. Can a community co-own a digital twin rather than just having it hosted by the government or run by a vendor? Can it represent cultural identities and emotional geographies instead of reducing urban life to utility consumption or movement data? Just as urban environments can be repurposed, reclaimed, or rebuilt, can it be audited, contested, and modified by the people it serves? Can it facilitate not only operational choices but also creative actions—imaginations of a city's potential rather than its current state?

How we decide to manage, create, and tell the story of these technologies will determine the answers to all these questions. A civic twin is characterized by its ability to empower multiple futures rather than by its code. It is not limited to technical excellence; it must also foster emotional resonance and ethical reflection. It enhances our capacity to understand and care for the city, not replace it.

Ownership and access must be rethought in light of this civic orientation. Even if a lot of digital twins are being created top-down by infrastructure agencies, tech companies, or municipal councils, public stewardship is essential to their long-term viability. Cooperative models, which are financed by shared investment, governed by public-private-civic partnerships, and created through participatory processes, may hold the key to the future of digital twins. Communities may soon push for increased participation in neighbourhood modelling, the transparency of predictive simulations, or the representation of local needs on city-wide platforms, much like they do when they advocate for public green space or call for improvements in public transportation.

The rise of civic digital twins has significant ramifications for design culture and urban pedagogy as well. This new reality requires us to change the way we educate design, planning, and government. Future professionals must learn to interact with digital twins as interpreters, storytellers, ethical agents, and data scientists in addition to software developers if they are to become the "living blueprints" of our cities. They must learn to ask not just "what is the system doing," but also "who benefits from the model's assumptions?" and "whose realities are represented?" Digital literacy turns into civic literacy in this situation.

Furthermore, the concept of cultural and emotional encoding in a digital twin creates a lot of creative opportunities. Imagine a digital doppelganger that records a neighbourhood's collective memory, including the music that used to be played in its plazas, the elders' stories, the rhythms of its festivals, and its protests, in addition to wind speeds and energy flows. Such a twin might serve as a storehouse of ancestry, a repository of life experiences, and a blank canvas for envisioning futures unconstrained by market forces or historical injustices.

Moving in this direction calls for a new ethics of representation in addition to technical standards. Digital twins run the potential of perpetuating current inequalities if their design is not intentionally inclusive, much how maps have traditionally distorted or excluded particular geographies and peoples. In digital form, exclusionary epistemologies, algorithmic prejudice, and data poverty can all encode unequal urban futures under the deception of impartiality. Deliberate inclusion of underrepresented data, marginalized voices, and alternate perspectives on the city is necessary to combat this.

As this book progresses, we will see how the generative dimension—AI's capacity to synthesise, propose, and learn—can enhance this civic role. By creating other urban futures, weighing moral trade-offs, and suggesting design changes that might not otherwise be thought of, generative AI holds the potential to help cities dream with data. This potential grows immensely when paired with digital twins. The twin turns become a co-creator of futures, a testing ground for the fusion of human creativity and machine learning, rather than merely a mirror of the present or a trend forecast.

However, as we consider the development and potential of digital twins, we may already see the emergence of a new urban paradigm. One in which intelligence is dispersed throughout systems, communities, and environments rather than being concentrated in a single machine. One in which care, co-creation, and accountability define governance rather than just control. One in which discussions and a common goal give meaning to data rather than mining it in a vacuum.

According to this concept, digital twins serve as a civic bridge connecting complexity and group action. They can help with ecological restoration, community empowerment, anticipatory governance, and spatial justice (Gaiba and Giovanardi 2024). But only if that is how we decide to design them. The question is not if technology will change—it will, without a doubt—but if our civic imagination will change with it. Ultimately, this chapter has demonstrated that digital twins are tools for creating urban meaning rather than just being tools for operational efficiency. They are a dynamic combination of human potential, environmental urgency, and technological competence. Reclaiming their potential as venues for ethical innovation, urban resilience, and the public good requires treating them as civic infrastructures.

In keeping with this, the upcoming chapters will explore in greater detail how generative AI and digital twins intersect, both as technological synergies and as drivers of climate-positive urban change. One fundamental realization guides our exploration of this next frontier: the twin is a dynamic process rather as a finished artifact, reflecting not just the city's physical features but also its essence.

References

Agostinelli S (2024) Optimization and management of microgrids in the built environment based on intelligent digital twins. https://iris.uniroma1.it/handle/11573/1699902

Cheshmehzangi A (2025) Advanced city: for the future of cities and opposing smart cities. Springer, Singapore

Emeakaroha VC, Fatema K, Healy P, Morrison JP (2015) Contemporary analysis and architecture for a generic cloud-based sensor data management platform. Sens. Transducers 182:100–112. https://repository.derby.ac.uk/item/933yy/contemporary-analysis-and-architecture-for-a-generic-cloud-based-sensor-data-management-platform
Gaiba A, Giovanardi M (2024) Towards interconnected "politically smart cities"? Rethinking participation from digital twins to translocal grassroots digital platforms. Riv. Digit. Polit. 4(3):485–511
Mazzetto S (2024) A review of urban digital twins integration, challenges, and future directions in smart city development. Sustainability 16(19):8337
Pal A, Hsieh SH (2021) A trend review on BIM applications for smart cities. In: Semeniv V. and Scherer R. J. (eds.) (2021) *ECPPM 2021-eWork and eBusiness in architecture, engineering and construction.* CRC, Boca Raton, pp: 391–398
Pourroostaei Ardakani S, Cheshmehzangi A (eds) (2024) Digital twin computing for urban Intelligence. Springer, Singapore
Saltelli A, Gigerenzer G, Hulme M, Katsikopoulos KV, Melsen LA, Peters GP, Pielke R Jr, Robertson S, Stirling A, Tavoni M, Puy A (2024) Bring digital twins back to Earth. Wiley Interdiscip. Rev. Clim. Chang. 15(6):e915
van Rees E (2013) Open geospatial consortium (OGC). Geoinformatics 16(8):28

Chapter 3
Generative AI: Principles, Potentials, and Ethical Dimensions

3.1 Foundations of Generative AI

From machines that only react to data to machines that can create, conjecture, and originate, the rise of generative systems represents a significant change in the development of artificial intelligence (AI) (Batty 2025). This change is not a coincidence. It signifies a fundamental shift in our perception of how robots contribute to information generation, artistic expression, and problem-solving. Fundamentally, generative artificial intelligence is a class of computational models that are intended to produce new content, such as text, images, spatial forms, or simulations. This content is not just a retrieval or interpolation of preexisting data, but rather a synthesis of patterns, structures, and relationships that can mimic, extend, or even outperform human output.

It is useful to compare generative systems to previous iterations of algorithmic intelligence to understand their importance. Explicit logic, symbolic reasoning, and preset instructions were the methods by which traditional AI systems operated, especially those employed in rule-based decision-making or predictive modelling. These systems were constrained by the completeness of their input data and the rigidity of their design logic. They couldn't really invent; they could only rank, optimize, or classify. Their performance, while occasionally astounding, was ultimately limited by what had been encoded into them, and they functioned within strictly regulated realms.

Generative systems are an exception to this rule. They use the statistical characteristics of big datasets to discover underlying structures and distributions rather than depending only on supervised mappings or deterministic rules. They serve as models for both the present and the future. In this context, the ability to synthesize coherent outputs that demonstrate novelty, diversity, and internal consistency—rather than replication—is what defines generativity. Numerous architectural advancements have enabled this increase in capabilities, each adding to a new lexicon of computational inventiveness. Large language models (LLMs), transformer-based models,

A. Cheshmehzangi, *Generative AI-Powered Urban Digital Twins*, Urban Sustainability,
https://doi.org/10.1007/978-981-95-4766-1_3

diffusion models, and generative adversarial networks (GANs) are some of the most significant. The capabilities of machines have been fundamentally altered by each of these architectures, not only incrementally.

Generative Adversarial Networks (GANs), announced in 2014, pioneered a new technique of training models (Bengesi et al. 2024) to produce synthetic data by staging a contest between two components: a generator and a discriminator. While the discriminator tries to discern between real and fake data, the generator aims to create data that resembles a training distribution. The generator learns to generate increasingly realistic outputs through iterative refining, such as representations of non-existent faces, architectural shapes that make sense based on material logic, or metropolitan layouts that adapt to limitations without being exact replicas of actual maps. GANs opened the door to a plethora of exploration in visual domains and spatial synthesis by demonstrating that machines could not only mimic but also innovate within limitations.

Transformer models introduced a new architecture that could model long-range dependencies in sequential data, and they initially appeared in the context of natural language processing. In contrast to earlier models that processed language in defined chunks, transformers use a self-attention mechanism that enables them to consider relationships between pieces in a sequence, regardless of their position. This capability allowed for revolutionary advancements in contextual reasoning, summarization, and translation by dynamically assigning meaning to different inputs. The foundation for generative systems that could generate coherent paragraphs, poems, policies, or spatial narratives that integrate planning logic, social restrictions, and environmental data was more significant.

Diffusion models, which have become more popular recently, approach generativity in a different way (Cao et al. 2024). Instead of directly mapping data, they learn to undo a slow process of noise corruption. The dynamics of order emerging from randomness are effectively learned by these models, which begin with pure noise and gradually learn to reconstruct structured data. Since order and form frequently arise through layered interactions rather than rigid hierarchies, their conceptual foundation—emergence through iteration—resonates intimately with complex systems thinking, including urbanism. Their applications have proved particularly intriguing in picture generation.

Large Language Models (LLMs) are currently the most visible type of generative AI (Barreto et al. 2023). These models, which have been trained on enormous amounts of human text, are able to predict and produce sequences that exhibit grammatical, logical, and even narrative coherence. Beneath their seeming fluency, however, is a statistical engine—a tool for mapping likely continuations using learned distributions. The importance of LLMs is found in both their cross-domain flexibility and text generation capabilities. Due to the fact that language encodes a wide variety of knowledge, including design discourse, socio-political narratives (Dhole 2023), and regulatory frameworks, LLMs act as a link between technical information and human interpretation.

These architectures work together to form the fundamental grammar of generative artificial intelligence. However, comprehending generativity is more than just a technical task. It is philosophical as well. What does the term "machine creation" mean? Is there a deeper logic of emergence at work here, or is it just recombination? Latent space, a mathematical construct where patterns, meanings, and traits are recorded in high-dimensional vectors, is where generative AI models function in real-world scenarios. The model can produce new outputs that are structurally similar to yet distinct from its training data by navigating this hidden space. The creative power of generative AI lies in its ability to work on continuous, fluid gradients of meaning and form rather than fixed categories.

Importantly, generativity is probabilistic as well. It is controlled by striking a balance between coherence and exploration. Incoherence results from too much randomness, while repetition results from too much rigidity. This balance—how much a system can innovate before becoming unintelligible, and how far it should deviate from norms—is frequently calibrated as part of the art of tuning generative models. This has significant ramifications in urban settings. When designing street networks or suggesting zoning configurations, a generative system must balance novelty and familiarity, surprise and stability, and innovation and viability.

Therefore, generative AI's roots are not just about learning to create; they are also about generating responsibly in a design space that is influenced by limitations, previous work, and desired results. These systems are collaborators with unique affordances rather than authors in the human sense. Their interface parameters, architectural presumptions, and training data all influence their outputs. If we want to effectively incorporate these principles into planning, design, and urban government, we must comprehend them.

The philosophical and architectural foundations of generative AI have been outlined in the first section of this chapter, establishing it as a new frontier in computational design and reasoning. It has demonstrated that generativity is an organized process based on teachable patterns, creative recombination, and iterative emergence rather than a mysterious phenomenon. Building on this foundation, the following sections will examine how these capabilities can be applied to urban challenges, how human oversight and collaboration can be rethought in the era of machine-aided creativity, and how ethical issues need to be addressed in the face of generative systems that are becoming more autonomous and persuasive.

3.1.1 From Algorithms to Creativity: What Makes AI Generative?

What separates a system that recognises patterns from one that creates them? A key difference between conventional AI and the emerging generation of generative models is this question, which lies at the core of generative artificial intelligence. While the latter is constructive and able to generate new combinations, scenarios, and outputs that were not present in its training data but are nonetheless logical and significant, the former is primarily reactive—classifying images, forecasting results, and identifying anomalies.

We must start with how a system learns to comprehend what makes it generative. The majority of conventional AI systems are trained using supervised learning, which involves exposing models to labelled datasets and teaching them to link particular inputs to predetermined outputs (Saravanan and Sujatha 2018). When the goal is to mimic established results, whether in fraud detection, language translation, or disease diagnosis, this method performs admirably. However, its ability to produce new information or to envision options outside training labels is constrained.

In contrast, generative AI makes extensive use of self-supervised and unsupervised learning methods. These models analyse raw data, such as millions of photos, text passages, or spatial layouts, and discover the statistical relationships contained therein, eliminating the need for labels. They create internal representations of how elements relate to one another in context rather than "memorizing" examples in the traditional sense. They can create something new and possibly unexpected by sampling from what is known through this learning process.

The idea of probabilistic sampling is a crucial component that makes this possible. Generative models produce results based on probability distributions over a large latent space rather than predetermined responses. The model chooses one path among many that strikes a balance between originality and coherence when asked to finish a sentence, sketch a building facade, or model a street network. This innate diversity is a strength rather than a weakness. It implies that every generation is a statistically informed invention rather than a deterministic replica. With the right guidance, such systems can produce an endless variety of plausible, context-aware designs.

The concept of latent space, a multidimensional mathematical abstraction that represents the characteristics, patterns, and semantic connections discovered in the training data, is essential to this procedure. Similar concepts are grouped together in a latent space, whereas dissimilar concepts are grouped farther apart. For example, different facade typologies may group together along gradients like formal symmetry, material texture, or openness in an architectural dataset. Generative models can interpolate between or beyond established styles by navigating this latent space, producing hybrid forms that are based on precedent but not constrained by it.

Additionally, creative recombination takes place in latent space. In contrast to rule-based design algorithms, generative systems have the ability to combine elements from many domains or typologies. For example, they can combine climate-responsive aspects with regional cultural themes or merge urban typologies from different regions. This recomposition of learned dimensions into new assemblages is synthesis rather than mimicry. This could entail creating building morphologies that are optimal for both daylighting and cultural orientation or suggesting zoning schemes that strike a balance between walkability, green infrastructure, and density.

Multimodal generation—the capacity of models to generate, translate, or align outputs across several data formats, including text, graphics, code, and geographical representations—represents another frontier in generativity. This ability broadens the applicability of generative AI well beyond discrete tasks. Now, a single model can produce an architectural plan, model environmental performance, or produce narrative visualisations for public interaction when given a written cue. For urban planning and design, which depend on the integration of several data types—quantitative and qualitative, visual and textual, metric and symbolic—this multimodal synthesis is especially important.

Therefore, the architecture of reasoning—the ability to model possibility spaces, navigate ambiguity, and optimize novelty without degenerating into chaos—is what distinguishes generative AI from mere output of new content. It effectively deals with uncertainty, producing outputs that are both organized and flexible, influenced by past data but not constrained by it.

A new way of thinking is required for this transition from recognition to creation and from classification to creativity. Systems are now being trained to ask new questions rather than to respond to well-known ones. This has significant ramifications for cities. It implies that AI can help with the co-design of other futures as well as the management of current urban situations. It can generate adaptive building configurations under future climate constraints, propose equitable land use scenarios, or develop culturally resonant designs from textual narratives and demographic data.

In conclusion, the dynamic interaction of probabilistic learning, latent representation, and multimodal synthesis is what distinguishes generative AI (Suzuki and Mutsuo 2022). These systems are trained to imagine within limits, to experiment within learned constraints, and to create meaningful alternatives; they are not programmed to follow orders. They offer new tools not only for automation, but for augmentation—enabling human designers, planners, and communities to explore more expansive, inclusive, and adaptive futures.

3.2 Generative AI in the Urban Context

In the urban sphere, where complexity, dependency, and uncertainty are constants, the advent of generative AI has created new opportunities. A fundamentally different paradigm is provided by generative AI, which supports speculative design, systems-level exploration, and real-time synthesis across urban scales, in contrast to traditional tools that react to fixed inputs or solve isolated tasks. Because it allows experts to ask better questions, explore broader decision spaces, and find design choices that might otherwise go unnoticed, its strength is in augmentation rather than automation. This entails changing the perception of computational tools in urbanism from passive instruments to active partners in creating more sustainable, inclusive, and adaptable cities.

Spatial design is one of the most recent fields where generative AI is becoming popular. Urban planning and architecture frequently work in very constrained environments, including scarce land, conflicting uses, legal requirements, societal expectations, and environmental imperatives (Cheshmehzangi 2022). These days, generative models—especially those trained on typological data, zoning regulations, and architectural plans—are being used to generate thousands of design variations that explore new spatial configurations while adhering to these limitations. Architects and planners can assess trade-offs between daylight and density, privacy and connectivity, and energy efficiency and cost at a never-before-seen speed and scale thanks to this method, called design space exploration.

Generative algorithms, for example, can suggest unit layouts in home design that maximize natural ventilation while satisfying fire egress and accessibility regulations. They can produce block layouts in wider precinct planning that adapt to pedestrian movements, sun access, and the distribution of green space—all in response to changing environmental goals or demographic demands. By traversing large solution areas, generative AI complements design agency rather than replaces it, providing a more creative and knowledgeable foundation for decision-making.

In addition to physical form, generative systems are also changing practice in the field of planning optimization. It can be challenging to react swiftly to changing urban conditions because traditional planning models frequently rely on static scenarios and incremental updates. On the other hand, alternative land use patterns, transportation systems, or zoning arrangements that support strategic objectives like social inclusion, transit-oriented development, or carbon neutrality can be simulated and suggested by generative models.

One such example is the redesign of transportation corridors using generative models and reinforcement learning. These systems investigate how alternative interventions, like redistributing road space, altering land use intensities, or implementing micro-mobility, might result in more resilient, equitable, or efficient outcomes rather than just projecting future traffic volumes. These simulations are strategic provocations rather than deterministic plans because they increase the number of conceivable possibilities and encourage more proactive forms of government.

Particularly promising is generative AI in the context of climate adaptation. Climate-responsive urbanism necessitates adaptable, context-sensitive tactics that change over time and space, such as stormwater management, heat mitigation, and green infrastructure. To suggest adaptation measures suited to regional vulnerabilities, generative models can synthesize data on land cover, topography, urban morphology, and climate projections. These could include scenario engines that assess the cooling effects of planting trees vs reflective surfaces in various metropolitan districts, generative shading studies for extreme heat, or synthetic terrain models to mimic flood-prone areas.

Crucially, reactive resilience strategies are not the only way to use these capabilities. Additionally, they advocate for proactive design for regenerative urbanism, which plans cities to improve socio-environmental well-being and restore ecological balance rather than just withstand change. In addition to suggesting ideas for productive landscapes or sponge parks, generative models can assist in identifying underutilized parcels for ecological retrofits and simulating their long-term impacts on urban metabolism. By combining data-driven knowledge with creative design, generative AI acts as a bridge between urban possibilities and urgency.

Mobility orchestration is another area where generative AI is being used increasingly. Managing the movement of people and products in extremely dynamic metropolitan environments is a challenging issue. Adaptive mobility strategies—from the best transit timetables to dynamic lane allocations or last-mile logistics configurations—are being produced by generative models that have been trained on mobility patterns, public transportation data, and real-time sensor inputs. Generative systems can respond to interruptions, adjust to changes in behaviour, and optimize for efficiency, equity, and emissions all at once, unlike standard transport models that assume stable demand.

Crucially, expert domains are not the only areas where generative AI can be used. The way communities interact with planning processes is starting to change as a result of its capacity to facilitate participatory co-design. Residents can express their preferences, investigate spatial alternatives, and comprehend the ramifications of policy decisions with the aid of generative tools, which include interactive scenario generators, visual simulations, and natural language interfaces. For example, a community member could articulate a need for more inclusive public spaces, and a generative system could provide park layouts that accept various users, adjust to climatic conditions, and integrate local traditions.

This fusion of synthetic generation and public dialogue represents a new phase of digital democracy—one where planning is not simply presented to the public but shaped in collaboration with them. It also tackles a crucial equity issue: generative AI can close knowledge gaps that historically influence planning decisions by producing synthetic data in places with a dearth of empirical data, such as marginalized neighbourhoods.

In sum, the use of generative AI in urban settings shows a move away from deterministic modelling and toward possibility mapping. These systems are instruments for investigating, putting forth, and improving alternate futures; they are not limited to optimization within predetermined parameters. They enable designers and decision-makers to deal with complexity by combining ideas rather than simplifying them. Generative AI can act as a catalyst for more imaginative, adaptable, and inclusive urban transformation by valuing diversity and accepting uncertainty. Building on these applications, the following section will critically analyse how algorithmic agency and human authorship are evolving and how human-machine collaboration is changing the process of design itself.

3.2.1 Co-Creation or Automation? Rethinking Human-AI Collaboration

The question of whether we are co-creating with machines or progressively handing over fundamental aspects of creativity, authorship, and judgment to automated systems arises when generative AI is incorporated into the field of urban design and planning. The distinction between a tool and a collaborator becomes increasingly blurred as AI systems participate more in ideation by creating options, scenarios, and future simulations. It is no longer adequate to think of AI as a passive extension of human intent in this changing environment. We must interrogate its emerging role as an active agent in shaping the way cities are imagined, evaluated, and transformed.

Historically, design has been regarded as a deeply human endeavour that is based on creativity, ethical consideration, contextual knowledge, and intuition. This process has long been aided by computational tools, but their functions were limited to calculation, visualization, and documentation. This established hierarchy is upset by generative AI. Instead, it makes suggestions, provides alternatives, assesses parameters, and presents new possibilities, some of which even the human designer finds surprising. This poses important problems regarding authorship: who is the creator when a design is created by navigating a latent space that has been influenced by data and encoded logic? Who was the planner that triggered the model? The group that trained it? The device that produced it?

The notion of co-authorship becomes essential here—not as a metaphor, but as a structural reality of contemporary design workflows. The generative model is more than just a responsive interface in co-authored design; it actively participates in brainstorming. It contributes a different kind of intelligence to the creative process, one that is synthetic, statistical, and non-human. This reframes the role of the human creator rather than diminishing it. The designer becomes more of a curator, director, and interpreter of generative results rather than just an idea creator. The interaction—between suggestion and intention, between framing and emergence—becomes the new site of creation instead of the mind.

This change creates new dynamics in the workflow. AI-augmented workflows are iterative, non-linear, and probabilistic, in contrast to traditional design, which frequently follows a linear process from brief to concept to refining. In just a few minutes, a designer may produce hundreds or even thousands of possibilities, assess them using performance indicators or user input, then reword the prompt and produce once more. The tempo and logic of design are changed by this cycle of creation, criticism, and regeneration. Timelines are shortened, the design space is increased, and a new kind of agility is introduced. However, it also increases the risk of overproduction, which includes an excessive number of options, a lack of reflection, and a deterioration of design thinking's narrative continuity.

The epistemic change brought about by generative AI is another important factor to take into account. Human designers use situated judgment, cultural knowledge, intuition, and precedent. On the other hand, generative systems work by finding patterns in high-dimensional spaces and creating extrapolations or interpolations. They encode links between form and function, density and access, and environment and usage, but they do not "understand" cities. This indicates that their outputs are believable, frequently graceful, but occasionally lacking in context. A roadway network may maximize flow while disregarding regional norms or unofficial uses, whereas a facade may be aesthetically pleasing but culturally inappropriate. Synthetic coherence devoid of cultural nuance is the danger here.

It is necessary to actively control this difference in epistemologies. Machine-generated recommendations are not always neutral or context-free. Training data, which represents prevailing paradigms and historical patterns, shapes their generativity. If not controlled appropriately, this might lead to the recurrence of spatial biases—amplifying car-centric design, repeating discriminatory zoning, or neglecting vernacular traditions. Therefore, in addition to actively guiding outputs, human designers also need to actively question inputs: what data was used to train the model? Whose values are encoded by it? What omissions could it hide?

Instead of picking between human and machine agency, it would be more beneficial to develop constructive asymmetry, which is a strategy that makes use of each party's advantages without erasing their differences. In addition to proposing new formal procedures and optimizing for multi-dimensional constraints, machines are capable of rapidly exploring large design areas. Humans contribute cultural fluency, aesthetic sensibility, moral reasoning, and contextual intelligence. When they engage in constructive tension rather than one replacing the other, the creative process gets richer.

But this is not just a technical link. Educational frameworks, professional conventions, and institutional cultures all influence it. Schools of architecture and planning must change if AI is to become a true collaborator. In order to encourage students to critically interact with generating systems rather than merely operate them, curricula must incorporate both technical literacy and ethical inquiry. Hierarchical authorship must give way to more distributed and iterative production models in professional practice, where concepts are discussed and agreed upon rather than imposed.

The wider implication is that the whole identity of design professions is called into question by co-creation with AI. It requires discernment—the capacity to assess, contextualize, and improve what machines produce—and humility—the understanding that creativity is no longer solely the purview of human minds. Additionally, it creates new areas for interdisciplinary collaboration, such as between data scientists and urban planners, between computational theorists and architects, and between communities and digital platforms. New kinds of authorship, such as situated, plural, and shared authorship, may arise in these hybrid spaces.

Ultimately, the question is not if AI will become a design partner—it has—but rather how we will shape that collaboration. Will it expand our creative potential or limit it by becoming overly dependent on it? Will it democratise design expertise, or consolidate it in the hands of platform owners and proprietary systems? Will it flatten urban life into globalized templates, or will it reflect its diversity?

These issues continue to be crucial as we go more into the moral implications of generative systems in the following section. Collaboration requires cultivation, governance, and ongoing questioning; it is not a given.

3.3 Ethical Frontiers: Bias, Opacity, and Autonomy in Generative Systems

Generative AI systems are not neutral tools when they enter the fields of urban planning, design, and governance; rather, they are agents with values, risks, and unexpected outcomes. These systems' ability to generate, propose, and simulate is unparalleled, but so are the moral conundrums they present. These issues are crucial to future cities' legitimacy, safety, and equity; they are not incidental. Therefore, a rigorous examination of generative AI's ethical frontiers—algorithmic bias, systemic opacity, disinformation, and the autonomy of machine-led decision-making—must go hand in hand with its implementation.

Perhaps the most obvious and well-documented risk in AI systems is algorithmic bias, and generative models are not an exception. They naturally inherit the hierarchies, inequities, and exclusions present in existing datasets since they pick up patterns from them. This has significant ramifications for the urban setting. A generative model is likely to replicate past planning choices that have marginalized racialized communities, excluded informal settlements, or favoured car-centric development in its outputs—often in the name of objective optimization or technical neutrality.

A generative design tool for housing distribution, for instance, can prioritize land-use efficiency and cost-effectiveness over social cohesiveness, accessibility for people with impairments, or extended family living customs. The model's recommendations will reflect the homogeneity of the training data if there is little variation in the types of dwellings or neighbourhood typologies. Even worse, even when the outputs contain blatant inequities, they may have an air of authority or reason that makes them hard to contest.

The risk in this case is not that the system will make mistakes, but rather that those errors will be concealed and encoded into outputs that seem to be socially detrimental but are technically sound. The decisions we make about who gets to live where, what is valued in the urban form, and whose needs are deemed legitimate are shaped by epistemic bias, which turns into an infrastructure. The issue of opacity is closely related to prejudice. Generative systems are frequently referred to as "black boxes," especially those that are based on deep learning architectures. Even the engineers who construct them find it challenging to understand how they operate internally. There are serious issues with accountability because of this lack of transparency. Decisions are discussed, recorded, and open to public review under conventional planning procedures. However, layers of algorithmic inference and probabilistic logic may mask the reasoning behind a zoning proposal or infrastructure plan that is based on an AI model.

Opacity is a democratic issue, not just a technological one. Communities cannot challenge or have an impact on decisions if they do not comprehend the decision-making process. This breaches procedural justice standards and erodes societal trust in public-sector applications. Furthermore, it becomes impossible to audit judgments, fix mistakes, or identify the causes of bad results in the absence of explainability procedures. This is particularly risky when generative systems are employed for predictive governance or policy simulation in addition to design inspiration.

The concept of hallucination—a term used to characterize generative outputs that seem believable but factually or logically incorrect—is another new ethical frontier. This can seem as fabricated citations or deceptive policy summaries in text-based systems. In spatial situations, hallucinations may result in designs that generate infrastructure parts that do not exist, violate building rules, or misrepresent environmental conditions. These hallucinations can cause harm in the real world when they infiltrate decision-making processes, whether through workflows that are not adequately supervised or over-trusted tools.

The stakes are particularly high in situations that are changing quickly, like climate adaptation or post-disaster recovery. A synthetic projection or hallucinated map could cause interventions to be directed in the wrong direction or mislead the allocation of vital resources. Additionally, the risk of disinformation is increased when artificial data is used to fill in the gaps in empirical datasets, which frequently occur in underrepresented communities. Despite its strength, synthetic urban data needs to be properly labelled, carefully evaluated, and integrated into governance frameworks that are able to discern between reality and approximation.

However, the autonomy of generative systems—especially when they start to inform or even make decisions about planning and governance—poses perhaps the most existential ethical conundrum. Any partial delegation of authority to an AI system necessitates a redistribution of power. Even though this redistribution may be effective, it also replaces reasoning, gut feeling, and group judgment. Algorithmic governance is already evident in several smart city projects, where real-time technologies manage zoning changes, energy pricing, and dynamic tolling with little human intervention.

Efficiency's appeal must be balanced with the decline of public reasoning. Cities are moral, social, and political ecologies in addition to being technical systems. Urban form, access, and mobility decisions include more than simply math; they also involve compromise, negotiation, and confrontation. The historical memory, lived experience, and ethical nuance required for such decisions cannot be replicated by generative AI. However, by structuring options, limiting possibilities, or giving preference to some logics over others, it can change the circumstances in which those judgments are made.

Although slight, this framing power is significant. Although a generative model may not recommend the construction of a high-rise, it does limit the options by omitting low-rise or mixed-use alternatives. Even though it might not advocate for the removal of informal settlements, if its optimization processes favor formal land tenure, that result is subtly included into the design space. These are subtle structures of exclusion created by omission rather than purpose; they are not overt forms of discrimination.

A more comprehensive ethical framework that incorporates algorithmic openness, data diversity, participatory monitoring, and regulatory safeguards is required to address these issues. This includes working with local communities to co-create training datasets, institutionalizing explainability criteria, and creating audit methods. It also necessitates a shift in mindset: from considering generative AI as a neutral tool to recognising it as a moral actor within bigger systems of power and injustice.

Ethical clarity is not a luxury in urban planning and design, since choices have a lasting impact on generations. Although generative systems may have remarkable possibilities, their implementation must adhere to values that prioritize civic agency in city-making, safeguard the most vulnerable, and reveal the invisible. As we turn to questions of governance and accountability in the next section, we carry forward this ethical imperative: that intelligence, no matter how advanced, must serve justice—not the other way around.

3.4 Governance, Accountability, and the Ethics of Urban Intelligence

Establishing governance frameworks that guarantee generative AI systems stay accountable, explicable, and in line with public values is becoming more necessary as these systems play a bigger role in determining urban futures—whether through modelling spatial scenarios, suggesting interventions, or influencing policy. The institutional structures that generative AI functions inside shape, mediate, and either restrain or exacerbate the ethical frontiers that were previously discussed: bias, opacity, and autonomy. Therefore, governance is not a post-mortem. It is the foundation upon which urban intelligence's morality and civic legitimacy are established.

Generative AI systems are flexible, adaptive, and frequently self-learning in contrast to traditional urban technologies, which are usually restricted in scope and subject to rules. They are both powerful and unpredictable due to their ability to synthesize across domains, change with new data, and quickly produce high-impact results. A multi-layered governance strategy that includes institutional norms, technological standards, legal regulation, and participatory oversight procedures is required due to this dual nature. Such governance must be especially strong, open, and inclusive in urban areas where decisions are influenced by infrastructure, identity, ecology, and equity.

Auditability is a fundamental tenet of AI system governance. This is the ability to track and examine a model's training process, data usage, decision-making process, and evolution over time. Auditability is crucial for institutional accountability when employing generative urban technologies, whether they are employed to create infrastructure layouts or model housing schemes. Urban planning is a public activity by nature, and when automated technologies are used, its inner workings must be transparent, especially when impacted groups want to understand, challenge, or appeal results.

But auditability isn't enough on its own. Additionally, systems ought to be explicable. Humans, particularly non-technical stakeholders, must be able to understand the technical choices made by generative models, such as choosing a design option, ranking interventions, or allocating resources. Explainable AI (XAI), which aims to give comprehensible explanations for model outputs, falls under this category. Explainability serves a democratic purpose in urban administration by allowing professionals, people, and politicians to evaluate the reasoning behind AI-generated suggestions and, if required, to contest them.

When AI judgments lack explainability, they turn into what sociologist Langdon Winner referred to as "technological politics"—decisions made by computers that have an impact on people but are not subject to democratic scrutiny. For instance, the justifications for a generative model's advice to reallocate park space to housing in a dense district must be understandable to elected officials, community organizers, and urban residents in addition to data scientists.

This leads directly to the question of public accountability. When a generative system generates an output that is harmful, incorporates exclusion, or turns out to be defective, who bears the blame? Legally speaking, accountability for AI-driven judgments is frequently ambiguous and divided among platform suppliers, developers, data sources, and the local governments that use them. The social compact between local governments and their citizens is weakened by such dispersal. Therefore, it is necessary to formalize accountability mechanisms, which entails defining liability, guaranteeing redress channels, and integrating institutional roles for supervision at every phase of the AI lifecycle, from acquisition and training to implementation and improvement.

Global regulatory frameworks are starting to take shape, which is encouraging. For instance, the EU Artificial Intelligence Act divides AI systems into risk categories and imposes more stringent regulations on high-risk systems, such as those utilized in public services, urban transportation, and essential infrastructure. Applications of generative AI in urban planning would probably come within this regulation's categories that demand strict documentation, transparency, and human monitoring. The EU AI Act is one of the most extensive legislative remedies to the problems presented by intelligent systems in the public domain, even though it is still being negotiated.

At the same time, city governments are developing civic charters and urban AI principles. Cities such as Helsinki, Barcelona, and Amsterdam have enacted digital rights charters that contain clauses pertaining to data sovereignty, algorithmic transparency, and participatory governance. These charters are not merely symbolic—they reflect a growing commitment to aligning technological innovation with democratic values. In order to reveal the locations and methods of algorithm usage in planning, public administration, and service delivery, some cities have now started to publish registries of automated decision systems. These kinds of registers aid in establishing trust and institutionalizing transparency.

However, even though legal and regulatory measures are important, participatory supervision mechanisms must be used in addition to them. Only from above can the ethics of urban intelligence be protected. They need systems that enable citizens to actively participate in the governance of AI systems, especially those that influence public space, housing, mobility, and spatial justice. Public hearings on the deployment of generative systems in sensitive areas, community co-design of training datasets, and citizen juries on algorithmic planning decisions are a few examples of participatory methods. From collective reasoning to machine-led simulation, these models broaden the definition of urban intelligence.

Furthermore, civic engagement contributes to epistemic richness in addition to legitimacy. Generative systems frequently lack access to the kind of local information that communities hold, such as historical memory, cultural customs, and everyday experience. The contextual accuracy and fairness of generative tools are improved when these ideas are incorporated into their training, assessment, and improvement. In this way, involvement is a benefit rather than a surrender.

To be truly ethical, governance must also be adaptive. The institutions that oversee generative systems also need to change quickly. Static regulations will not suffice. Dynamic feedback loops are required, including cross-sectoral learning platforms, continuous review procedures, and regulatory sandboxes that permit risky experimentation without sacrificing accountability. Urban AI needs to develop into a living governance domain that adapts to changing public values and sociopolitical demands in addition to technical advancements.

In conclusion, institutional architecture will have just as big of an impact on the ethics of generative AI in cities as technical design. The nexus of algorithmic power and democratic principles is governance. AI's ability to make cities more inclusive, resilient, and just will depend on our ability to integrate intelligence into strong ethical frameworks rather than just how well models perform. This framework needs to be reflective, participatory, legal, and procedural—it should be designed for people as well as for systems. In this chapter's last section, we turn to the future and examine what it means to create reflective, regenerative, and civically imaginative urban intelligences rather than just smart or ethical systems.

3.5 Toward Reflective and Responsible Urban Futures

It is evident as we wrap up this chapter on the fundamentals, possibilities, and moral implications of generative AI that speed, scale, or technological superiority by themselves will not determine the future of intelligent cities. It needs to be driven by introspection—a purposeful, continuous investigation into the types of urban futures we are creating, for whom, and with what resources. Generative AI has the potential to speed up problem-solving, broaden creative perspectives, and reveal hitherto unthinkable answers (Cheshmehzangi and Ardakani 2024). However, that power runs the potential of being misused—to reinforce inequality, automate injustice, or put efficiency ahead of compassion—in the absence of a thoughtful civic framework.

Reflective AI urbanism is a new paradigm that is starting to take shape. Responsible AI governance is only one aspect of this; another is incorporating deeper values into the development and application of generative systems. It challenges us to think of intelligence in a pluralistic way, moving past the human versus machine dichotomy. Cities are places of meaning, memory, conflict, and care in addition to being technical systems. Therefore, the diversity of urban knowledge—from climate science to cultural history, from lived experience to Indigenous worldviews—must be acknowledged and respected when designing AI in urban settings.

To do this, automation must give way to augmentation. Instead of displacing urban knowledge or civic discernment, generative AI could be viewed as enhancing them. Its strength is its ability to expand our perspective, allowing us to see more options, variables, and configurations. However, this abundance necessitates the use of discernment, or what Daniel Kahneman referred to as "slow thinking". Reflectiveness slows us down in the right places during our haste to innovate: when it comes to democratic duty, ethical ambiguity, and spatial consequences. It challenges us to consider not just what the model is capable of, but also whether we ought to act upon its recommendations and whether they are in line with the general welfare.

This also means embracing *plural epistemologies*. The understanding that every city is covered with various ways of knowing and being must take the place of the myth of a universal, objective metropolis. Despite their strength, generative systems are frequently trained on normative information and dominant narratives. They run the risk of homogenizing urban variety if nothing is done. The question of whose data is incorporated is one that reflective urban AI raises. What are the modelled realities? Who is excluded? The governance, instruction, and use of generative tools must be influenced by the responses to these questions.

When used properly, generative AI can foster both civic creativity and operational efficiency. Cities can use it to test audacious ideas, practice other futures, and investigate flexible approaches to uncertainty. However, human hands must continue to control imagination. The objective is to create cities that become increasingly sensitive to the intricacies and paradoxes of urban life, not ones that react automatically to preset measures. This entails creating structures that encourage communication, highlight trade-offs, and provide room for dissent, flexibility, and innovation.

Our urban future, which is characterized by social disintegration, the climatic catastrophe, and technological disruption, calls for tools that are not just clever but also inclusive, responsible, and modest. The goal of reflective AI urbanism is not to solve the city's problems. Instead, it strengthens our ability as a group to manage it: to balance conflicting demands, to make room for disputed ideals, and to respect the dynamic nature of urban life.

In this way, generative AI transcends its status as a technological innovation and becomes a social initiative. It is a tool for envisioning what might be as well as a mirror of what is. Not merely a prediction system, but also a reflection companion. Additionally, it serves as a catalyst for moral, inclusive, and regenerative urban transformation in addition to being a solution engine. This is our time's (shared) opportunity and responsibility.

References

Barreto F, Moharkar L, Shirodkar M, Sarode V, Gonsalves S, Johns A (2023) Generative artificial intelligence: opportunities and challenges of large language models. In: Balas V E, Bhaskkar Semwal V, and Khandare A. (eds.) (2023) *International conference on intelligent computing and networking*. Springer Nature Singapore, Singapore, pp 545–553. https://link.springer.com/chapter/10.1007/978-981-99-3177-4_41

Batty M (2025) Generative AI. Environ Plan B Urban Anal City Sci 52(5):1031–1034

Bengesi S, El-Sayed H, Sarker MK, Houkpati Y, Irungu J, Oladunni T (2024) Advancements in generative AI: a comprehensive review of GANs, GPT, autoencoders, diffusion model, and transformers. IEEE Access 12:69812–69837

Cao H, Tan C, Gao Z, Xu Y, Chen G, Heng PA, Li SZ (2024) A survey on generative diffusion models. IEEE Trans Knowl Data Eng 36(7):2814–2830

Cheshmehzangi A (2022) Exploring prospects to strengthen the nexus between ICT, cities, and positive peace: limitations, challenges, and future directions. In: Cheshmehzangi A (2022) *ICT, cities, and reaching positive peace*. Springer Nature Singapore, Singapore, pp 219–235.

Cheshmehzangi A, Pourroostaei Ardakani S. (2024) Embracing the digital twin paradigm for urban sustainability. In: Pourroostaei Ardakani S. and Cheshmehzangi A. (eds.) (2024) *Digital twin computing for urban intelligence*. Springer Nature Singapore, Singapore, pp 1–11.

Dhole K (2023) Large language models as sociotechnical systems. In: Proceedings of the big picture workshop, December 2023, pp. 66–79

Saravanan R, Sujatha P (2018) A state of art techniques on machine learning algorithms: a perspective of supervised learning approaches in data classification. In: 2018 second international conference on intelligent computing and control systems (ICICCS). IEEE, pp 945–949

Suzuki M, Matsuo Y (2022) A survey of multimodal deep generative models. Adv Robot 36(5–6):261–278

Chapter 4
Integrating AI with Urban Digital Twins: Architecture and Infrastructure

4.1 Converging Systems: The Architectural Logic of Integration

It takes more than just technological convergence to integrate generative AI with urban digital twins; it requires architecture. It necessitates the meticulous assembling of systems that vary in logic, temporality, and epistemology in addition to shape and function. One uses inference, pattern synthesis, and prediction, while the other uses simulation, feedback, and representation. Data interchange alone is not enough to coordinate these systems. It requires architectural coherence—a common framework that allows them to communicate, react, and change together.

To ensure that cities are sensed, modelled, and understood consistently across technical layers, there are two imperatives at the core of this integration: first, synchronizing computational architectures across AI models and digital twin systems; and second, harmonizing knowledge frameworks. Intelligent urban infrastructures are built on this dual integration of meaning-to-meaning and machine-to-machine. It makes cognitive compatibility—a mutual intelligibility between the intricacies of the city and the logics of code—possible in addition to functional interoperability.

The understanding that generative AI and digital twins are physically distinct but operationally complimentary is the first step in the architectural logic of integration (Gebreab et al. 2024). Digital twins have temporal and spatial anchors. As dynamic, data-rich models, they depict the operational, behavioural, and physical aspects of urban systems, including buildings, transportation patterns, energy grids, and demographics. Their reactivity and fidelity—the capacity to simulate future conditions and reflect the city in real-time—are their strongest points.

In contrast, generative AI is not bound by the real world or even the present. It is focused on what is feasible. It uses learnt patterns to generate novel configurations, scenarios, or hypotheses by drawing from large latent spaces. A new urban operational layer is created when both capacities are combined—when the twin's reactive

A. Cheshmehzangi, *Generative AI-Powered Urban Digital Twins*, Urban Sustainability,
https://doi.org/10.1007/978-981-95-4766-1_4

intelligence and AI's speculative intelligence come together. One that is both realistic and creative, rooted in the present while having the ability to suggest flexible, innovative possibilities.

However, such convergence is not a natural occurrence. It needs to be designed. Building interfaces and pipelines that enable AI models to seamlessly interact with digital twin environments is what this entails on a computational level. The live, structured data streams that twins generate—from satellite feeds to IoT sensors, from BIM models to traffic logs—are necessary for generative AI to access (Filippova et al. 2025). On the other hand, the twin needs to be able to absorb, contextualize, and visualize AI-generated outputs, whether they are policy scenarios, synthetic data, or spatial designs. The integration stays surface-level—two systems operating in parallel but not communicating—in the absence of strong data orchestration and model alignment.

At this point, the synchronization architecture becomes crucial. Digital twins work on geographical and infrastructure realities, while AI models work on abstracted, frequently high-dimensional feature spaces. Mapping between these layers is necessary for integration in order to guarantee consistent alignment of temporal resolutions, units of measurement, spatial references, and semantic labels. If the twin operates at the parcel level, the generative model's district-level zoning suggestion may need to be translated, layered, or interpolated in order to be useful. Accuracy in this translation is not just technical; it is essential to the reliability of decisions made by AI.

Deeper integration at the epistemological level is required, going beyond just synchronizing computational systems (Vallverdú i Segura 2009). This entails bringing the presumptions, classifications, and interpretive frameworks that support each system's perception of the city into line. Urban knowledge is diverse and includes social behaviours, natural processes, political purposes, cultural histories, and engineering logics. AI, which has been primarily trained on patterns and proxies, may introduce biases or blind spots into this mix that run counter to the logic inherent in the twin.

A local twin could need to take into account indigenous land uses or informal economies, whereas a generative model trained on global datasets might prioritize formal infrastructure (Xu et al. 2024). The integrated output runs the danger of being deceptive or incompatible if semantic alignment is not maintained, which guarantees that terms like "public space," "resilience," and "mobility" have the same meaning across systems. Achieving this requires ontological harmonisation: the creation of shared vocabularies, taxonomies, and data schemas that bridge the diverse epistemologies of urban knowledge and machine learning.

This is an act of translation, negotiation, and co-production rather than just data organization. To make sure that complexity is visible, actionable, and just rather than flattened out, engineers, planners, sociologists, and data scientists must collaborate. Integration thus becomes both a cultural and a technical barrier. "How do we connect the systems?" "Whose knowledge do they represent?" and "How do we make the city intelligible to both humans and machines without erasing its multiplicity?" are some of the questions it poses.

Ultimately, coherence across systems, scales, and modes of knowing is what the architectural logic of integration is all about. It involves creating shared infrastructures of meaning rather than merely interfaces, where synthetic imagination enhances urban representation and generative possibility is linked to actual circumstances. We explore how this architecture manifests itself across cities and systems in the ensuing chapters and sections, moving from this conceptual underpinning into the infrastructural realities of sensing, computing, and interoperability.

4.2 Data Pipelines and Urban Sensing Ecosystems

A strong, ongoing, and flexible data pipeline is essential to any significant fusion of generative AI with urban digital twins. The promise of intelligent and responsive cities remains aspirational in the absence of a consistent supply of high-quality, well-structured, and context-aware data. Data is the glue that holds sensing, modelling, and decision-making together to form a dynamic, generative ecosystem. It is more than just fuel. It makes it possible for AI to make sense of a moving metropolis and for the digital twin to develop into a dynamic, learning system rather than a static representation.

Data is produced in urban settings from an astounding variety of sources, modes, and scales. This data must be collected, cleaned, converted, and contextualized using pipelines that are carefully designed in order to feed a generative AI model that can make a significant contribution to a digital twin. As the city itself changes, this process is not linear; it requires constant iteration, feedback loops, and calibration to preserve accuracy and usability.

The initial link in this chain is data acquisition. Today's urban settings are teeming with sensors, which are found in wearable technology, cell phones, automobiles, infrastructure, and buildings. Granular, time-stamped data on temperature, air quality, traffic flow, energy use, noise levels, and other topics are produced by these Internet of Things (IoT) devices. Simultaneously, mobile sensing platforms—such as personal mobile phones, drones, or bus fleets—offer distributed and adaptable sensing capabilities that enable real-time micro-level pattern detection. Increasingly available through commercial providers and open data initiatives, satellite imagery and aerial photogrammetry offer citywide views at regular intervals, facilitating large-scale environmental monitoring, land use detection, and change analysis.

A crucial layer of social and behavioural knowledge is added by crowdsourced data, despite its more changeable structure and dependability. Residents can add local knowledge, give meaning to space, and draw attention to things that automated systems might overlook, like unofficial transit routes, public opinion, or the lived experience of infrastructure deterioration, by using platforms like OpenStreetMap, Google Reviews, and participatory planning tools (Akkaya et al. 2024). These human-sourced signals are frequently more reliable and timely than official records in metropolitan settings that are unstable or undergoing fast change.

But cleaning, enriching, and synchronizing data from disparate sources is just as difficult as gathering it. Data streams frequently arrive in partial states, different units, and inconsistent formats. Time latency, data sparsity, and sensor drift can all add bias and noise. To be feasible in real-time systems, cleaning necessitates extensive pre-processing, including noise filtering, outlier detection, temporal alignment, and imputation of missing values. All of these steps must be automated at scale. Spatial-temporal tagging, integration with contextual layers (such demographic profiles or zoning data), and conversion into formats that may be used by models are all part of enrichment (Niu and Silva 2023). In actuality, this entails not just standardizing sensor logs but also adding metadata, such as the source, degree of confidence, and frequency of updates.

When designing efficient data pipelines, the issue of temporal and spatial granularity is crucial. From local junctions to regional transportation corridors, from minute-by-minute mobility patterns to multi-decade climate projections, generative AI and digital twins' function at numerous scales at the same time. Data must be appropriately aggregated or disaggregated. While a planning simulation might use weekly averaged socioeconomic variables at the neighbourhood level, a model forecasting heat island effects might need thermal data at 10-meter resolution and 15-min intervals. Advanced data fusion techniques, which merge datasets with varying resolutions without causing distortion or deleting important detail, are necessary to align these granularities.

Urban intelligence also needs to deal with unpredictability. No sensor is error-proof, and no dataset is flawless. To measure and manage uncertainty, probabilistic models—such as ensemble methods or Bayesian networks—are crucial for finding areas of inadequate data coverage, generating confidence intervals, and flagging abnormalities. In order to make uncertainty a recognized and traceable aspect of every analytical output, these models must be included into the data pipeline itself rather than added after the fact. This is particularly crucial in urban settings because choices have practical repercussions; for instance, a poorly predicted flood risk may result in disastrous planning errors.

There are two aspects of uncertainty in the context of generative AI. On the one hand, it is a limitation, reducing the accuracy of model results and the dependability of forecasts. It is a generating opportunity, however. Instead of being anchored to a particular projected route, it enables models to investigate a range of conceivable futures. AI can use techniques like scenario generation, stochastic sampling, and multi-model simulation to approach uncertainty as a design area to explore rather than as a problem to solve.

This leads to questions of data governance. Controlling who owns, accesses, and uses data is increasingly important as it becomes more and more integral to AI-twin systems. The demands of privacy and openness, security and usefulness, and public value and commercial interest must all be balanced in urban data governance. Data justice must be taken into consideration, making sure that underprivileged groups are not unfairly surveyed, misrepresented, or left out of the data that influences their surroundings. The lineage of data—how, by whom, for what purpose, and under what conditions—must be addressed by governance. This openness is essential for the verifiability and reliability of AI-generated results in addition to maintaining ethical integrity.

The establishment of data trusts or civic data commons—organizations that manage urban data as a shared resource with collaborative accountability and participatory oversight—is an emerging best practice in this field. These groups help to institutionalise transparency, restrict platform access, and guarantee that data practices match with civic values rather than economic motivations alone. Any AI-twin integration's capacity to succeed ultimately rests on how robust, flexible, and inclusive its sensing environment is. A smart data pipeline is a municipal infrastructure, not only a piece of technology. Equality, openness, and responsiveness must be prioritized just as much as speed, resolution, or scalability. When properly planned, these pipelines enable the city to sense itself—across movement and memory, across air and stone—and to convert that awareness into thoughtful, creative action.

We examine the processing, computing, and operationalization of these data flows in the following part, outlining the computational framework supporting scalable, intelligent, and responsive AI–digital twin ecosystems.

4.3 Computation at the Edge and in the Cloud

In addition to complex algorithms and rich data ecosystems, the confluence of generative AI and urban digital twins necessitates robust and flexible computing infrastructure. Cities must function across a distributed computing landscape in order to digest the massive, ongoing, and diverse streams of urban data—and to produce insights in real time. Cloud computing, edge computing, and increasingly hybrid architectures that allow for high-speed responsiveness while guaranteeing scalability, security, and efficiency define this environment.

Data-driven urbanization has long relied on cloud computing. Centralised cloud platforms offer high storage capacity, scalable compute power, and access to advanced AI models that require significant GPU and memory resources. Cloud servers can hold generative models that learn from multi-year, multi-modal urban datasets, handle historical data archives, and oversee large-scale simulations in the context of digital twins. Coordination is also made easier by cloud environments, which give researchers, developers, and city departments remote access to twin platforms' dashboards, visualizations, and analytical tools.

However, latency is a significant drawback of cloud-based computing. The delay caused by sending data to and from distant servers can reduce the efficacy of applications that require instant feedback, like autonomous vehicle routing, emergency response coordination, or traffic signal optimization. In these situations, speed is essential rather than a luxury.

At this point, edge computing becomes crucial. The term "edge computing" describes the placement of computational resources nearer to the actual data source, such as a local controller integrated into a building's HVAC system, a street sensor, or a security camera. By processing data at or near the point of collection, edge systems reduce the time between sensing and response, enabling real-time decision-making that does not rely on constant cloud connectivity. Without waiting for commands from a central server, an edge-enabled camera at a pedestrian crossing, for instance, can recognize activity and initiate a safety procedure in milliseconds.

Edge computing acts as a link between digital abstraction and physical reality in urban digital twins. It enables the twin to maintain responsiveness even in situations when localized processing is necessary due to data privacy concerns or when cloud connection is sporadic. By sending just summarized or prioritized data into the central twin model, edge devices can perform fundamental AI tasks on-site, such as item recognition, anomaly detection, or environmental monitoring. While maintaining a certain level of intelligence at the urban periphery, this hierarchical architecture reduces the strain on central systems. However, the full spectrum of computing needs imposed by AI-twin ecosystems cannot be met by either cloud or edge alone. Most cities need hybrid architectures that integrate distributed edge intelligence with centralized cloud storage. According to this concept, the edge facilitates lightweight inference, quick reaction, and pre-filtering, while the cloud houses the generative models, deep learning pipelines, and intricate simulations. Careful coordination is needed to synchronize these layers, making sure that feedback loops, model versions, and data schemas stay in sync throughout time and space.

Federated learning, a method that enables AI models to be trained across numerous edge devices or local nodes without aggregating the data in a central repository, is also made possible by this hybridization. Each device trains a model using its local data in federated learning, and only the model updates—not the data itself—are shared and combined in the cloud. This method has several benefits, including protecting data privacy, cutting down on network bandwidth, and enabling models to learn from various urban settings without distorting local facts.

In regional or multi-jurisdictional metropolitan systems with disparate data governance policies or unequal internet connectivity, federated solutions are especially pertinent. Digital twins in these networks can function somewhat independently while still adding to a common learning framework, facilitating intercity cooperation without enforcing central authority. For example, a federated AI that adjusts to local topographies, climatic patterns, and infrastructure weaknesses can be informed by flood prediction models that have been trained in several coastal cities.

The energy footprint of AI computing must be taken into account in addition to technological architecture. Large-scale generative models require a lot of resources to train and run, and as cities strive for net-zero status, computational sustainability becomes a design requirement in and of itself (Cheshmehzangi and Ardakani 2024). While cloud providers are investing more in green data centers and carbon-conscious workload management, edge computing can cut down on pointless data transfers and idle compute. High performance and environmental accountability are both necessary for the ethical integration of AI and digital twins.

Lastly, resilience needs to be considered when designing computational infrastructure. Power outages, cyberattacks, or natural disasters can all interrupt the flow of data and the ongoing computation in a city. By decentralizing operations, distributed computing models add a certain amount of redundancy and fault tolerance. Local processing can sustain minimum operations when networks go down, and other nodes can compensate when one fails. This decentralization is consistent with the city's networked, diverse, and adaptable logic.

In conclusion, more than just computational skill is required for the AI-twin integration. Its foundation is a quick, adaptable, and context-aware computational architecture that facilitates both long-term learning and real-time response. Cities can create a foundation for intelligent operations that are both technologically sound and rooted in civics by integrating cloud and edge, central and distributed, generative and reactive systems. The standards, protocols, and interoperability frameworks that enable such integration to be inclusive, transparent, and scalable across various urban contexts are discussed in the section that follows.

4.4 Standards, Protocols, and System Interoperability

Interoperability becomes crucial as urban digital twins develop from isolated pilots into intricate, citywide platforms and as generative AI becomes increasingly integrated into planning, simulation, and governance procedures. Fundamentally, interoperability is the ability of various actors, devices, and systems to cooperate—to exchange, understand, and use data in a meaningful way across institutional and technical barriers. It is the architecture of collaboration, not just a characteristic of technical systems. Integration is unsustainable, fractured, and superficial without it.

A common language, established by technological standards, ontologies, and data schemas, is essential to interoperability. These frameworks guarantee the efficient communication and modularity of various components, including sensors, models, software platforms, and governance tools. Such standardization is essential for preventing duplication, lowering friction, and facilitating scaling in AI-twin ecosystems, where data flows are continuous and cross-sectoral.

Ontologies specify the classification and relationships between urban things, including roads, buildings, users, and events. They provide a semantic framework that enables digital twins and AI systems to "understand" the context of data generation and interpretation. For instance, a generative model that suggests new land use allocations needs to be able to make references to ecological buffers, transit systems, and zoning categories in a way that is consistent with the internal organization of the digital twin. Collaboration between human and machine intelligences is made feasible by this semantic alignment.

The structural blueprints for data sharing and storage are known as data schemas. Widely used formats for representing three-dimensional city objects, geospatial data, and building information models (BIM) are offered by open schemas like CityGML, GeoJSON, and IFC. More sophisticated interoperability initiatives include the Open Geospatial Consortium's (OGC) SensorThings API, which provides standardized methods for integrating and accessing real-time sensor data across platforms (Cheshmehzangi et al. 2024). These tools establish the framework for composable systems—systems that can expand, adapt, and interconnect without proprietary lock-in.

But there are disparities in the interoperability landscape. Different technical regimes and governance frameworks control the operations of cities, vendors, and regions. Whereas a digital twin in Dubai might be constructed on a closed proprietary stack with little external integration, one in Helsinki might adhere to open standards and make use of interoperable APIs. Departments may employ incompatible systems, even within a single city. For example, environmental data may be stored in one format while transportation data may be in another, and there may not be a translation layer between the two. These divisions create obstacles to institutional flexibility, public transparency, and technical integration.

The conflict between monolithic design and modularity is one of the recurring issues in this field. Some suppliers provide all-in-one platforms that combine visualization, AI, simulation, and sensing into one package. Although this can make deployment easier, it frequently reduces flexibility and makes future system integration more challenging. On the other hand, cities can construct their systems piece by piece using open architectures that employ standard protocols (such as MQTT, WMS/WFS, and RESTful APIs), choosing best-in-class tools and changing over time without losing coherence.

Governance and versioning present additional difficulties. Cities require long-term stability and predictability in their infrastructure investments, but standards must be updated as technology advances (Razaghi and Finger 2018). Collaborative organizations that coordinate standard development while preserving backward compatibility, like the OGC, ISO committees, or regional urban data alliances, are necessary to manage this tension. These organizations are essential to preserving the interoperability ecosystem's integrity and trust.

Crucially, interoperability is a civic issue as well as a technical one. Standards are not neutral; they are a reflection of power dynamics, presumptions, and priorities. Interoperability frameworks unintentionally reduce urban diversity to unduly restrictive schemas when they disregard local categories, indigenous knowledge, or informal behaviours. Maintaining inclusive, transparent, and flexible norms is important for justice as well as efficiency as cities depend more on AI-driven intelligence. Moving from theoretical frameworks to practical instances of inclusive interoperability, we examine how open standards and cross-sectoral coordination might facilitate more democratic, scalable, and resilient AI-twin infrastructures in the following subsection.

4.4.1 *Open Standards and Cross-Sectoral Coordination*

Open standards serve as the foundation for long-term interoperability, innovation, and institutional resilience in the growing ecosystem of AI-powered urban digital twins. As generative AI systems are increasingly integrated into digital twins, which are becoming essential for city management and planning, the need for open, transparent, and widely recognized standards is becoming more than just a technical convenience; it is a civic imperative. Without them, platforms become siloed, integration becomes fragmented, and cities run the risk of being forced to use vendor-dependent solutions that hinder development and prevent participation.

Publicly accessible specifications created through cooperative methods are known as open standards. They specify the structure, description, and intersystem exchange of data. Cities can combine various tools, suppliers, and technologies without compromising control or coherence thanks to open standards, which are accessible, flexible, and vendor-neutral in contrast to proprietary formats. They enable departments within the same municipality to work together effortlessly using common protocols, or they enable a generative AI system trained on one dataset to function meaningfully within the digital twin of another city.

These foundations have been laid in large part by important organizations like the International Organization for Standardization (ISO) and the Open Geospatial Consortium (OGC). For spatially grounded digital twins, the OGC in particular has taken the lead in developing geospatial interoperability standards. For instance, the SensorThings API offers a standardized interface for real-time access to and integration of sensor data from various sources. This eliminates the need for specialized middleware or translation layers by allowing environmental data, traffic flow data, and energy measurements to be delivered straight into a twin and analyzed by AI.

Likewise, an OGC standard called CityGML provides a geometric and semantic data format for 3D urban environment representation. It enables the functional as well as visual description of landscape, vegetation, buildings, and roads, making them understandable to generative algorithms and simulation engines alike. Applications ranging from noise simulation to climate adaptation are supported by CityGML, which offers the framework for sharing, updating, and expanding city models over time. These models provide a basis for scenario-based design generation that is both structurally sound and context-aware when combined with generative AI.

At the same time, openBIM, which is supported by buildingSMART International, encourages the architecture, engineering, and construction (AEC) sectors to adopt non-proprietary standards. At the precinct or district level, openBIM facilitates the interchange and integration of building models with urban twins through formats such as IFC (Industry Foundation Classes). This makes it possible for generative systems to move across scales, from facade morphologies to infrastructure coordination, establishing a smooth connection between architectural design, construction management, and citywide planning.

These standards facilitate governance cooperation and are more than just technical artifacts. Aligning planning logics, simulating cross-sectoral impacts, and coordinating responses in real time are made possible when the transportation, housing, energy, and environment agencies adopt a single set of schemas and interfaces. Additionally, it facilitates more flexible regulatory frameworks that allow policy scenarios to be created, tested, and disseminated among several agencies without causing errors or duplication of effort.

Open standards also encourage market diversity and innovation. By lowering entrance hurdles, they allow academic institutions, civic tech projects, and smaller technology suppliers to connect to pre-existing platforms without having to deal with proprietary obstacles. This promotes a more inventive, competitive, and locally responsive ecosystem and democratizes access to infrastructure development. By doing this, open standards give cities the flexibility to develop their digital capabilities on their own terms, independent of static models or monolithic platforms.

Most importantly, open designs promote long-term resilience and civic transparency. Publicly stated standards facilitate knowledge transfer, citizen participation, and external auditing. They guarantee that a system's reasoning is open to scrutiny. This visibility is a democratic safeguard in a time when digital twins and AI models are influencing decisions that have long-term effects.

However, cross-sectoral cooperation is just as important to the success of open standards as their technical soundness. To agree on common frameworks, keep domains aligned, and modify standards as technology advances, city agencies, software providers, civic actors, and others must collaborate. This is a continuous institutional practice rather than a one-time endeavour. Standards must be reviewed, discussed, and updated in response to the evolving needs and values of urban communities because they are living agreements. In the upcoming chapters, we will see how these principles are operational realities rather than theoretical aspirations, and how cities may create intelligent systems that are not only efficient but also ethical, inclusive, and resilient by design thanks to open and coordinated infrastructures.

4.5 Toward a Unified Urban Intelligence Infrastructure

As generative AI moves from a peripheral innovation to embedded capability and digital twins develop from static models into dynamic engines of real-time urban simulation, it becomes imperative—not just aspirational—to integrate these systems as part of a single urban intelligence infrastructure. Software compatibility and the layering of technical components are insufficient explanations for this convergence. It necessitates a more thorough reconsideration of how we plan, construct, and oversee the fundamental pillars of the digital city.

Ad hoc connections are used to patch together AI and digital twins that are often developed in parallel by various teams and governed by distinct standards. Short-term usefulness can be achieved with these methods, but they frequently lack the cohesiveness needed for long-term scalability, durability, and public legitimacy. Co-evolution—a paradigm where AI and digital twins are not only compatible but symbiotic, co-designed from the ground up to learn, adapt, and reflect together—is what the future demands in addition to connection.

Systemic thinking is where this vision starts. It is impossible to design urban intelligence in isolation. It requires the cooperation of architecture, governance, and technology. In order for what we construct to physically reflect what we model computationally and for what we govern socially to be informed by what we simulate intelligently, the built environment, digital infrastructure, and civic systems must all be in harmony in both form and function. Cities can transition from reactive planning to anticipatory design—where infrastructure, policy, and adaptation change dynamically in response to shifting circumstances and group demands—thanks to this alignment.

To achieve this, cities must embrace a set of foundational principles for infrastructure development (See Fig. 4.1):

Resilience comes first. Distributed, redundant, and fault-tolerant systems are essential components of a unified intelligence infrastructure. It shouldn't rely on just one vendor, server, or data source. Rather, it ought to function across public and private networks, cloud and edge, and federated and centralized learning systems. Here, redundancy is strength rather than waste. Intelligent systems need to be able to degrade gracefully, recover rapidly, and adapt continuously in a world full of political unrest, climate shocks, and digital threats.

The second is design ethics. As much as intelligence is engineered, it also needs to be regulated. Instead of being added as regulatory afterthoughts, privacy, transparency, and accountability must be ingrained in the design. The system should provide public explanation mechanisms, data lineage, and auditability as standard features rather than exceptions. Twins must be contestable rather than black-boxed,

Fig. 4.1. Summary of four suggested foundational principles of infrastructure development

and AI models must be interpretable rather than opaque. Building public trust in the mechanisms that increasingly influence life at all scales is more important than merely adhering to regulations.

Third, specificity combined with scalability. Cities operate within distinct cultural, ecological, and political contexts, despite the fact that they face similar issues. Modular and flexible, a unified intelligence infrastructure may extend across precincts, cities, and regions without enforcing consistency. Interoperable APIs, open standards, and adaptable ontologies allow systems to expand while maintaining local relevance and autonomy.

Civic alignment comes last. The integration of AI and digital twins must continue to be grounded in human values. These infrastructures are civic institutions rather than just technological resources. They must be created with communities in mind, not just for them. Co-creation, inclusive governance, and participation are structural requirements rather than merely polite phrases. Instead of automating complexity, an intelligent city assists its citizens in interacting with, comprehending, and influencing it collectively.

To facilitate meaningful integration between generative AI and urban digital twins, we have described in this chapter how architecture, sensing, computing, and standards come together. However, these layers are just the beginning, not the end. They serve as the foundation for a new paradigm of urban infrastructure that is principled yet adaptable, strong yet inclusive, and clever yet modest. Such a paradigm does not replace the city—it reflects its intelligence back to itself. It provides a window into how cities can thrive as well as how they operate. We continue to examine how these foundations can help with community resilience, climate action, and the creation of smarter—but wiser—city designs in the upcoming chapters.

References

Akkaya M, Özçevik Ö, Tepe E (2024) A machine learning application to Google Maps reviews as a participatory planning tool. Int J Urban Sci 28(3):379–402

Cheshmehzangi A, Ardakani SP (2024) Embracing the digital twin paradigm for urban sustainability. In: Digital twin computing for urban intelligence. Springer Nature Singapore, Singapore, pp 1–11

Cheshmehzangi A, Batty M, Allam Z, Jones DS (2024) Conclusions and the future of city information modelling (CIM). In: City information modelling. Springer Nature Singapore, Singapore, pp 249–253

Filippova E, Hedayat S, Ziarati T, Manganelli M (2025) Artificial intelligence and digital twins for bioclimatic building design: innovations in sustainability and efficiency. Energies 18(19):5230. https://www.preprints.org/frontend/manuscript/95958065cb06561c20c2e5e72c1028e8/download_pub

Gebreab S, Musamih A, Salah K, Jayaraman R, Boscovic D (2024) Accelerating digital twin development with generative AI: a framework for 3D modeling and data integration. IEEE Access 12:185918–185936

Niu H, Silva EA (2023) Understanding temporal and spatial patterns of urban activities across demographic groups through geotagged social media data. Comput Environ Urban Syst 100:101934

Razaghi M, Finger M (2018) Smart governance for smart cities. Proc IEEE 106(4):680–689
Vallverdú i Segura J (2009) Computational epistemology and e-science: a new way of thinking. Minds Mach 19(4):557–567
Xu H, Omitaomu F, Sabri S, Zlatanova S, Li X, Song Y (2024) Leveraging generative AI for urban digital twins: a scoping review on the autonomous generation of urban data, scenarios, designs, and 3D city models for smart city advancement. Urban Inform 3(1):29

Part II
Environmental Solutions and Urban Sustainability

Chapter 5
Designing Cooler Cities: AI-Driven Climate Simulation, Urban Heat Mitigation, and the Pursuit of Thermal Justice

5.1 Urban Heat as a Design Challenge

The contemporary city is warming. Not just because of global warming, but also because of the way we plan, construct, and live in cities. In addition to being a noticeable sign of unsustainable urbanization, the urban heat island (UHI) effect—where cities get noticeably hotter than nearby rural areas—has become a difficult design problem for planners, architects, and legislators (Cheshmehzangi et al. 2023). The heat island is a spatial representation of how density, concrete, asphalt, and design decisions influence the microclimates of daily life rather than a technical oddity. The UHI has emerged as one of the most pressing and significant manifestations of ecological imbalance in the built environment in the era of climate volatility.

The causes of UHI are well established. Building geometries trap heat in urban canyons; the lack of vegetation lowers evapotranspiration; human activities, such as air conditioning and transportation, increase the thermal load; and dense concentrations of dark, impermeable surfaces absorb and re-emit solar radiation. These factors work together to intensify temperature extremes, producing hot spots that can last all night and get worse during heatwaves. Extreme heat events are becoming more often and intense due to climate change, making them existential concerns rather than seasonal annoyances, especially for cities already struggling with aging infrastructure, socioeconomic inequity, and ecological degradation.

The effects of UHI are extensive. In terms of public health, heat is widely acknowledged as one of the deadliest climate-related hazards in urban settings, contributing to increases in respiratory and cardiovascular diseases, heat stroke, dehydration, and death, particularly among small children, the elderly, and outdoor workers (Shahmohamadi et al. 2011; Buscail et al. 2012; Heaviside et al. 2017; Singh et al. 2020). The strain on emergency response networks, social services, and healthcare systems increases as heat stress increases. In contrast to floods or hurricanes, which occur quickly and overtly, heat spreads gradually and unevenly, frequently going unnoticed until it overwhelms people who are least prepared to handle it.

A. Cheshmehzangi, *Generative AI-Powered Urban Digital Twins*, Urban Sustainability,
https://doi.org/10.1007/978-981-95-4766-1_5

In terms of ecology, urban heat strengthens the emissions cycle that causes global warming by hastening soil deterioration, influencing local biodiversity, and raising energy consumption through a greater reliance on cooling systems, which are frequently driven by fossil fuels. In this feedback loop, local discomfort and global emissions come together to turn the city into a heat-producing engine. Higher temperatures also have an impact on water systems, stressing stormwater infrastructure, increasing evaporation rates, and decreasing the efficiency of natural cooling through green-blue corridors.

The UHI effect exacerbates spatial inequity on a social level. The urban fabric does not disperse heat uniformly. According to studies, the poorest, most racially separated, and least vegetated neighbourhoods are frequently the hottest. Low-income neighbourhoods in many international cities are found in places with fewer trees, fewer parks, more buildings, and less-than-ideal insulation. This thermal disparity is not a coincidental phenomenon; rather, it is a legacy of redlining, infrastructure neglect, zoning decisions, and disinvestment. Therefore, combating urban heat is more than just a design issue; it is a political and moral necessity that goes right to the core of our conception of justice in the built environment.

A new type of intelligence—one that can precisely map, forecast, and intervene—is required due to the spatial dimensions of UHI (Liu et al. 2024). Even though they are crucial, traditional heat mitigation techniques like planting trees, installing cool roofs, and modifying buildings are frequently used in a reactionary, one-size-fits-all way. A predictive and adaptable strategy is required, one that views heat as a highly localized phenomenon that changes across time, geography, and sociopolitical context rather than as a universal condition.

This is where the combination of urban climate modelling and generative AI becomes an ally for revolutionary design. Cities can no longer afford to speculate about who will be impacted, where the heat will settle, or which mitigation techniques will have the most co-benefits. We need to be able to map temperature flows across rooftops and street canyons, simulate thousands of spatial scenarios, predict how tree canopy growth will alter thermal profiles over decades, and optimize interventions based on intersecting criteria, such as land availability, energy cost, cooling efficiency, and demographic vulnerability.

In this context, urban heat is framed as a design challenge in the most profound sense, rather than merely a material science or meteorological problem. It poses the question, "How can we set up space to support life under stress?" How can cities be retrofitted for thermal dignity as well as efficiency? How can we layer ecology, culture, and infrastructure to reduce harm and create opportunity?

In this chapter, we examine how generative AI might be used as a climate intelligence tool, allowing cities to react not just quickly and accurately but also creatively and thoughtfully. We explore how data-driven creativity might make cities cooler, more equitable, and more responsive through anything from high-resolution temperature mapping to AI-guided cooling interventions, from climate-just zoning to thermally sensitive architecture design.

But let us be clear: technology is not a panacea. No algorithm can reverse decades of spatial exclusion or cool a concrete jungle on its own. AI provides a fresh perspective—a means of observing invisible heat patterns, testing plans before putting them into action, and broadening the creative imagination beyond trial and error. The challenge is to improve our ability to make informed decisions in the face of rising temperatures, not to replace human judgment. This chapter encourages a change in the way we envision, model, and cool the cities of the future by redefining urban heat as a spatial, ecological, and justice-oriented design challenge (Allam et al. 2023). Regaining the right to live, breathe, and prosper in the future urban climate is more important than merely cutting degrees.

5.1.1 Climate Justice and Thermal Inequity

Despite being a climatological occurrence, the urban heat island effect has profoundly human—and unequal—repercussions. Cities do not experience uniform heat distribution. It traces the lines of racial segregation, economic inequality, and infrastructure neglect. The hottest neighbourhoods are frequently the poorest in every major city on the planet. A crucial reality is shown by this spatial distribution of thermal risk: heat is a question of justice as much as temperature.

The idea of climate justice highlights the systemic injustices that influence susceptibility to environmental risks (Zahnow et al. 2025). All cultures are impacted by global warming, but the effects are dispersed according on privilege, power, and policy. The urban microclimate is the one place where this is most noticeable. Neighbourhoods with little tree cover, poor insulation, lots of concrete and asphalt, and restricted access to public cooling facilities like parks or community centers are more likely to be inhabited by low-income communities (Fraser et al. 2017). These same neighbourhoods frequently experience chronic underinvestment, increased noise pollution, and poor air quality, which adds to the burden and increases the risk of heat-related disease and mortality.

Particularly vulnerable groups include the elderly, those with disabilities, those who work outdoors, migrants, and the homeless. Many people don't have access to air conditioning in their buildings or can't afford the energy expenditures of continuous use. During heat emergencies, some people do not have access to information or transportation. A heatwave can be fatal for these communities, making it more than just uncomfortable. The discourse of adaptation in this context needs to go beyond resilience and toward reparative design—strategies that address the socioeconomic conditions that have made certain lives more disposable than others while also acting as a buffer against climate risk.

Here, generative AI has the potential to be a game-changer—not as a neutral optimizer, but as a tool for tailored, data-driven urban solutions that address environmental injustice. Artificial intelligence (AI) can assist planners and policymakers in precisely identifying high-risk locations by learning from geographical patterns of heat exposure, demographics, infrastructure quality, vegetation cover, and health effects. It can replicate the effects of interventions, such as cooling centers, reflective pavements, and tree planting, both in terms of equity and temperature. Where will people most benefit from a green corridor? In underprivileged areas, how might a rooftop garden program change the exposure to heat? Which cooling techniques best suit behavioral patterns or cultural preferences?

More significantly, AI can support the transition from a reactive to an anticipatory justice planning paradigm. Conventional heat mitigation measures are frequently implemented after a crisis—a severe heatwave that causes political urgency or public outcry. However, scenario forecasting made possible by generative models enables cities to detect "thermal time bombs" before they explode. By producing artificial microclimate data for regions without sensors, they can close knowledge gaps that usually keep marginalized people hidden from decision-makers.

However, this potential will only be realised if the tools are governed with inclusive ethics. Safeguards must be incorporated into generative AI systems to stop the replication of biases present in past data, such as zoning regulations, housing evaluations, or service delivery. They need to be transparent, auditable, and receptive to community feedback. Co-creating thermal maps with people who live in hot climates is preferable to simply superimposing them on cities.

Heat equity is more than just a technical result. It is a political pledge to acknowledge that every life counts and that every degree matters. Trees and cooling materials are not the only ways to mitigate heat. It's about taking back the right to live in the city with honour. The spatial inequities that determine who perspire, who suffers, and who lives can be revealed by generative AI. But what is needed to turn understanding into impact is civic action and care-based design. We shall examine how these technologies might be used to chill not just the air in cities but also our urban conscience in the upcoming chapters. The difficulty lies in modelling a more equitable city rather than just a cooler one (Cheshmehzangi and Butters 2017). Heat turns become both a lens and a hazard in that quest.

5.2 Generative AI and Climate Modelling

In order to understand how heat, moisture, and air flow through the built environment, climate simulation has historically depended on physics-based models, specifically computational fluid dynamics (CFD). These models, which provide high-precision insights into how structures, materials, and urban layouts affect microclimate, are fundamental to the field of environmental engineering and architecture. However, the need to extend and supplement traditional modelling with more adaptive, scalable, and generative methodologies is developing as cities become more complex and climatic dynamics become more turbulent. Enter generative AI, a potent addition to CFD that can simulate climate conditions at scales, speeds, and scenarios that were previously impossible to handle with just traditional techniques.

Climate modelling adopts a completely new paradigm thanks to generative AI. Generative AI models learn patterns, correlations, and latent structures from large datasets, whereas traditional models depend on explicitly programmed physical laws and boundary conditions. After training, these models can yield new outcomes—possible microclimatic futures—based on modifications to urban form, material composition, or vegetation covering, in addition to reproducing established situations. Their power resides in their capacity to synthesize huge, diverse datasets and identify significant patterns within them, especially in cases when conventional modelling data is insufficient or inconsistent.

Neural networks, especially convolutional neural networks (CNNs) and graph neural networks (GNNs), are among the most promising model classes in this field. CNNs are utilized to identify and forecast spatial heat trends in satellite images or urban form maps because of their reputation for processing image-like data. On the other hand, GNNs are especially well-suited to depicting urban environments as interconnected systems, in which edges capture relationships like proximity, shading, and airflow, and nodes represent spatial elements like buildings or street segments. These graph-based models are very useful for localized climate forecasting and focused mitigation because they are excellent at simulating the spread of temperature over intricate urban geometries.

Diffusion models, a type of generative models that represent the gradual change of one spatial state into another, are another novel breakthrough. Planning professionals can see how actions, such as planting trees or upgrading materials, may change the heat dynamics of a neighbourhood over days, seasons, or decades by using diffusion models to represent how temperature fields change over time. These models may take into consideration both short-term variations and long-term trends, and they perform very well in situations when transitions are neither linear nor predictable.

When incorporated into multimodal frameworks, large language models (LLMs), which are usually connected to text generation, also contribute to climate modeling. LLMs can interpret descriptive metadata, annotate climate initiatives, and communicate with design experts using natural language prompts when paired with vision models and spatial datasets. Users can now ask sophisticated questions like "Which street in this district will benefit most from additional canopy cover by 2030?" or "Simulate the thermal impact of reducing road surface area by 20%", creating new opportunities for participatory planning.

The ability of generative AI to facilitate the creation of scenarios at the urban scale is arguably the most fascinating area of its application in climate modelling. Depending on various input assumptions, such as shifts in albedo, tree cover, building orientation, or traffic patterns, AI models can produce hundreds or thousands of variations instead of doing a single deterministic simulation. These scenario ensembles assist cities in investigating a variety of futures—under various design configurations, policy directions, and climatic scenarios. Crucially, they enable planners to visualize uncertainty, assess trade-offs, and pinpoint solid tactics that work effectively in a variety of scenarios.

But generative AI's strength extends beyond its ability to make predictions. Additionally, it makes possible a radically different epistemology that values multiplicity, complexity, and uncertainty. In open systems, where numerous interacting variables evolve in nonlinear ways, generative models flourish, whereas CFD models strive for physical precision in confined systems. Generative AI enables us to model the city as a living system that is sensitive, adaptive, and indeterminate, as opposed to modelling it as a machine.

However, generative models work best when combined with simulations that are based on physics. CFD provides precise physics understanding of radiation, conduction, and airflow, particularly at the building or block scale. In contrast, generative AI is very good at identifying patterns at the meso- and macro-scale, which helps put local phenomena in the perspective of larger urban systems. When combined, these models provide a hybrid intelligence that blends specificity with generalization, as well as accuracy and flexibility.

Generative AI creates new opportunities for proactive, multi-scalar design thinking as cities struggle with increasing heat stresses. It makes it possible to not only analyze the state of affairs now but also to creatively envision different possibilities. It promotes design as an act of anticipation based on facts, creativity, and moral foresight rather than merely as a response to heat. By doing this, it recasts climate modelling as a proactive tool for creating cities that are more resilient, equitable, and cool rather than as a technical back-end function.

5.3 Data Inputs and Sensing the Urban Microclimate

The accuracy and richness of the data that algorithms use to generate their output are just as important to the efficacy of AI-driven climate simulation as the complexity of the algorithms themselves. Generative models need to be trained on large and varied datasets that capture the complex nature of urban microclimates to learn, infer, and produce thermal scenarios across urban contexts with accuracy. This section explores the fundamental function of data in creating insightful urban heat models, describing the various types of measurement, observation, and sensing needed to allow AI to "see" the city in thermal terms.

Urban microclimate modelling requires fine-grained, high-resolution data, both spatially and temporally, in contrast to global climate models that function at coarse resolutions and continental scales. The difference between a dangerous hotspot and a liveable street can be determined by a few degrees of thermal variation. The line separating discomfort from heatstroke can be drawn after a few hours of exposure. Therefore, it is essential to gather and combine accurate data regarding the absorption, storage, and emission of heat across structures, surfaces, plants, and infrastructure.

One of the most reliable and accessible data sources for analyzing surface temperature is satellite thermal imagery. Researchers can map broad patterns of urban heat islands (UHIs) using the use of satellites like Landsat, Sentinel, and MODIS, which provide periodic thermal readings throughout cities. Systemic heat inequalities between metropolitan cores, suburban fringes, and rural peripheries can be identified with the use of these satellite pictures. However, their use for fine-scale operations is limited by their spatial resolution, which normally ranges between 10 and 100 meters.

Furthermore, abrupt weather changes like heatwaves may cause satellite passes to miss rapidly changing thermal dynamics.

Urban sensor networks—ground-based systems of temperature, humidity, and wind sensors installed on lampposts, buildings, cars, and mobile platforms—are being used by cities more and more to close this gap. AI models may be calibrated with real-world ground truth thanks to these real-time sensors, which capture dynamic shifts in temperature conditions with far better realism. Micro-scale comparison and hyper-local intervention planning are made possible by sensors positioned in shaded streets, crossroads with a lot of asphalt, or courtyards with vegetation. These networks, however, are frequently dispersed unevenly, favouring wealthier or more visible regions, and they can be costly to set up and maintain.

Weather stations, which record wind speed, sun radiation, air temperature, and dew point, offer trustworthy meteorological baselines to supplement sensor data. Weather stations provide long-term data sets that are useful for training generative models to identify seasonal rhythms and climate trends, despite their often more sparse spatial distribution. They offer calibration and continuity across datasets with varying update frequencies when combined with other inputs.

LiDAR (Light Detection and Ranging) scanning is another potent input source that provides intricate three-dimensional representations of urban morphology. Surface geometry, vegetation height, building envelope properties, and material textures are all captured by LiDAR and have an impact on the absorption and dissipation of heat. Where shadows fall, how breezes circulate, and where reflecting versus absorptive materials predominate can all be inferred by AI models trained on LiDAR-enhanced urban maps. When modelling vertical heat gradients—between street level, rooftops, and canyon-like passages between buildings—this is especially crucial.

An increasingly useful and democratic element of microclimate sensing is crowd-sourcing data. Residents themselves can record temperature measurements, thermal comfort levels, and felt heat stress using wearable technology, smartphone apps, or participatory mapping platforms. By adding emotive and experience elements to thermal modelling, this human-centric layer of data highlights not only hot spots but also areas that feel dangerous or intolerable. Additionally, it assists in identifying official monitoring blind spots, especially in migrant districts, public housing, and informal settlements that are frequently excluded from institutional datasets.

There are still significant obstacles in spite of this increasing amount of data. The first is spatial resolution, or the degree to which urban information is captured by the data. Although urban datasets are frequently fragmented or unevenly gridded, generative AI models work best when trained on consistent, high-resolution inputs. Temporal sensitivity presents another difficulty. Hourly variations in heat are caused by the sun's angle, wind speed, and patterns of activity. The quick escalation of heat stress during an acute wave may not be captured by data that is updated on a daily or weekly basis.

Interoperability is another problem; different data sources have different coordinate systems, formats, and semantic labelling, which makes integration a challenging technological endeavour. Last, but not least, data governance is still a major issue:

who gathers, owns, and has access to microclimate data? The ethical and transparent use of thermal sensing must be protected if it is to be used as a tool for public policy.

The ultimate objective is to create extensive, multi-layered datasets that enable AI algorithms to envision what might be in addition to reproducing current circumstances. Combining satellite, sensor, LiDAR, and participatory data makes a city machine-readable in ways that facilitate inclusive, responsive, and well-informed action. The urban microclimate is a real experience rather than merely a theoretical concept. AI can recognize that experience and create designs to better it thanks to data.

5.4 Designing for Cooling: AI-Guided Interventions

There has never been a more pressing need to develop efficient, scalable, and context-sensitive cooling solutions as cities deal with the growing threat of excessive heat. Conventional urban planning techniques frequently use time-consuming modelling technologies, expert judgment, and historical data to assess design alternatives. This capability is drastically increased by generative AI, which allows planners, architects, and legislators to investigate hundreds of heat mitigation alternatives while balancing practical limitations like cost, land usage, aesthetics, and social impact.

The ability to combine intricate spatial, climatic, and socioeconomic factors into logical solutions is at the heart of AI-guided intervention design. The thermal impact of installing urban trees along important corridors, switching from asphalt to permeable paving, or putting green roofs on top of various building types, for example, can be quickly simulated using generative models. These models map knock-on effects like evapotranspiration, albedo shifts, shading, and airflow redirection in addition to visualizing temperature decreases. The AI becomes a co-creative collaborator by learning from pre-existing datasets and climatic responses, testing, improving, and suggesting contextually relevant tactics that would be impossible to assess manually.

Singapore's use of AI-enhanced urban twins to determine the best places for tree planting based on population density, wind routes, and land availability is a well-known example (Trigka and Dritsas 2025). Across districts, the system dynamically assesses the effects of shade trees on walkability, daytime surface temperatures, and even mental health metrics. Similar to this, researchers in Barcelona have mapped the cooling potential of renovated rooftops using machine learning. They have done this by comparing rainwater retention systems, green roof layers, and solar reflectance to find the best combinations under various future climatic scenarios.

AI is being tested to determine which informal settlements are most at risk from heat stress and to provide technically sound and socially acceptable solutions in quickly expanding cities like Nairobi or Dhaka. Models might, for instance, recommend a combination of reflective roof coatings and interventions in public green spaces, which are intended not only for cooling but also for community usage and teaching on climate resilience. To guarantee that design concepts are regionally relevant and have a higher chance of being accepted, generative models can take into account behavioural data, governance restrictions, and cultural preferences.

The capacity of generative AI to optimize across several goals at once is what makes it particularly useful. It is uncommon to select a cooling intervention based only on thermal performance. In addition, it must be reasonably priced, low maintenance, free from the demands of gentrification, and blend in seamlessly with the current urban landscape. A subset of techniques that work well under many, sometimes conflicting constraints can be identified by using AI models, which can score thousands of iterations across different factors.

Designing for cooling so becomes a civic opportunity as much as an issue of climatic logic. In order to help cities make wise decisions now so they can survive and prosper tomorrow, generative AI turns urban heat mitigation into an inclusive, responsive, and iterative process.

5.4.1 From Simulation to Implementation: Closing the Feedback Loop

Generative AI is just the first step in creating intelligent cooling strategies. The real test is putting simulation into practice and making sure that knowledge acquired in virtual spaces results in observable, quantifiable enhancements to the actual city. AI runs the risk of becoming just another layer of theoretical techno-solutionism without this shift, disconnected from the practical realities of building, planning, and government. Climate-responsive urbanization thus depends on closing the feedback loop between AI-generated scenarios and executed actions.

A number of innovative cities have started to operationalize this loop in recent years. AI-powered simulations are being directly integrated into adaptive planning tools in pilot projects, enabling decision-makers to see the results of interventions in real time and modify their plans as necessary. For example, in Los Angeles, vulnerable neighbourhoods have been identified and prioritized for reflective pavement rollouts using AI-supported models (Gaiba and Giovanardi 2024). These simulations were not merely theoretical; they translated data into coordinated urban operations and influenced public outreach, worker deployment, and procurement.

The incorporation of urban digital twins—real-time, spatially anchored platforms that continuously mirror and monitor the changing city—is a crucial facilitator of this translation. Digital twins provide as a link between AI forecasts and urban systems, offering a monitoring dashboard for evaluation after deployment and a dynamic testing ground for suggested solutions. A digital twin can demonstrate, for instance, how the construction of green roofs impacts local temperature readings over time, how it changes the energy demand in nearby buildings, or whether it changes the patterns of pedestrian movement in public areas when it comes to urban heat mitigation.

AI-driven insights become a part of an iterative design-governance-monitoring cycle through this type of coupling, rather than being static outputs. This methodology is being tested in cities like Seoul and Vienna, where cooling measures are implemented gradually, assessed using community reporting and sensor data, and then modified in response to actual performance. This method views urban heat mitigation as a living experiment that is sensitive to climatic conditions, social feedback, and policy priorities rather than as a set blueprint.

However, institutional and regulatory innovation is also necessary to close the gap between simulation and execution. The speed and diversity of AI-driven insights are frequently too great for traditional planning frameworks, which are either too inflexible, siloed, or delayed. Planning procedures must become more flexible and iterative in order to accommodate mid-course adjustments and evidence-based policy updates when real-time intelligence is used to inform public investment, zoning regulations, or procurement requirements. This necessitates interoperable data systems, agile yet accountable governance models, and agency-wide capacity building.

Furthermore, without community involvement and trust-building, implementation cannot be successful. AI models should not be used to dictate design; instead, they should be discussed in public and be subject to criticism, improvement, and contextualization. Participatory urban labs have been established in cities such as Medellín, where people are able to discuss, co-interpret, and apply the results of simulations to inform choices. Participatory feedback loops like these provide implementation more social legitimacy and increase its resilience, justice, and grounding.

Measurement is another important feature. Cities must have systems in place to evaluate whether cooling actions are having the desired effect to close the feedback loop. Long-term sensor deployment, comfort and health surveys, energy usage monitoring, and even qualitative assessments of urban experience are all part of this. In order for AI models to gradually recalibrate, learn, and provide better recommendations, these observations must then be fed back into them. In this way, implementation marks the start of a new learning cycle rather than the conclusion of the design phase.

Finally, closing the feedback loop turns AI into a governance partner rather than a predicting tool. It encourages more responsive, moral, and democratic urban transformation in addition to more intelligent planning. This ability to act, observe, learn, and adapt in real time will determine which cities survive—and which take the lead—as the climate crisis intensifies.

5.5 Multi-Scalar Coordination and Governance

The level of cooperation across several governmental scales is just as important to the success of AI-enabled urban heat reduction as technological sophistication. Cities are intricate political environments where local laws, private development plans, community needs, and federal policies all interact. Climate resilience is a governance requirement rather than only a design or data challenge, particularly when it comes to heat. Cities must create institutional architectures that facilitate shared data infrastructures, cooperative decision-making, and flexible policy frameworks in order to fully utilize generative AI and climate simulation.

Jurisdictional boundaries are not respected by urban heat. Intensified by road design, land use patterns, construction materials, and tree canopy distribution, it spans neighbourhoods, districts, and regions. However, the government's duties to mitigate heat are frequently dispersed. While local councils are in charge of zoning, the distribution of green space, and construction codes, national governments may establish emissions objectives and infrastructure financing priorities. Communities suffer the most from overheating, while developers determine the shape and scope of initiatives. Even the most sophisticated AI models run the risk of producing solutions that no one has the power—or motivation—to put into practice if coordination is lacking.

Three fundamental aspects of multi-scalar governance must be in harmony: accountability procedures, decision rights, and data systems. At the data level, cross-sectoral, integrated, high-resolution data is what generative AI thrives on. Access to information owned by utilities, transportation agencies, health authorities, insurers, and even social services is necessary for heat mitigation techniques that maximize environmental performance and social equality. To create the data commons that AI can function on, coordinated data-sharing agreements supported by privacy protections and common standards are required. Shared urban data platforms, which combine heat-related facts to guide public and commercial initiatives, have been explored by cities including Toronto and Amsterdam.

Governance at the decision-making level must shift from divided planning departments to cross-sectoral and interagency cooperation. AI-powered insights can be used to estimate cost-benefit trade-offs, prioritize cooling treatments, and locate heat hotspots. However, putting those insights into practice calls for cooperative frameworks in which various stakeholders—such as public health specialists, housing authorities, transportation planners, and environmental agencies—can decide together using common resources. Although scaling these models is still difficult, early examples of such integrated governance initiatives include Paris' Climate Action Plans and Melbourne's Resilient Melbourne initiative.

Governance at the local level needs to be responsive, inclusive, and participatory. If AI systems are to be successful in real-world settings, they cannot be seen as technocratic or top-down. The types of interventions that are pursued, such as street trees, reflective pavements, or shaded transportation stops, must be decided by the locals, particularly those who live in heat-vulnerable areas. The use of citizen climate councils, co-design workshops, and participatory mapping to include community perspectives in the governance process is growing. This is a matter of efficacy as well as justice; solutions that take into account community ownership and local knowledge have a higher chance of succeeding.

Adaptability is also necessary for governance, especially in light of the increasing and unpredictable threats associated with climate change. The frequency, severity, and unpredictability of heat waves are increasing. Policy frameworks must be able to adapt their policies in response to changing circumstances by using real-time data and continuous assessment. This adaptive ability is supported by generative AI and digital twins, which make scenario testing, feedback loops, and predictive modelling possible. However, policies must change with them, adopting flexible rules, iterative cycles of implementation, and reflective tools that take into account lived urban realities.

Involving the private sector adds even more complication. In order to implement AI tools and construct heat-resilient infrastructure, developers, energy companies, and technology providers are frequently essential. However, their incentives could not be in line with sustainability or equality objectives in the absence of legal frameworks or public interest mandates. To leverage private innovation while maintaining public responsibility, public-private governance models are required, such as green construction rules, climate risk disclosure laws, or incentive programs for cool roofs and green spaces.

Lastly, trust and legibility must be the foundation of multi-scalar cooperation. Heat governance, particularly with AI systems, needs to be open about its presumptions, clear about its suggestions, and responsible for its results. Cities ought to make their models publicly available, reveal the weights and data inputs, and allow the public to examine the outcomes. Regardless of how "smart" its systems are, a city will find it difficult to retain legitimacy if it is unable to justify why it grows trees in one district but not another.

In conclusion, smart institutions are needed for AI-enabled heat mitigation, not just smart tools. Organizations that can integrate many data sources, engage local communities, coordinate across jurisdictions, and make real-time policy adjustments. Cities must face this governance challenge with bravery, openness, and collaboration as climate risks increase, and urban overheating worsens. Only then will AI be able to function as a civic infrastructure for equitable and resilient urban futures, rather than merely as a technological advancement.

5.6 The Climate-Responsive City: Intelligence, Equity, and Design in a Warming World

The city's intelligence must increase in tandem with the planet's heat. This chapter has examined how generative AI presents new opportunities for comprehending, reducing, and eventually changing our relationship with climatic stress, especially in the form of urban heat, when integrated into the urban planning process. However, the potential of these tools only materializes when based on a more comprehensive idea: a new paradigm of climate-responsive urbanism, where simulation, sensing, and spatial justice come together to rethink the fundamental reasoning behind city-making.

Urban heat is a social and moral concern, not just a technical or environmental one. It exacerbates already-existing disparities, interferes with daily living, and makes cities less livable for present and future generations. It turns into a slow violence that disproportionately affects those least accountable for climate change if it is not controlled. However, this difficulty also creates an opportunity to reconsider what cities can become. The urban fabric itself can be made intelligent, adaptive, and regenerative with the correct partnerships between ecology, technology, and community.

The ability of urban systems to identify climatic stress in real time, model potential futures, and inform design and policy choices is 'responsiveness', which is at the core of this change. Here, generative AI acts as a catalyst. It enables us to transition from reactive to proactive and anticipatory planning. Cities may test thousands of cooling techniques without waiting decades for data, identify vulnerable zones before a crisis occurs, and optimize treatments based on equality, cost, and community acceptance in addition to thermal performance. However, AI is insufficient on its own. The insights of lived experience, local knowledge, and place-based wisdom must also be included into a climate-responsive metropolis.

It is now essential to incorporate green infrastructure, such as parks, trees, water features, green roofs, and permeable surfaces (Mitra et al. 2024). These are climate technologies in and of themselves, not only beautification initiatives. They provide psychological respite, enhance air quality, promote biodiversity, and chill the city and urban environments (Butters et al. 2024). Their deployment becomes more impactful, efficient, and strategic when paired with AI-driven modelling. The secret is to approach these interventions as vital parts of urban metabolism—systems that breathe, absorb, and regenerate—rather than as stand-alone conveniences.

Additionally, thermal equity needs to be promoted as a key indicator of urban development. We need to start evaluating cities based on how fairly they shield their residents from climatic damage, just as we do with their GDP, infrastructure, or housing supply (Baker 2012). This entails making sure that cooling techniques are implemented not only in business districts or affluent neighbourhoods, but also in informal settlements, rental apartments, schoolyards, and senior care facilities. If generative AI is directed by inclusive governance and public ideals, it can be a potent ally in achieving this goal thanks to its ability to simulate minute details and create focused designs.

The key to creating climate-responsive cities in the future is carefully weaving intelligence. Adaptive planning, real-time sensing, and computational foresight are examples of intelligence (Noor 2013). Long-term stewardship, cultural awareness, and community involvement are examples of care. The most developed cities are those that learn, listen, and change in response to their surroundings and citizens, not those that automate the most decisions.

As demonstrated in this chapter, the combination of artificial intelligence, urban sensing, and regenerative design represents a cultural and institutional change rather than merely a technological advancement (Cheshmehzangi 2025). It demands new responsibilities for designers and technologists, new roles for civil society, and new capacities within governments. A climate-responsive city is developed gradually through iteration, feedback, and a steadfast dedication to justice.

The question as we proceed is not if we can construct such cities, but rather if we will decide to do so. The urgency increases with each degree of warming. However, so does the chance to create cities that not only endure the heat but also foster health, hope, and group resilience.

References

Allam Z, Cheshmehzangi A, Jones DS (2023) Climate and social justice in the political landscape of urban resilience and mercantilism: a concluding note. In Allam Z, Cheshmehzangi A, Jones DS (2023): Climate and social justice: the political economy of urban resilience and mercantilism. Springer Nature Singapore, Singapore, pp 103–110

Baker JL (ed) (2012) Climate change, disaster risk, and the urban poor: cities building resilience for a changing world. World Bank Publications, Washington

Buscail C, Upegui E, Viel JF (2012) Mapping heatwave health risk at the community level for public health action. Int J Health Geogr 11(1):38

Butters C, Cheshmehzangi A, Bakhshoodeh R (2024) Sustainable construction: the embodied carbon impact of infrastructures and landscaping. Urban Sci 8(3):76

Cheshmehzangi A (2025) Advanced city: for the future of cities and opposing smart cities. Springer, Singapore

Cheshmehzangi A, Butters C (eds) (2017) Designing cooler cities: energy, cooling and urban form: the Asian perspective. Palgrave Macmillan, Singapore

Cheshmehzangi A, He BJ, Sharifi A, Matzarakis A (2023) Climate change, cities, and the importance of cooling strategies, practices, and policies. In Cheshmehzangi A, He BJ, Sharifi A, Matzarakis A (eds.) (2023): Climate change and cooling cities. Springer Nature Singapore, Singapore, pp 2–19

Fraser AM, Chester MV, Eisenman D, Hondula DM, Pincetl SS, English P, Bondank E (2017) Household accessibility to heat refuges: residential air conditioning, public cooled space, and walkability. Environ Plann B Urban Analytics City Sci 44(6):1036–1055

Gaiba A, Giovanardi M (2024) Towards interconnected «Politically smart cities»? Rethinking participation from digital twins to translocal grassroots digital platforms. Riv Digit Polit 4(3):485–511

Heaviside C, Macintyre H, Vardoulakis S (2017) The urban heat island: implications for health in a changing environment. Curr Environ Health Rep 4(3):296–305

Liu C, Lu S, Tian J, Yin L, Wang L, Zheng W (2024) Research overview on urban heat islands driven by computational intelligence. Land 13(12):2176

Mitra S, Madhuvanthi S, Sabumon PC (2024) Nature-based urban resilience: integrating green infrastructure. In Singh P, Srivastava P, and Sorokin A. (eds.) (2024): Nature-based solutions in achieving sustainable development goals: harmonizing nature and progress. Springer Nature Switzerland, Cham, pp 167–205

Noor A (2013) Envisioning engineering education and practice in the coming intelligence convergence era—a complex adaptive systems approach. Open Eng 3(4):606–619

Shahmohamadi P, Che-Ani AI, Etessam I, Maulud KNA, Tawil NM (2011) Healthy environment: the need to mitigate urban heat island effects on human health. Procedia Eng 20:61–70

Singh N, Singh S, Mall RK (2020) Urban ecology and human health: implications of urban heat island, air pollution and climate change nexus. In Verma P, Singh P, and Raghubanshi A.S. (eds.) (2020): *Urban ecology: Emerging Patterns and Social-Ecological Systems.* Amsterdam: Elsevier, pp 317–334. https://doi.org/10.1016/B978-0-12-820730-7.00017-3

Trigka M, Dritsas E (2025) Wireless sensor networks: from fundamentals and applications to innovations and future trends. IEEE Access 13:96365–96399. https://ieeexplore.ieee.org/abstract/document/11008746/

Zahnow R, Yousefnia AR, Hassankhani M, Cheshmehzangi A (2025) Climate change inequalities: a systematic review of disparities in access to mitigation and adaptation measures. Environ Sci Policy 165:104021.

Chapter 6
Hydrological Intelligence: Digital Twins, AI, and the Regenerative Future of Urban Water Systems

6.1 Water Under Pressure: The Urban Hydrological Challenge

The way that cities relate to water—both its abundance and its scarcity—is changing dramatically. Urban hydrological systems, which were once thought to be predictable and controllable, are currently under tremendous strain from a combination of factors (Abera 2025), including growing urbanization, climate change, and the gradual deterioration of aging infrastructure. There is less space for absorption or delay when droughts last longer, rainfall episodes are more intense, and impermeable surfaces proliferate. Cities all around the world are stuck between water abundance and water insecurity, and they are both drowning and running dry. Static infrastructure and conventional planning methods are becoming less appropriate in this unstable new normal.

One of the main accelerators is climate change. The hydrological balance of cities is significantly impacted by rising global temperatures because they change precipitation patterns, amplify the urban heat island effect, and increase the frequency of extreme weather events. Rainfall is becoming more unpredictable in some areas, with heavy downpours overtaxing stormwater systems and flooding city streets (Cheshmehzangi et al. 2024). In others, protracted droughts cause aquifers and reservoirs to be depleted, endangering the supply of water and escalating competition between users and sectors. These two pressures—too much and too little water—are now structural hazards that require constant preparation rather than sporadic response. They are no longer seasonal aberrations.

Urbanization trends that harden the landscape and detach cities from their biological bases further compound the problems. The natural ability of soil and vegetation to absorb water is reduced when concrete and asphalt spread. Once-infiltrated rainfall now rushes across sealed surfaces, causing streams to erode, runoff to accelerate, and combined sewer systems to overburden. Inadequately planned developments, frequently found in informal settlements or floodplains, put a pressure

A. Cheshmehzangi, *Generative AI-Powered Urban Digital Twins*, Urban Sustainability,
https://doi.org/10.1007/978-981-95-4766-1_6

on legacy infrastructure and make people more vulnerable. Stormwater drainage systems in many cities were created using antiquated climatic and land-use assumptions decades ago. These systems are currently overworked, underfunded, and more likely to malfunction.

The invisible catastrophe of aging water infrastructure exacerbates this. Every day, billions of litres of treated water are lost through underground pipe networks. In many areas, pumping stations, treatment facilities, and reservoirs are nearing the end of their design lives and need significant investments. However, changes are frequently postponed or implemented piecemeal because of the high costs, protracted timescales, and political challenges involved, leaving cities with fragile, opaque, and reactive systems. As a result, there is an increasing discrepancy in institutional capacities to handle urban water realities.

A new, integrated, predictive, and adaptable paradigm for water governance in cities is required in light of these intertwining issues of obsolescence, overload, and scarcity. By treating drinking water, wastewater, stormwater, and natural hydrological systems as interdependent flows rather than as distinct engineering domains, integration entails breaking down silos between them. Prediction is the process of using machine learning and high-resolution data to detect vulnerabilities, predict flood episodes, and model the results of interventions. Enabling systems to change with the times and react quickly to variations in rainfall, consumption trends, and societal demands is known as adaptation.

In this regard, AI-powered digital twins are becoming indispensable instruments for urban water management in the twenty-first century (Ndubuisi et al. 2025). Digital twins offer a dynamic, real-time depiction of water systems that is connected to sensor data, able to simulate, and sensitive to intervention, in contrast to static GIS models or one-off flood maps. They provide a means of visualizing the intangible, such as stormwater catchment zones, underground pipes, real-time flow rates, or the consequences of infrastructure failure. They establish an environment where planners, engineers, emergency managers, and even people can comprehend, predict, and influence hydrological behaviour at various scales by coordinating computer models with physical reality.

AI further augments this potential. Machine learning models are capable of simulating thousands of rainfall-runoff scenarios under various climate conditions, predicting pipe bursts, optimizing pump schedules, and identifying anomalies in flow patterns. These features transform water management from a reactive to a proactive business when incorporated with digital twins. Cities can go from overdesigning infrastructure to precisely and strategically adjusting it; they can go from reacting to floods to preventing them entirely.

However, technology is not the answer on its own. An ecosystem of funding, governance, community involvement, and ecological regeneration must surround the use of AI and digital twins. Rebuilding equitable, resilient, and regenerative urban interactions with water is the aim, not merely better water management. When digital tools facilitate this larger shift—when they assist cities in transitioning from hydrological catastrophe to hydrological intelligence—they take on significance.

Digital twins are already being utilized to optimize stormwater networks, model floods, coordinate infrastructure across agencies, and inform early warning systems, as we will discuss in the sections that follow. A change from fragmented risk management to holistic water stewardship, where every drop is seen, sensed, and protected, is the deeper opportunity that rests not only in their ability to calculate but also in their ability to catalyze it.

6.2 Predictive Modelling and Flood Simulation with AI

One of the most damaging and common effects of climate variability in urban settings is flooding. Flood management has become a major concern for modern cities due to its unpredictable nature, quick onset, and compounding effects on ecosystems, infrastructure, and human lives. Despite having strong theoretical foundations, traditional hydrological modelling tools frequently fail to capture the complexity, dynamic nature, and spatial heterogeneity of urban settings. Accuracy is necessary, but so is flexibility: models that can change in real time, integrate large and varied data sources, and replicate the cascade impacts of runoff, rainfall, and infrastructure response under many future conditions. This is where the paradigm shift is occurring due to the convergence of digital twin technology and artificial intelligence.

A novel rationale for urban hydrological forecasting is introduced by AI-enhanced digital twins. They can adjust as conditions change because, in contrast to static models, they are constantly updated by sensor feeds, satellite data, and weather forecasts. In addition to predicting where water will collect during a storm, they can also predict how flows may change over time, which roadways might become impassable, and which vital services would be interrupted. They are essential for both long-term urban planning and operational flood management due to their ability to be dynamic in both space and time.

Rainfall prediction, an infamously difficult problem, is at the core of this system. Traditional statistical methods are unable to account for the subtleties of real-time weather data, and climate models frequently lack the granularity required for local-scale precipitation forecasting. Recurrent neural networks (RNNs) and temporal convolutional networks (TCNs), two generative and predictive AI models, have demonstrated significant promise in this field. These models can more accurately predict short- and medium-term rainfall distributions by using satellite imagery, sensor inputs, and historical weather trends. This allows for proactive measures to be taken in areas that are most likely to be affected.

The difficulty of modelling water flow based on terrain extends beyond rainfall. A complex matrix of surfaces, slopes, obstacles, and absorptive capabilities shapes runoff in a developed environment. This spatial complexity is particularly well-represented by AI models, especially graph neural networks (GNNs). GNNs replicate the flow of water between urban surfaces under various conditions by treating them as interconnected nodes, such as streets, rooftops, and green spaces. This method is an effective tool for simulating urban flood dynamics because it maintains spatial linkages while taking into account the uneven geometry of cities.

Simultaneously, hybrid AI-CFD (Computational Fluid Dynamics) models are starting to close the gap between AI-driven flexibility and physics-based accuracy. Although very accurate, traditional CFD simulations are time-consuming and computationally costly. They are frequently impractical for real-time use, necessitate extensive datasets, and require meticulous calibration. Cities may achieve significantly faster processing rates while maintaining the accuracy of physical modelling by using CFD data to train AI models. These artificial intelligence surrogates, often referred to as emulators or reduced-order models, are capable of simulating thousands of flood scenarios in a matter of minutes, examining the effects of minor modifications to precipitation, land use, or infrastructure layout on water dynamics.

The ability to create flood scenarios under future climatic conditions is a significant achievement in this discipline. Because of the potential for increased rainfall, altered seasonal patterns, and the emergence of new weather extremes, climate change poses significant uncertainty to hydrological planning. AI algorithms can create probabilistic flood maps that represent a variety of potential futures by ingesting ensembles of downscaled data and climate projections. This makes it possible for planners to go beyond historical baselines and create emergency plans and infrastructure that are resilient in a variety of situations.

AI-enhanced digital twins, for instance, simulate storm surge interactions with rainfall events in Rotterdam, a city well aware of its susceptibility to sea level rise and river flooding (Zhao et al. 2025). This helps to identify weak places in the dike system and suggests adaptive floodplain techniques. In Jakarta, real-time flood risk projections that direct evacuation and response activities are generated using deep learning models trained on topography, meteorological, and social vulnerability data. Hybrid models have been used in Brisbane to assess how future densification can make flash flooding worse unless permeable design (Cheshmehzangi 2022) and green infrastructure are implemented to mitigate it.

These forecasting abilities represent epistemological shifts as much as technological accomplishments. They alter how cities interact with their citizens, plan investments, and perceive risk. Instead of depending on antiquated flood maps created once every ten years, towns can use dynamic risk surfaces that change every day in response to fresh data. Minutes before a storm occurs, emergency managers can model inundation zones, allowing for quicker and more focused alerts. The way that street-level interventions, such as raised crossings, rain gardens, and swales, change the water flow in a particular microclimate can be investigated by urban designers. Developers, utility businesses, and insurance firms may all assess risk profiles with fine-grained spatial accuracy.

Predictive power needs to be balanced with institutional capability and moral awareness, though. The judgments that AI models are used to inform determine how helpful their output is. Priorities can be misdirected if black-box models are overused without validation or explainability (Hassija et al. 2024). Even worse, the models that are produced could reinforce environmental injustice if the data sources are skewed, leaving out informal settlements or neglecting to include temporary populations. Therefore, governance systems that place a high priority on openness, public accountability, and social inclusion must incorporate flood risk predictions (Alexander et al. 2016).

The potential of AI in flood simulation is in its capacity to learn, adapt, and iterate—to develop with cities rather than against them. When incorporated into digital twins, these models transform from forecasting instruments into learning infrastructures that assist cities in adapting to both the today's floods and the future's unpredictable waters.

6.3 Designing Smart Water Infrastructures: Reuse, Retention, and Release

The design and implementation of intelligent water infrastructure has become a fundamental necessity for urban resilience as cities encounter increasing hydrological stresses, ranging from flash floods to protracted droughts. Contemporary water-sensitive urban design emphasizes diffuse, flexible, and ecologically integrated solutions, moving away from rigid drainage systems and hard-edged engineering. Smart stormwater management systems, rain gardens, bioswales, retention basins, green roofs, and permeable pavements are no longer merely auxiliary measures (Tota-Maharaj et al. 2024). They create a dynamic infrastructure of reuse, retention, and release that serves as a crucial interaction between urban form and the hydrological cycle.

In this paradigm change, digital twins are used as computational frameworks for planning and optimizing nature-based water infrastructures in intricate urban terrains, rather than just as digital copies of drainage networks. By combining spatial models, behavioural simulations, and real-time environmental data, a digital twin helps cities develop, test, and refine their infrastructure plans over time. This platform further develops when generative AI is added, going from a descriptive system to a design engine that can suggest and improve solutions based on site-specific information, long-term climate projections, and public goals.

The foundation of sustainable urban water management is the idea of reuse. Stormwater and greywater reuse technologies present a competitive alternative to conventional water supply infrastructures as freshwater becomes more scarce. However, it is frequently challenging to identify the best site, architecture, and operating regime for such systems. By simulating various reuse situations, AI-enhanced digital twins can compare the effects of variables like as maintenance costs, evapotranspiration rates, water demand profiles, and rainfall variability on performance over time. They can suggest dispersed networks of small-scale reuse facilities, such greywater recycling units or rainfall harvesting tanks, that are positioned thoughtfully to service entire precincts or building clusters. By simulating natural hydrological cycles in the built environment, these devices assist cities in "closing the loop" and lowering their dependency on drinkable water.

Retention is equally vital. Cities built to withstand flooding must have the capacity to temporarily retain water, which will restrict its flow across hard surfaces and allow it to soak, seep, or evaporate. A new breed of green and hybrid retention systems, including as sponge parks, vegetated ponds, green medians, and bioswales, have replaced traditional culverts and detention basins. These systems not only hold water but also temper the microclimate, increase biodiversity, and improve public space. When used in a digital twin setting, generative AI can analyze rainfall data, topography, land use, and subsurface conditions to identify the best locations for these kinds of systems. It can strike a compromise between avoiding culturally sensitive places, improving pedestrian experience, and maximizing retention volume while protecting buildable land.

Stormwater management's release phase is becoming more complex, particularly in urban areas that are battling aged drainage infrastructure or combined sewer systems. Smart stormwater systems combine predictive AI models that predict impending storms or pinpoint system bottlenecks with real-time telemetry, such as flow sensors, valve actuators, and water-level gauges. By rerouting flows to alternate holding zones, adjusting pump activity in response to downstream river levels, or postponing discharge during periods of high rainfall, this data enables dynamic control of water release inside a digital twin. These millisecond-fast decisions rely on continuous feedback and high-speed data integration, two capabilities that digital twins are uniquely suited to offer.

In this infrastructure design process, generative AI plays a revolutionary role. It can investigate thousands of potential infrastructure configurations—changing size, location, materiality, and operational rules—to maximize performance under a variety of future circumstances by learning from historical and simulated datasets. It helps with multi-objective decision-making, assessing trade-offs between cost, carbon footprint, ecological gain, and social benefit, in addition to automating engineering computations. A generative model might, for example, recommend a bioswale alignment that maximizes runoff capture, enhances walkability, and places shade trees along streets that are prone to heat. Alternatively, it might reorganize a retention pond to accommodate both recreational and hydrological purposes, suggesting design changes that improve accessibility and safety without sacrificing technical functionality.

Additionally, cities can use generative technologies to customize microclimate interventions, adjusting plans for regions with limited tree canopy, high imperviousness, or sensitive populations. Digital twins allow for spatial precision rather than the use of general solutions, such as the deployment of porous surfaces where infiltration is feasible or green roofs in areas with strong solar exposure and little ground-level space. Feedback loops can be used to track, assess, and modify these interventions over time. The twin receives performance data from sensors, such as pollution levels, water depth, and soil moisture, which enable real-time learning and adaptation by the models. Infrastructure evolves in response to shifting weather patterns, urbanization, and community demands rather than being static.

There are important planning and governance ramifications. Cities can transition from reactive maintenance to proactive planning and reallocate resources from damage repair to risk prevention by utilizing digital twins and artificial intelligence.

The ability to test infrastructure portfolios prior to allocating resources makes capital planning more flexible. Additionally, public participation is improved. Through the use of impact dashboards and visual simulations, residents can observe how suggested changes affect their neighbourhoods, providing information about areas that are vulnerable to flooding, areas that require repair, or local values that need to be maintained.

These talents are starting to spread over the world. A cloud-connected stormwater system in Copenhagen reduces combined sewer overflows by opening and closing valves in real-time in response to rainfall forecasts. Digital twin platforms are used in Singapore to model the hydrological impacts of detention tanks and green roofs in congested urban areas. Based on factors like slope, street width, and water quality objectives, planners in Los Angeles can find the best spots for rain gardens with the aid of AI-driven siting tools.

These examples mark a turning point. Water-sensitive infrastructure, created with AI and integrated into digital twins, is no longer secondary or experimental; rather, it is increasingly essential to climate-adaptive urbanism. Expanding access to these tools, standardizing their incorporation into planning processes, and enhancing institutional capacity to decipher and act upon their insights are increasingly critical. Because infrastructure needs to do more than just channel water in this era of climate unpredictability. It needs to respond, regenerate, and hold on.

6.4 From Data to Decision: Real-Time Management and Early Warning Systems

Climate change has made extreme weather occurrences more unpredictable, necessitating more than static preparations or post-disaster responses. Real-time operational information is increasingly necessary for cities to effectively coordinate reactions among various stakeholders, manage water systems dynamically, and foresee issues before they become more serious. Digital twins are particularly useful in this transition from reactive to anticipatory governance, as they function as active operational platforms that integrate data, computation, and action in addition to being planning tools.

A digital nervous system made up of IoT sensors, hydrological telemetry, and AI-enabled feedback loops is at the center of this change. Water levels, flow rates, rainfall intensity, valve positions, pump pressures, and even groundwater saturation are all recorded by sensor networks that are installed throughout urban watersheds, stormwater drains, rivers, retention tanks, and treatment facilities. The city's digital counterpart receives this information directly and processes them almost instantly.

Data is not just visualized once it is captured; it is also analyzed, correlated, and used. Adaptive algorithms detect emergent abnormalities, identify deviations from expected baselines, and initiate machine-learned or rule-based responses. For instance, if downstream capacity permits, the system may automatically start drainage through a downstream channel when stormwater levels in a detention basin get close to critical thresholds. Upstream inflow can be controlled by smart valves or diverted into temporary holding tanks if the intensity of the rainfall exceeds forecasts.

Often called dynamic infrastructure control, this capability marks a significant advancement over conventional water engineering, which has depended on manual supervision and static standards. It makes it possible for infrastructure to act in a flexible, context-aware way, modifying its operations on a minute-by-minute basis in response to both the present and the future. By successfully "thinking with the weather," these systems are able to adjust to sudden changes that might otherwise overwhelm inflexible hydraulic systems.

Importantly, digital twins also make it possible for several agencies to coordinate during situations involving water. A digital twin can give a single operating view of the hydrological system by combining data from emergency services, utilities, urban planning departments, and meteorological organizations. This facilitates coordinated responses, such as setting off alarms, notifying people to evacuate, or directing the positioning of emergency pumps and sandbags. Decision-makers can monitor the impact of interventions on the network and make necessary adjustments to plans because the system is updated continuously.

These systems' efficacy is dependent on interface design in addition to algorithmic intelligence and data fidelity. Complex hydrological dynamics must be easily and clearly communicated by digital twins to a variety of audiences, including emergency responders, city engineers, urban planners, and, increasingly, the general public. It is possible to visualize where water will accumulate, how long it will last, and which assets or communities are most at risk by using interactive simulation tools, visual dashboards, and predictive heatmaps.

Participatory risk awareness and citizen participation are made possible by this communication dimension; these will be discussed in more detail in the following subsection. However, the real-time affordances of digital twins encourage quicker, more transparent, and more assured decisions even at the institutional level. Policymakers can evaluate how a rainfall event has impacted underprivileged neighbourhoods; infrastructure managers can predict when pumps will require maintenance based on system load; and first responders can deploy resources based on hydrodynamic projections rather than just field reporting.

This expanding paradigm is demonstrated by notable cases from around the world. To coordinate flood defence measures in real time, Rotterdam's digital twin combines pump telemetry, tidal gates, and rainfall sensors (Morales Ortega 2023). Water utilities in Melbourne balance flood management and water reuse by adjusting stormwater collection infrastructure throughout precincts using AI-enhanced twins. In Seoul, vulnerable subway exits are proactively closed during heavy monsoons thanks to real-time flood forecasting dashboards connected to the urban twin.

As urban flooding increases in frequency and severity, real-time water intelligence is no longer optional. Digital twins create a predictive infrastructure that can prevent harm, save lives, and save long-term recovery costs when combined with AI-powered adaptive systems. They represent a shift in water administration from static to intelligent systems, from blind spots to collective vision.

Ultimately, better timing is just as important as having better tools. Seconds can be the difference between a disaster and a nuisance flood in hydrological management. A real-time decision platform's worth is not solely derived from its volume of data or aesthetic appeal, but also from its capacity to align action with demand, assisting cities in managing water resources not only effectively but also intelligently and precisely.

6.4.1 Engaging the Public and Democratizing Risk Awareness

Expert systems and institutional actors alone will not be sufficient for successful flood management as cities become more complex and climate hazards increase. It has become clear that behavioural resilience and public awareness are equally important aspects of urban water governance. At this point, digital twins can become civic tools rather than just technical ones, acting as interfaces for community empowerment as well as infrastructure monitoring. Digital twins provide new ways to include citizens in comprehending, anticipating, and responding to hydrological hazards through interactive storytelling, accessible alarms, and real-time visualisations.

A digital twin's capacity to convert ambiguity into clarity is what gives it its communication power. By their very nature, hydrological systems are dynamic, spatial, and frequently undetectable until a disaster occurs. Residents can "see" the city below when digital twins make these systems visible, for as through drainage capacity indicators, flood risk maps, or water flow simulations. For both experts and regular users of urban space—commuters, students, business owners, and vulnerable people residing in flood-prone areas—this visibility is essential. Geospatial layers and visual dashboards transform abstract danger into concrete knowledge.

Here, interactive interfaces are essential. Users can examine localized flood forecasts, drainage conditions, and emergency alerts via dashboards integrated into public websites, mobile apps, or community kiosks. By providing scenario-based visualisations, some systems go one step further. For example, "What happens to your street in a 100mm rainfall event?" or "If this canal overflows, where will the water flow?" These simulations, which are based on actual data but are displayed in easily comprehensible formats, allow people to make proactive decisions, such as moving cars, cleaning drains, or selecting a safer route.

However, digital twins also open up possibilities for two-way communication in addition to top-down communication. Citizens can contribute data to the system through participatory platforms, including real-time rainfall observations, clogged stormwater grates, and flood photos. The twin is enhanced by this community-based sensing, which provides firsthand knowledge, particularly in places that are not well-monitored or developed. By making locals co-observers of the urban water system, it bridges the gap between predicted outcomes and actual experiences.

In this situation, the concept of open dashboards becomes crucial. Cities promote a transparent and trustworthy culture by making urban water statistics publicly available. Understanding the rationale behind decisions increases the likelihood that people would support flood adaptation strategies, participate in early action, and heed notifications. Additionally, open data encourages outside innovation, enabling grassroots organizations, developers, and designers to create new tools, maps, or educational initiatives centered around the essential digital twin infrastructure.

Crucially, digital twins facilitate spatial storytelling as well, which has the potential to change how communities view water risk. Twin platforms can animate the stories of previous floods, future projections, and local coping mechanisms instead of displaying flood maps as static layers of hazard. These narratives might overlay resident accounts and illustrate how new initiatives will prevent a repetition of the 2011 neighbourhood school floods. Spatial storytelling humanizes risk and strengthens the emotional bond with adaptation efforts by fusing data with memory and foresight.

International examples highlight this civic dimension's potential. Informal settlements in Jakarta have been able to push for better drainage thanks to flood maps that have been augmented with crowdsourced inputs and historical photos. Residents of Copenhagen can experience flooding from a street-level perspective thanks to immersive simulations, which has sparked cooperative design workshops about urban blue-green infrastructure. Block-by-block flood susceptibility metrics are available on public dashboards in New York City, which assist communities in implementing localized resilience strategies and submitting funding applications.

Additionally, digital twins can be used in schooling. Children can learn about climate change, stormwater infrastructure, and the water cycle in schools using interactive urban models. Simplified interfaces can facilitate neighbourhood-level flood drills or home preparedness training in community centers. By integrating water literacy into the social fabric of urban life, these interactions foster long-term resilience.

However, fair access is equally essential to the democratic promise of digital twins. Not every community has the time to interact with complicated interfaces, digital literacy, or dependable internet access. Twin-based engagement initiatives must therefore be multi-modal, integrating online dashboards with offline community mapping sessions, printed risk maps, SMS alerts, or local language radio broadcasts. Instead of being an afterthought, inclusivity needs to be ingrained in the structure of participation.

Finally, using digital twins to engage the public is about redistributing awareness, agency, and responsibility rather than just spreading knowledge. It involves fostering a civic culture in which water risk is viewed as a shared urban reality that is recognized, anticipated, and addressed collectively rather than as a remote expert concern. By bridging the gap between infrastructure intelligence and collective resilience, digital twins transform from control systems into civic platforms. These tools revolutionize how cities interact with themselves and provide care for those most vulnerable to the effects of climate change by making flood risk visible, relevant, and actionable.

6.5 From Risk to Regeneration: Rethinking Urban Water Futures Through AI

As discussed in this chapter, the use of generative AI and digital twins in urban water management represents a significant change in how cities perceive, anticipate, and address hydrological risk. However, our aspirations must go beyond astute observation and accurate forecasting if we are to meet the full scope of the climate crisis. A regenerative paradigm that reimagines urban water systems as living, adaptable, and community-nurtured ecologies is required, in addition to more effective water governance. This change necessitates a close coordination of social justice (Allam and Cheshmehzangi 2024), ecological restoration, and technological intelligence.

A shift in perspective is the first step toward regeneration. Water was viewed as a linear resource over a large portion of the industrial and contemporary planning eras: taken, consumed, treated, and released. To manage it, infrastructure was created to push it away from populated areas, channel it into pipes, and temper its unpredictable nature. However, this model is breaking under the strain of climate fluctuation. These days, cities deal with both too much and too little water—spatially, seasonally, and concurrently. Rather than opposing complexity, regenerative water urbanism welcomes it. By reestablishing the disrupted cycles that originally let water to be retained, filtered, slowed, and reused within the landscape itself, it completes the circle.

In order to construct such flexible, circular water systems, digital twins are essential (Sabharwal and Murari 2025). They can direct the planning and administration of facilities that not only reduce risk but also restore capacity because they are real-time reflections of urban hydrology. A digital twin, for instance, can assist in the strategic placement of bioswales, rain gardens, and subterranean retention tanks—each of which contributes to both risk reduction and ecological enrichment—by modelling seasonal water supply, soil absorption, and storm surge scenarios. With the use of these tools, planners can evaluate not only what is technically feasible but also what can thrive in a given context—interventions that take into account local ecosystem dynamics, cultural practices, and topographies.

Participatory design is also essential to regenerative water futures. Every community pattern, floodplain, and watershed is distinct, making urban hydrology incredibly place-based. No matter how advanced the technology, no top-down approach can completely account for or predict these subtleties. The ability of digital twins to facilitate co-creation is where they excel in this situation. Communities can actively participate in reshaping their water environments through interactive scenarios, spatial visualization, and easily available data layers. The digital twin becomes a common platform for group decision-making, from testing distributed reuse techniques to co-mapping flood memories.

Equally crucial, urban water needs to be socially inclusive in the future. Water stress and floods affect different residents. Vulnerable populations, including as elderly people, low-income neighbourhoods, and informal settlers, frequently reside in places that are most at danger and have the fewest resources available for recovery.

Thermal and hydrological equality are included into the planning process through a regenerative approach. It guarantees that funds for cooling parks, retention basins, or real-time alarm systems are dispersed where the greatest need exists rather than concentrated in affluent precincts. By detecting overlaps between flood and heat exposure and demographic vulnerability, generative AI can help achieve this goal and make sure the twin does more than just mimic systems—it can also indicate when justice needs to be served.

Furthermore, regeneration takes time. Instead of only responding to the next crisis, it calls for governance structures that may change across decades. Digital twins provide a link between long-term planning and real-time operational control. They become learning systems that assist cities in adapting their water strategy as circumstances change by recording historical occurrences, monitoring performance indicators, and feeding into adaptive feedback loops. This necessitates cross-sectoral commitment and institutional will, with people, utilities, environmental agencies, and urban planners all working toward a common, open, and updated platform.

However, digital twins must also change to fully support a future with regenerative urban water. They need to transition from infrastructure monitoring tools to ecological intelligence systems. This entails combining land use change models, watershed health measurements, and biodiversity markers. It entails being transparent in terms of governance, ethics, and community accessible in addition to technological interoperability. A regenerative twin is a civic infrastructure that reflects and supports the changing city life, not just a high-performing algorithm.

Ultimately, the urban water dilemma is about separation rather than just excess or lack. Disconnection between people and the waters that influence their lives, between data and decision-making, and between ecosystems and infrastructure (Bell 2015). With the help of AI and digital twins, regenerative design provides a way to return to wholeness. It re-establishes creativity with justice, stewardship with technology, and flow with form.

Cities must develop into places that not only withstand the flood but also get stronger as we confront the impending storms, both literal and figurative. They have to rehabilitate, adapt, and learn. Water is not an enemy to be controlled in this future; rather, it is a teacher to be heard, a lifeline to be preserved, and a shared duty to be carried—yes, digitally modelled, but ultimately lived together.

References

Abera L (2025) The growing role of artificial intelligence in tomorrow's urban hydrological infrastructure. Institute for Homeland Security. Huntsville, Texas: Sam Houston State University. https://shsu-ir.tdl.org/items/f2eadd8c-5419-4a88-a256-17cb87d411eb

Alexander M, Priest S, Mees H (2016) A framework for evaluating flood risk governance. Environ Sci Policy 64:38–47

Allam Z, Cheshmehzangi A (2024) Theoretical and international perspectives on sustainable futures. In Allam Z, Cheshmehzangi A (2024): Sustainable futures and green new deals. Springer Nature Switzerland, Cham, pp 29–53

Bell S (2015) Renegotiating urban water. Prog Plann 96:1–28
Cheshmehzangi A (2022) Green infrastructure and urban sustainability: an editorial. In Cheshmehzangi A (ed.) (2022): Green infrastructure in Chinese cities. Springer Nature Singapore, Singapore, pp 1–17
Cheshmehzangi, A., Sedrez, M., & Flynn, A. (2024). Stormwater management: issues, opportunities, and challenges in cities and communities. In: Cheshmehzangi A, Sedrez M, Flynn A (eds) Rethinking stormwater management through sustainable urban design, (pp. 1–22). Springer Nature Singapore, Singapore
Hassija V, Chamola V, Mahapatra A, Singal A, Goel D, Huang K, Scardapane S, Spinelli I, Mahmud M, Hussain A (2024) Interpreting black-box models: a review on explainable artificial intelligence. Cogn Comput 16(1):45–74
Morales Ortega LR (2023) A digital twin for ground water table monitoring. Master's thesis, University of Twente, Enschede
Ndubuisi OG, Amaka C, Aku Ugah T, Agbakhamen CO, Ali SE, Nesiama O (2025) Integrated water resource management in a changing climate: assessing adaptive strategies, technologies, and policies for resilient water system. Int J Innov Scientific Eng Technol Res 13(2):264–277. https://www.seahipublications.org/wp-content/uploads/2025/04/IJISETR-J-24-2025.pdf
Sabharwal D, Murari UK (2025) AI-driven solutions for sustainable urban development: smart cities and resource management. In Çağrı Yıldırım D, Yıldırım S, Kandpal V. (eds.) (2025): Effects of digitalization and circular economy on sustainable policy and climate change prevention. IGI Global Scientific, Hershey, pp 351–378
Tota-Maharaj K, Karunanayake C, Kunwar K, Chadee AA, Azamathulla HM, Rathnayake U (2024) Evaluation of permeable pavement systems (PPS) as best management practices for stormwater runoff control: a review. Water Conserv Sci Eng 9(1):32
Zhao T, Song C, Yu J, Xing L, Xu F, Li W, Wang Z (2025) Leveraging immersive digital twins and AI-driven decision support systems for sustainable water reserves management: a conceptual framework. Sustainability 17(8):3754

Chapter 7
Cities as Living Systems: Circular Metabolisms, Climate Intelligence, and the Architecture of Regeneration

7.1 Rethinking Urban Metabolism

Cities must be viewed as metabolic systems; organisms that absorb, alter, and expel matter and energy in intricate, interrelated ways, rather than merely as constructed settings in the era of resource shortage and climatic crises. By redefining the city as a living system with inputs and outputs, similar to an ecosystem or biological creature, the idea of urban metabolism is presented (Zou et al. 2022). The energy fuels that illuminate our homes, the materials that shape our buildings, the water that nourishes our bodies and green areas, and the associated outputs—carbon emissions, solid waste, heat, wastewater—that are frequently externalized or disregarded are all made apparent by it. Rethinking urban metabolism is a prerequisite for rethinking urban sustainability.

Cities have historically functioned according to a linear metabolic model, in which resources are harvested, used, and then wasted. Water is pumped, processed, and flushed away; food is transported in and wasted; fossil fuels are consumed for transportation and electricity. Although this strategy has provided short-term convenience, it has come at a significant long-term cost. It exacerbates systemic inefficiencies and produces a cascade of environmental problems, including greenhouse gas emissions, ecological deterioration, and contamination of the air and water. Additionally, it strengthens reliance on centralized infrastructures and extractive supply chains, which are becoming more fragile due to the stresses of urbanization and climate change.

In light of this, the idea of the circular economy shows up as a revolutionary substitute. Circularity proposes a cradle-to-cradle approach to resource consumption, in which materials are recycled, remanufactured, regenerated, and reintegrated into the system. Waste turns into a resource. Stewardship is the result of consumption. Instead of lines, cities turn into loops. In terms of metabolism (Cui et al. 2019), the objective is to rewire the city's digestive logic—how it processes, circulates, and metabolizes matter and energy—in addition to curbing its desire for virgin resources.

A. Cheshmehzangi, *Generative AI-Powered Urban Digital Twins*, Urban Sustainability,
https://doi.org/10.1007/978-981-95-4766-1_7

Designing out waste, keeping materials at their best value, and regenerating natural systems are the tenets of the ‘circular economy’, which provide a potent framework for changing urban metabolism (Domenech and Borrion 2022). However, circularity includes more than just increasing recycling and composting. It necessitates a complete overhaul of urban systems, including the planning and demolition of buildings, the production and distribution of food, and the coordination of materials, energy, and mobility throughout space and time. It takes more than excellent intentions to bring about this systemic change. It requires intelligence, namely the ability to monitor, simulate, and act in real time throughout the entire range of urban flows.

This is where the combination of digital twins and generative AI offers significant new possibilities. AI-powered digital twins highlight the hidden facets of urban metabolism by simulating intricate situations, modelling interconnected systems, and visualizing resource paths (Ranawaka et al. 2024). They enable communities, engineers, and planners to understand where resources could be recovered, where energy is being lost, where emissions are highest, and where interventions could have the biggest effects. In addition to mapping current fluxes, these systems offer fresh ideas on how cities could rewire their metabolic loops to be more flexible, circular, and equitable.

Importantly, this more comprehensive metabolic approach cannot be separated from carbon reduction and climate action. Carbon emissions are the result of broken urban systems, thus they are not a singular issue (Hong et al. 2022). A building leaking energy, a truck sitting in traffic, or a factory with manufacturing goods that are thrown away after a few weeks are all signs of metabolic inefficiency more than just carbon issues. Cities must address the underlying causes ingrained in their transportation, manufacturing, growth, consumption, and disposal practices if they are to meet net-zero ambitions or become carbon neutral.

Recasting emissions through a metabolic lens allows us to view carbon as both an indicator and a result of consumption patterns, infrastructural legacies, and design decisions, as well as an indicator of urban health. Redesigning the flows that generate emissions is therefore necessary to reduce them. Rethinking supply chains, moving toward renewable and local energy sources, or incorporating green-blue infrastructure—which restores habitats while lowering urban heat and energy consumption—could all be part of this.

Additionally, metabolic thinking promotes a cross-scale perspective on urban change (Cheshmehzangi 2025). Although a single building may have net-zero emissions, how does it relate to the city’s, the region’s, or the precinct’s larger resource loops? In a similar vein, a recycling program may be successful in a particular neighbourhood, but what are the consequences for upstream materials and is it possible for the model to scale without unanticipated rebound effects? By enabling simulations at different dimensions, digital twins assist in navigating these issues and help cities identify ripple effects and create system-wide, context-sensitive responses.

Building circular cities involves more than just implementing technology, as this chapter will examine; it also entails rethinking how we perceive and manage urban systems. Generative AI-informed digital twins offer a set of tools for bringing the invisible to life, facilitating cross-sector coordination, and establishing aspirational objectives—such as carbon neutrality and regenerative development—in concrete, data-driven practice. The transition from extraction to regeneration, from control to co-evolution, and from cities as machines to living metabolisms capable of healing, adapting, and thriving, is fundamentally philosophical.

7.1.1 From Linear to Circular: Principles of the Circular Economy

The fundamental ideas of circular cities—designing out waste, reusing materials, and regenerating natural systems—are defined in this subsection. It highlights how AI and digital twins can operationalize circularity at the urban scale and connects these ideas to net-zero carbon goals. One of the most significant paradigm shifts of our time is the move from linear to circular urbanism. The circular economy advocates for a comprehensive overhaul of how cities handle resources, trash, and ecological linkages, in contrast to the prevalent "take-make-dispose" paradigm that has guided urban growth since the Industrial Revolution (Fletcher 2019; Dąbrowski et al. 2025; Shinde 2025). Three fundamental ideas form the basis of this model: regenerating natural systems, minimizing waste and pollution, and preserving goods and resources. In addition to reorienting urban planning and architecture, each principle directly promotes social justice, biodiversity restoration, and climate mitigation.

To design out waste, one must change their perspective from considering waste as an unavoidable byproduct to acknowledging it as a design failure; hence, a mental shift is essential. Materials are chosen and systems are set up in a circular city to minimize waste before it even occurs. Food systems are designed to minimize spoiling; buildings are built with disassembly in mind; and packaging is either biodegradable or recyclable. This idea pushes engineers, designers, architects, and legislators to incorporate circularity from the beginning rather than as an afterthought. Imagining the end of life of every material and process from the beginning is an act of prefiguration.

The importance of looping fluxes within the urban system is emphasized by the second principle, which is to keep materials and products in use (Mohan et al. 2020). Through recycling, remanufacturing, repair, and reuse, the circular economy aims to preserve value rather than allowing resources to move linearly from source to disposal. This idea serves as the foundation for the urban mining concept, which views the city as a dynamic storehouse of materials—buildings, cars, and infrastructure—that can be reused and reintegrated rather than as a terminal consumer of resources. To prolong the lifecycle of assets and lessen the need for the extraction of virgin resources, it promotes shared-use platforms, materials banks, reverse logistics, and circular supply chains at the systems level.

Regenerating natural systems is the third and possibly most revolutionary principle. The circular city restores, whereas the linear economy depletes and extracts. Urban forests, wetlands, green roofs, and bioswales are examples of green and blue infrastructure that is no longer considered decorative but rather necessary since it purifies the air and water, cools neighbourhoods, stores carbon and restores ecological function. In this way, circularity is more than just a technical solution. It is an ethic of environmental reciprocity and stewardship. Regeneration proposes a beneficial contribution to the biosphere—designing systems that give back more than they take—as opposed to "net-zero", which is a balancing act of emissions accounting.

However, putting these ideas into effect in urban settings is a difficult task. Cities are cluttered, complex, and politically intertwined. Circularity necessitates long-term vision, real-time intelligence, and coordination at the systems level; it cannot be accomplished by a single actor or action. Digital twins driven by AI are useful in this situation.

In its more sophisticated form, digital twins allow cities to simulate circular circulation in both space and time. They may mimic the effects of various intervention tactics and track material stocks and flows, such as organics in food chains, water in systems, and steel in buildings. They enable urban planners to evaluate the effects of water harvesting networks, material reuse warehouses, and decentralized composting hubs in relation to larger systems rather than in isolation. To put it briefly, they translate the circularity vision from an abstract notion to practical understanding.

This capability is improved by generative AI, which suggests new system configurations. Generative models can envision thousands of future paths based on changing inputs, such as a shift in the climate, an increase in population, or a new material discovery, as opposed to merely depending on past data or deterministic models. They can create logistics chains that maximize reuse with little energy input or optimize urban layouts that minimize construction waste. To facilitate circular transitions, they can even create prototypes, regulations, or communication plans. In a world of increasing interdependence and uncertainty, this creative, anticipatory intelligence is essential.

Furthermore, there is a close connection between carbon neutrality and circularity. Cement manufacture, energy use, and garbage incineration are just a few of the linear processes that contribute to greenhouse gas emissions. Circularity lowers emissions at the source by regenerating nature, minimizing waste, and preserving material value. AI-powered twins are able to compute embodied carbon savings, create carbon budgets that are in line with global boundaries, and monitor these reductions across initiatives. As a result, digital twins not only encourage circularity but also quantify its climate advantages, making it understandable to communities, financiers, and policymakers.

Crucially, circularity isn't only a technocratic goal. Politics, values, and practice cultures are all involved. AI and digital twins should be used to promote inclusive co-design rather than impose top-down optimization. Community-generated information, open data platforms, and participatory dashboards can democratize circular planning by empowering neighbourhoods to map their own metabolic fluxes and imagine regenerative futures. As this chapter goes on, we'll see how cities are transitioning from linear excess to circular intelligence thanks to the convergence of AI, digital twins, and circular design. It is a shift in worldviews as well as systems, moving toward cities that are ecologically giving, metabolically aware, and able to learn how to coexist peacefully within boundaries.

7.2 Emissions Intelligence: Tracking Carbon in Real Time

This section examines the measurement and visualization of greenhouse gas emissions in urban areas using AI-powered digital twins. It covers remote sensing, embedded IoT devices, and data sources (such as energy grids, transportation networks, and industrial output). Additionally, it looks into how cities may use digital twins to pinpoint emissions hotspots and track decreases over time. With more than 70% of global carbon emissions attributed to urban activity, cities are at the center of the climate catastrophe due to the rapid pace of urbanization. However, if cities can precisely measure, localize, and reduce their emissions, they are also in a unique position to serve as decarbonization engines. In this regard, the combination of real-time emissions intelligence and AI-powered digital twins marks a significant advancement in urban climate governance. Digital twins are helping cities create a detailed, spatially explicit understanding of their greenhouse gas (GHG) footprints by combining dynamic data from energy grids, transportation networks, industrial processes, and human activity. This is a crucial first step in managing what cities can no longer ignore.

Data integration is at the heart of emissions intelligence, and digital twins are uniquely suited to this task. Conventional emissions inventories are frequently out of step with spatial reality, aggregated at annual or sectoral levels, and backward-looking. On the other hand, by integrating emissions data into dynamic, geographic city models, digital twins give the data life. From high-resolution satellite observations and remote sensing platforms to building energy consumption logs, smart meters, vehicle telematics, and IoT-enabled infrastructure, they absorb and integrate a variety of data sources. Every layer of data adds to a more comprehensive understanding of the locations, patterns, and causes of emissions.

For example, hourly energy consumption by source, such as rooftop solar versus fossil fuel-based electricity, can be reported via smart building systems. Transit data can show the carbon intensity of morning commutes or delivery patterns by reflecting emissions by mode and time of day. Waste management sensors monitor methane emissions from landfills or anaerobic digesters, while embedded Internet of Things devices in industrial zones can measure emissions from processes. Remote sensing platforms such as Sentinel-5P and GHGSat offer a top-down perspective of air concentrations at the urban fringe, providing wider trend analysis and external confirmation.

One of digital twins' most revolutionary contributions is the visibility of multi-scalar emissions (Islam 2025). It makes it possible to pinpoint pollution hotspots at the building, block, or even district level. Cities can now identify individual emitters or inefficient areas rather than depending on sector-wide proxies or average emissions per capita. An outdated diesel bus depot, a public housing complex with inadequate insulation, or a garbage plant that isn't performing up to par can all be mapped, tracked, and targeted for intervention. Not only is this spatial accuracy useful technically, but it is also strategically important politically, allowing for more open prioritization, focused funding, and community involvement.

Furthermore, tracking emissions in real time creates new opportunities for adaptive governance. Digital twins can give almost immediate feedback on the effectiveness of therapies when they are equipped with machine learning models and constant data inputs. Emissions curves can be used to model and track changes in building codes, congestion pricing schemes, or the adoption of electric buses, with real-time responses. Cities can use this capability to set dynamic targets, develop baselines for emissions, and iteratively adapt their plans over time. This is especially important when cities try to meet net-zero targets, which call for not just ambition but also measurable progress.

In this situation, generative AI acts as a catalyst. AI models are capable of more than just data aggregation; they can also identify correlations, non-linear patterns, and system relationships that human planners might overlook. They can predict how emissions will change under various energy and growth scenarios, or they can suggest design and policy alternatives that are best suited for reducing carbon emissions. AI can also quantify uncertainty through probabilistic modelling, highlighting data anomalies or providing confidence intervals around projections. As a result, emissions intelligence becomes more robust and richer, facilitating responsive and accountable policy actions.

Remarkably, the digital twin's visualisation layer converts complicated emissions data into easily understood formats. From urban managers to citizens, stakeholders can comprehend and analyze the carbon landscape with the help of interactive maps, temporal heatmaps, emissions dashboards, and scenario visualisations. Both external transparency and internal planning coordination depend on this accessibility. Emissions can be controlled once they are visible, have shape, time, and context.

However, ethical data governance must go hand in hand with this visibility. If emissions intelligence is not distributed fairly, there is a chance that it will reinforce surveillance methods or misrepresent communities. It is imperative that data fairness, consent, and accessibility be incorporated into emissions tracking systems. What data is gathered, how it is used, and which actions are prioritized must all be shaped by community input. Otherwise, the very instruments intended to facilitate urban climate action can perpetuate the disparities they aim to alleviate.

In conclusion, the abstract issue of urban pollution is becoming a concrete, geographical, and actionable topic thanks to AI-powered digital twins. They are helping cities go from emissions accounting to emissions responsibility, where choices are supported by data, advancements are precisely monitored, and climate plans are continuously improved. This combination of real-time sensing, AI analytics, and spatial computing may define the new frontier of climate intelligence in the rapidly developing subject of urban sustainability. As we move forward, the following part will examine how integration of emissions intelligence into circular economy systems expands and intensifies these capabilities, allowing for not only reductions but also regenerative advances in urban metabolism.

7.3 Modelling Circular Urban Flows with AI

The ability of circular cities to minimize waste, restore natural systems, and shut resource loops holds great potential. However, it takes more than just ambition to accomplish this on an urban scale—it takes brains. When combined with urban digital twins, generative AI provides a revolutionary way to model, plan, and optimize cyclical flows in intricate biological, material, energy, and water systems. A new paradigm of urban metabolism—one that is dynamic, adaptive, and actively regenerative—is emerging because of this convergence.

Fundamentally, a circular city is one that rethinks its systems as interconnected cycles where the products of one process become inputs for another, rather than as linear channels of input and discard. Urban digital twins are living maps of flows that track, predict, and forecast the movement of resources across the built environment, making such interdependencies visible and actionable. Then, generative AI takes over as the creative force, investigating different patterns, suggesting system redesigns, and maximizing resource use in both temporal and spatial dimensions.

The construction and demolition (C&D) industry, a significant contributor to urban waste, is one of the most potential sectors for AI-powered modelling. To predict the kinds and amounts of materials that will be produced during demolition, artificial intelligence (AI) can identify materials from architectural drawings, site scans, and sensor data using computer vision and natural language processing. Various reuse scenarios, such as matching deconstructed timber to new housing developments or routing salvaged steel beams to modular fabrication plants, can be simulated by generative models. Urban mining, in which cities recover resources from their current building stock rather than extracting new raw materials, is supported by this level of granularity.

In a similar vein, AI is being utilized more and more to predict demand and manage supply for recycled materials. For instance, digital product identities and material passports can be connected to digital twin platforms in circular building ecosystems, enabling suppliers and planners to instantly match reuse markets and predict demands. Recycling systems can increase in line with demand thanks to deep learning models' ability to predict future material flows based on zoning changes, urban growth trends, and regulatory changes. This lessens the inefficiencies and emissions related to logistics and the extraction of virgin resources by preventing both shortages and surpluses in secondary material streams.

In addition to materials, circular urban flows include food-waste-energy systems, which divert organic waste into nutrient recovery loops, composting, or biogas production. By modelling various collecting tactics, transportation routes, processing setups, and the physical arrangements of decentralized facilities, generative AI aids in the optimization of these systems. An AI model might, for example, locate neighbourhoods with a high potential for food waste, pair them with anaerobic digesters in the area, and recommend routing schemes that maximize energy yield while minimizing fuel consumption. Planners can target circular interventions where the greatest environmental and social benefits can be achieved by layering socio-economic data on top of these simulations in digital twin environments.

Another area where AI and circularity collide is in water reuse. AI models can forecast greywater availability, model storage requirements, and suggest the installation of treatment systems like constructed wetlands, decentralized filtration units, or industrial reuse loops using real-time telemetry from weather stations, smart meters, and water sensors. In order to ensure that water systems are spatially integrated into the city fabric without interfering with current functions or aesthetics, these models consider both technological viability and urban form.

Importantly, generative AI imagines what may be rather than merely simulating what is. Under various inputs, such as population expansion, the effects of climate change, consumer trends, or regulatory limits, planners can test thousands of circular economy scenarios. AI can be used, for instance, in regenerative neighbourhood planning to simulate the long-term interactions between modular recycling hubs, nearby composting facilities, and green roofs to cut waste, produce energy, and improve soil health. In addition to environmental performance, these scenarios can be assessed for community acceptance, maintenance requirements, and co-benefits like biodiversity enhancement or local employment.

This frontier is already being explored by several cities. As part of the city's circular economy roadmap, Amsterdam uses AI-powered digital twin models to map and optimize material flows in the built environment. The idea of "smart circularity" is being used in Singapore to integrate water recycling and waste-to-energy systems into a single urban twin. AI-powered dashboards in Tokyo track food waste streams from eateries and marketplaces, providing information to composting initiatives and redistribution networks.

However, systems thinking, cross-sectoral cooperation, and strong data governance are necessary for operationalizing such intelligence. Bureaucratic silos and jurisdictional boundaries are not respected by material flows. AI-twin systems need to work together across supply chains, government agencies, and community members to be successful. Additionally, they have to manage trade-offs between decentralization and economies of scale, between circularity and carbon, and between system efficiency and public acceptance.

In summary, using AI to model circular urban flows is a structural rethinking of how cities source, use, and renew their material base rather than just a technical improvement. Digital twins supply the context, fidelity, and feedback, while generative AI supplies the creativity and computational power. When combined, they provide a potent framework for regenerative urbanism in which every movement can be tracked, every intervention can be tested, and any potential future state can be designed.

7.4 Scenario Design for Carbon Neutrality and Net-Positive Development

The debate is no more whether cities should transition, but rather how to do so in a way that is equitable, methodical, and future-proof as they struggle with the increasing demands of decarbonization. Scenario design made possible by digital twins and generative AI is becoming a vital planning tool in this pressing environment. Urban decision-makers may now model, test, and repeat decarbonization paths in silico before allocating resources on the ground, removing the need for static masterplans or compartmentalized solutions. The outcome is a more flexible and comprehensive strategy for reducing carbon emissions, one that can be both large-scale and impactful.

Planners can create intricate and dynamic decarbonization scenarios that incorporate various systems, including buildings, energy, transportation, land use, and ecosystems, into a single simulation environment by combining digital twins with generative models. These models project into conceivable futures while remaining rooted on historical and real-time data. Planners can use this feature to examine the effects of different treatments in combination rather than separately. For example, what would happen to thermal resilience and carbon emissions if a district switched to electric buses, required green roofs, and planted a lot of trees? What are the trade-offs between operational savings over a 30-year period and the embodied carbon from retrofits? What is the impact of densification strategies on per capita mobility emissions?

These kinds of inquiries are no longer rhetorical. Digital twin platforms are already being used to model multi-sectoral decarbonization initiatives in places like Singapore and Helsinki. By creating and improving thousands of potential interventions by varying variables like building orientation, materials, transit frequency, or photovoltaic coverage, generative AI supports these initiatives. Planners can identify optimal or nearly ideal pathways by traversing through this enormous design space. These pathways balance additional limitations like cost, equity, and land availability in addition to reducing emissions.

Building retrofits, which offer one of the biggest unrealized carbon reduction potentials in developed metropolitan contexts, are among the most potent applications of this scenario design approach. To suggest customized retrofit packages, generative AI can analyze thermal performance, occupancy patterns, material aging, and grid interactions. Replacement windows, improved insulation, intelligent HVAC systems, and the incorporation of renewable energy sources are a few examples. Cities can then prioritize interventions for the greatest impact per dollar invested by simulating the total carbon and energy benefits throughout a district using the digital twin.

Similarly, AI-generated scenarios are being used to reinvent transportation networks, which have long been regarded as recalcitrant emitters. Digital twins provide for real-time visualization of how mobility changes impact emissions, traffic, noise, and access, from switching to active modes for private vehicles to planning routes for electric buses and micro-mobility networks. By adding behavioural data and urban morphology, these simulations start to represent the lived experience of decarbonized urban living, going beyond simple logistical tools.

But decarbonisation is not the final horizon. Cities are increasingly using a net-positive approach, whereby the urban environment actively promotes ecological and atmospheric regeneration in addition to minimizing harm. According to this concept, cities absorb more greenhouse gases than they emit through a combination of natural and artificial means, turning becoming carbon sinks rather than generators. By incorporating urban forests, blue-green corridors, building-integrated carbon-capture systems, and soil-enhancing green spaces, scenario models can test such regenerative futures. In addition to producing carbon offsets, they enable cities to evaluate how various designs can enhance biodiversity, enhance air quality, and restore ecosystem services.

Net-positive urbanism is a philosophy that extends beyond conventional carbon accounting. It sees cities as proactive planetary healers that use their capital, density, and intelligence to generate surplus advantages for neighbouring ecologies and future generations. In this sense, digital twins are more than just operational dashboards; they are creative tools that let communities, planners, and legislators experiment with different urban restoration scenarios in a range of cultural, climatic, and economic contexts.

Naturally, the ability of scenario design to democratize foresight is just as powerful as its technical accuracy. Residents can co-explore possibilities, comprehend trade-offs, and argue for pathways that match with their beliefs when digital twin interfaces are made accessible through participatory tools like visual dashboards, immersive virtual reality experiences, or deliberative platforms. Decarbonization plans are guaranteed to be effective, equitable, contextual, and resistant to climatic and political upheavals thanks to this participatory foresight.

All things considered, scenario design for net-positive development and carbon neutrality is a paradigm shift in how cities operate, plan, and respond. We are no longer limited to reactive planning or dispersed mitigation because to the combination of generative AI and urban digital twins. Alternatively, cities can be modelled as living labs of the future, where sustainability is continuously improved, scaled, and recalibrated. Cities can genuinely become centers of regenerative potential and decarbonization engines by adopting this iterative and systemic perspective.

7.4.1 Governance for Circular and Low-Carbon Cities

The shift to low-carbon and circular cities is essentially a governance challenge rather than just a technical or infrastructure redesign issue. Institutions must abandon fragmented silos and embrace coordinated, cross-sectoral strategies that incorporate industrial, waste, water, mobility, land use, and energy systems into a unified urban metabolism in order to achieve systemic change. The architecture that institutionalizes, oversees, and integrates circular principles into routine urban operations and decision-making is governance.

However, the linear paradigms that contemporary governance systems are intended to change are frequently reflected in them. Building regulations might not take embodied emissions or material reuse into consideration; procurement rules might inadvertently penalize circular approaches by giving preference to the cheapest, single-use alternatives; and energy departments might function separately from transportation authorities. As a result, the systems that implement sustainability goals are not in line with them. More than just new policies are needed to overcome this; interagency cooperation and a reorganization of institutional logics are also necessary.

Policy integration is a crucial component of this change. Effective governance must integrate several areas, including land-use regulation with material recovery, water-sensitive planning with low-carbon mobility, and energy transition strategies with waste valorization. This integration needs to take place horizontally, between departments and sectors, as well as vertically, across municipal, regional, and national scales. Using performance indicators that transcend conventional policy bounds, cities such as Amsterdam and Copenhagen are experimenting with urban governance frameworks that specifically need circular economy thinking in strategic planning and budgeting procedures.

For circular business models to succeed, government must simultaneously establish favourable conditions. This can involve providing incentives to businesses that implement zero-waste supply chains, product-service systems, or material reuse; encouraging local production using recycled materials; or providing funds to innovation hubs that support circular startups. To move capital toward circular value creation, financial tools like impact investment vehicles, tax incentives, and green bonds are being used. In this situation, governance turns becomes a tool for creating new, intentionally regenerative economic ecosystems.

Importantly, the circular transition cannot be imposed from above through technocratic means. It needs to be co-produced by local businesses, communities, and residents. This need participatory governance structures that allow for localized experimentation, grassroots creativity, and public imagination. Circularity can be rooted in lived experience through cooperative ownership models, neighbourhood-scale material exchanges, community repair projects, and participatory budgeting. In addition to facilitating these practices, policies must guard against incumbent systems absorbing or diluting them.

Digital twins are useful tools for governance in this situation. They can serve as shared civic platforms, allowing a variety of actors to access, visualize, and act upon data that reflects the flows of materials, emissions, and value throughout the city, rather than being merely technical systems for engineers. These platforms can simulate the effects of cross-sectoral alignment, find synergies, and test policy interventions when integrated with generative AI. More significantly, they can help individuals comprehend how garbage moves, how emissions build up, and how actions made in one area of the city impact other areas when they are designed with inclusive interfaces. By doing this, digital twins turn into tools for openness, cooperation, and group vision.

Resilience and adaptation are also necessary for the governance of low-carbon and circular cities. Shocks to urban systems will include supply chain interruptions, political upheaval, and climatic change. Real-time learning, resource reallocation, and target revision are all necessary for governance structures. This agility is supported by generative tools and digital twins, which keep living models of the urban system that are updated with new information on a regular basis and can adapt to changing circumstances. In this context, governance ceases to be a set plan and instead becomes an ongoing act of intelligent adaptation.

In conclusion, low-carbon and circular city governance is not a side issue; rather, it is the foundation upon which change either accelerates or stagnates. It necessitates an openness to experimentation, a dedication to justice, and an integrated culture. It must democratize access to knowledge, cross disciplines, and align incentives. Only then will AI-powered digital twins enable the full potential of circular economy principles to be realized as a just and sustainable urban change.

7.5 Regenerative Urban Metabolisms: A New Compact with the Planet

Efficient waste management and emission reduction are no longer sufficient as the global crisis worsens and urban footprints grow. Reimagining the city itself as a regenerative organism that fixes, restores, and replenishes the ecological systems it depends on, rather than as a machine that extracts, consumes, and discards, is the challenge. The fundamental idea behind regenerative urban metabolism is to plan cities for ecological healing as well as sustainability. This idea necessitates a new agreement between the earth and cities.

We have looked at how generative AI and digital twins can be used to measure, model, and optimize energy, material, and emission flows in urban systems throughout this chapter. Although these technologies are strong enablers, their revolutionary potential is limited by the paradigms that govern their use. A regenerative metabolism is more than just an efficient one. It requires that we rethink urban systems to close loops for planetary stewardship as well as performance and ethical reasons.

A regenerative city starts with a new awareness of itself. It employs real-time data to understand its own entanglement with the environment, not just to optimize, but to reflect as well as to govern. Emissions maps are ecological mirrors that show the scope and nature of urban impact, not compliance dashboards. In addition to tracking input-output, material flow models also identify dependencies, leaks, and chances to reconnect urban metabolism with natural cycles. According to this theory, digital twins serve as cognitive tools for ecological literacy, enabling cities to "see" themselves as metabolic systems that are a part of larger living systems.

However, sensing is only the first step. The metabolic fluxes of the regenerative city must also be rewired. This entails transforming grey infrastructure into green-hybrid systems that breathe with the rhythms of soil, air, and water, waste into inputs, and emissions into resources. It entails creating neighbourhoods that act as micro-ecosystems, streets that grow food and filter water, and buildings that produce more energy than they use. These flows can be simulated and coordinated by AI-powered digital twins, which can synchronize actions across spatial and temporal scales, forecast demand peaks, and optimize energy balances (AIOTI WG Energy 2024). Their strength, however, resides in their capacity to assist citizens and planners in envisioning integrated futures in which ecological logic and material cycles coexist.

A new sort of foresight, one that embraces complexity, plurality, and intergenerational responsibility, is also necessary for the regenerative city. Cities must prepare for resilience, rehabilitation, and undoing of past harm in addition to efficiency and growth. Digital twins with scenario engines can be used to model long-term trade-offs, such as how biodiversity corridors are impacted by green retrofits, how urban air chemistry is affected by fewer vehicle kilometers, and how thermal and hydrological regimes are altered by rewilded zones. With AI tools that learn from the past and project ethical paths forward, these possibilities are not merely theoretical; they can be tested, visualized, and improved.

Importantly, regenerative urbanism is a cultural and philosophical aim as well as a technological one. It challenges us to adopt a reciprocal worldview rather than one of dominance over nature. Cities must become net-positive forces that sequester more than they emit, clean more than they pollute, and heal more than they injure. They cannot simply aim to be carbon neutral. This calls for intelligent values—justice, equity, humility, and care—that are ingrained in the very norms, regulations, and practices of urban governance, in addition to intelligent systems.

Digital twins can aid in institutionalizing these values if they are created inclusively and with responsible governance. They can promote accountability across sectors, facilitate participatory simulation of ecological futures, and democratize access to difficult knowledge. However, they must be viewed as platforms for co-creation rather than as tools of control; they are tools that can hold the contradictions of urban life while pointing in the direction of change.

Therefore, the city of the future is an open system of metabolic consciousness rather than a closed circuit of data and gadgets. It pays attention, adjusts, and reciprocates. It is not made against nature, but with it (Allam and Cheshmehzangi 2024). It does not externalize its expenses or outsource its garbage. It redistributes value throughout inclusive loops, replenishes water through its streets, and regenerates soil beneath its foundations. Thus, regenerative urban metabolism envisions a city that actively increases the ecological space for all life to flourish, rather than merely existing within the bounds of the planet. It is a city that enacts a new agreement with the planet—one based on renewal rather than extraction—through civic engagement, AI-powered intelligence, and circular design.

References

AIOTI WG Energy (2024) Edge driven digital twins in distributed energy systems: role and opportunities for hybrid data driven solutions. https://aioti.eu/wp-content/uploads/2024/01/AIOTI-Edge-driven-Digital-Twins-in-distributed-energy-sy (Accessed online on 17 June 2024)

Allam Z, Cheshmehzangi A (2024) Technological innovation and sustainable transitions. In Allam Z, Cheshmehzangi A (2024): Sustainable futures and green new deals. Springer Nature Switzerland, Cham, pp 55–79

Cheshmehzangi A (2025) Verticality and the metabolic city: Chongqing's adaptive urbanism in the heights. In Cheshmehzangi A (2025): City walks in Chongqing: mapping a multi-layered, multi-identity, and multi-locality city that never sleeps. Springer Nature Singapore, Singapore, pp 51–65

Cui X, Wang X, Feng Y (2019) Examining urban metabolism: a material flow perspective on cities and their sustainability. J. Clean. Prod. 214:767–781

Dąbrowski M, Van den Berghe K, Williams J, van Bueren E (2025) Going circular: unlocking the potential of regions and cities to drive the circular economy transition. Taylor & Francis, Abingdon-on-Thames

Domenech T, Borrion A (2022) Embedding circular economy principles into urban regeneration and waste management: framework and metrics. Sustainability 14(3):1293

Fletcher CA (2019) Towards zero waste: the search for effective waste management policy to support the transition to a circular economy. Doctoral dissertation, Manchester Metropolitan University

Hong S, Hui ECM, Lin Y (2022) Relationship between urban spatial structure and carbon emissions: a literature review. Ecol. Indic. 144:109456

Islam FS (2025) Artificial intelligence-driven smart waste-to-energy networks for climate-resilient circular resource management in vulnerable megacities. Int. J. Environ. Clim. Chang. 15(7):381–415

Mohan SV, Amulya K, Modestra JA (2020) Urban biocycles–closing metabolic loops for resilient and regenerative ecosystem: a perspective. Bioresour. Technol. 306:123098

Ranawaka A, Alahakoon D, Sun Y, Hewapathirana K (2024) Leveraging the synergy of digital twins and artificial intelligence for sustainable power grids: a scoping review. Energies 17(21):5342

Shinde P (2025) Innovative polymeric waste management systems to enhance circular economy. Digital Repository of Theses-SSBM Geneva

Zou T, Cheshmehzangi A, Dawodu A, Mangi E (2022) Designing an urban food system for achieving circular economy targets: a conceptual model. Eco-Archit. IX 210:15–27

Part III
Governance, Engagement, and Implementation Pathways

Chapter 8
AI and Digital Twins for Participatory Urbanism: Co-creating Cities Through Collective Intelligence

8.1 Rethinking Participation in the Age of Urban Intelligence

For many years, the idea of involvement in urban planning has been cited as a moral requirement—a goal toward fairness, inclusivity, and a democratic process. However, the restrictions of analogue-era administration, such as town hall meetings, static designs plastered to walls, comment boxes, and rigid planning cycles, limited involvement for a large portion of the twentieth century. Despite their good intentions, these techniques were exclusive, episodic, and frequently symbolic. Participation was mostly reactive, influenced more by bureaucratic rhythms than by community needs, and happened late in the process (Rosener 2015), after important decisions had been taken. The city was created for people, not with them, according to this model.

However, the concept of participatory urbanism is undergoing a fundamental redefinition as cities have become more complex and the tools for interacting with complexity have become more potent. Participation as a supplementary rite is giving way to participation as an ongoing and essential aspect of urban administration. This change has been accelerated by the development of generative artificial intelligence and digital twins. In addition to providing new ways to analyze and simulate urban systems, these technologies also open up new channels of communication between the public and the city.

A significant reorientation in epistemology lies at the core of this change. The digital shift creates a space for multiple knowledges to inform decision-making in real time, whereas analogue participation valued expert knowledge and considered public input as complementary. People may see and engage with the forces reshaping their neighbourhoods through urban digital twins, which are dynamic, data-driven reflections of the built environment. They transform spatial data into readable form that people who inhabit its boundaries can examine, challenge, and even redesign.

A. Cheshmehzangi, *Generative AI-Powered Urban Digital Twins*, Urban Sustainability,
https://doi.org/10.1007/978-981-95-4766-1_8

This change is further compounded by generative AI. It allows communities to create alternate futures rather than just visualizing current circumstances or extrapolating patterns. Consider a group of locals discussing potential designs for a new park in real time, working with an AI-powered system that takes into account their input, values, and preferences. Consider a neighbourhood business association using a generative model to model street activation tactics that balance social gatherings, pedestrian traffic, and economic activity. In many instances, AI functions as a creative collaborator integrated within the municipal fabric rather than as a remote intelligence influencing the city.

This shift from consultation to co-creation is conceptual as well as technological. It necessitates redefining participation as an iterative, contextual, multi-scalar activity. Today, participation needs to work at many levels, from the systemic (a city's climate adaptation plan) to the hyperlocal (a sidewalk redesign). It must traverse timelines, enabling both long-term planning inputs and instantaneous feedback loops. Additionally, it needs to be firmly rooted in the sociocultural landscape of the area rather than detached from it.

This is where the most revolutionary potential lies in combining generative AI with urban digital twins. When combined, they allow for a relational, as opposed to extractive, kind of urban intelligence. Participatory AI systems can establish feedback loops in which data-generated insights are given back to communities in ways that are understandable, useful, and powerful, as opposed to collecting data from communities and putting it into black-box models. This reciprocity is essential. If power is not changed, participation is meaningless. In the era of urban intelligence, authority is derived from the capacity to create, model, and make decisions.

But in order to fulfill this promise, we must face enduring obstacles. One of the biggest obstacles to participation is still the digital divide (Cheshmehzangi et al. 2024). What happens to people who don't have access to, know how to use, or trust digital platforms as a medium for civic engagement? Additionally, digital interfaces that permit surface-level interaction without real impact on results run the risk of being tokenism. Under the guise of inclusion, participatory digital twins and generative systems have the potential to repeat the exclusions of their analogue forebears if they are not carefully designed and managed.

As a result, in the era of artificial intelligence and digital twins, participatory urbanism requires more than just the implementation of new technologies. Institutional imagination is needed. Participatory architectures that are both digitally inclusive and epistemically diverse—able to include cultural memory, emotional geographies, and local knowledge into the planning process—must be constructed by cities. It is important to view participation as an act of co-authorship in which communities are asked to co-create, co-evolve, and debate predetermined visions in addition to validating them.

This broader perspective on involvement is already being tested in a few locations. Residents of Helsinki may evaluate the effects of development and visualize zoning changes thanks to the city's digital twin. The Decidim platform from Barcelona makes it easier to collaborate on policymaking (Aragón et al. 2017; Cardullo et al. 2023). Predictive hydrological models in Jakarta use public data through participatory flood mapping. These illustrations suggest a participatory future where people and algorithms collaborate to think, plan, and act rather than just using representation.

Participatory urbanism becomes a dynamic process in this setting, a civic activity driven by design, data, and discussion. It turns into a dynamic dance between the digital and the physical, the present and the future, the expert and the commonplace (Artopoulos and Costa 2019; Gün 2023). Most significantly, it serves as a way to recover agency in an urban environment that is increasingly influenced by factors outside the purview of conventional democratic processes.

We will examine how this change is implemented in practice as we move through this chapter, including how inclusive interfaces are created, how local narratives can be used to train generative AI, and how procedural justice, ethics, and power must inform every stage of this participatory revolution. For the time being, let's ground this change in the straightforward but radical notion that urban futures should be envisioned and created—collectively—rather than foreseen or enforced.

8.2 Interfaces of Inclusion: Tools for Civic Visualisation and Engagement

The tools that people use to see, comprehend, and shape the city must be created with the same consideration, purpose, and inclusivity as the actual spaces they are intended to influence if they are to be co-authored by its residents. The interfaces that link the public to these intricate systems are becoming increasingly important from a civic standpoint as generative AI and urban digital twins become more capable. They are more than just information carriers; they are interpretive lenses, translational acts, and empowerment tools.

The most effective participatory interfaces turn intangible data into concrete urban futures. They transform technical inputs, such as traffic patterns, microclimate simulations, and zoning laws, into forms that can be challenged, altered, and rethought. While virtual reality (VR) simulations and augmented reality (AR) overlays offer spatially contextualized previews of suggested modifications (Shahbaz Badr 2023), immersive dashboards provide easy-to-understand overviews of real-time urban dynamics. An AR-enabled gadget might be used by a citizen standing on a street corner to visualize a future flood intervention or green corridor over their current surroundings. Residents may explore a virtual reality (VR) version of a renovated plaza in a community hall (Chen et al. 2024), modifying elements and expressing preferences that are immediately fed into a generative design cycle.

But these tools need to be more than just impressive; they need to be inclusive. Furthermore, in the context of civic technology, inclusiveness is never a given. It calls for design that takes into account differences in age, aptitude, language, and digital confidence. Both an adolescent who is proficient in technology and an elderly person who is hesitant about it should be able to use the interface. They must function on a variety of platforms, including smartphones, public library printed visualisation boards, and touchscreens. In order to allow people with various skills or disabilities to actively engage in the moulding of their environment, they must be multilingual, multimodal, and multisensory when necessary.

This is a political problem as well as a technical one. Assumptions regarding who is considered a stakeholder and how knowledge is valued are encoded in the design of participation tools. Thermal injustice is not captured by a map that shows emissions data but leaves out the lived experience of heat. A 3D model that ignores housing precarity and displays property values but not rent burdens may represent market dynamics. Interfaces must incorporate qualitative narratives—stories, memories, aspirations, and fears—as well as quantitative data to genuinely support inclusion.

Another crucial frontier is digital literacy. People need to be able to access and comprehend participatory technologies in order for them to be effective. This calls for funding for workshops, public education, and hybrid participation strategies that combine digital and analogue platforms. A community is more likely to trust the process and use it again if it sees its input represented in a developing model. For participatory urbanism to be legitimate and vibrant, feedback loops that close the circuit—where input results in noticeable change—are crucial.

Recognizing that civic interfaces are not necessarily digital is equally crucial. Additionally, interactive murals, paper-based simulations, and tactile models are interfaces of participation. Such hybrid approaches continue to be invaluable in many situations, particularly those where access is unequal or trust in digital systems is poor. The ability of communities to envision themselves in the futures being modelled, the transparency of the process, and the significance of the interactions are more important than the technological complexity.

Lastly, AI-enhanced interfaces have potential for both interactivity and visualization. Communities may explore alternatives, evaluate trade-offs, and iterate designs in real time with the aid of generative technologies that respond to user feedback. When a homeowner offers a communal garden, an interactive twin might recalculate after demonstrating the advantages of a tree canopy in terms of reducing heat. Interfaces become sensitive, teachable, and reflective of the community will because of this dynamic involvement.

The interfaces of digital twins, as they develop into platforms for creativity and governance, will dictate not only who can participate but also how democracy is mediated in the future city. Therefore, the design of those interfaces needs to be based on civic ethics—inclusion, empathy, and care—rather than just technological feasibility.

8.2.1 *Designing the Digital Commons: Accessibility and Representation*

The dangers of exclusion in AI-enabled urbanism are covered in this subsection. It investigates how decisions about language, visualization techniques, and data privacy impact who is able to contribute in a meaningful way. It promotes open data principles, inclusive UX/UI design, and protections against algorithmic marginalization in civic ICT settings. A new frontier of public space has developed as cities move into the era of AI-augmented urbanism; it is not one that is surrounded with trees or paved with concrete, but rather one that is represented by data, code, and dynamic simulations. This digital common has transformational potential and is embodied in participatory platforms and urban digital twins. It gives communities the power to not only see but also influence how their neighbourhoods will develop in the future. However, the politics of control, representation, and access apply to these digital spaces just as they do to real public ones. The design of these systems determines who can see, hear, and speak; it is not just a matter of connectivity.

Accessibility is at the heart of this problem—not as a feature to be added, but as a fundamental idea. Language is the first step toward accessibility in AI-enabled urbanism. Residents who speak different languages or lack formal planning literacy are alienated by planning models and twin dashboards' frequent default to technical jargon or English-centric design. A young person in Cape Town, an old person in Brisbane, or a street seller in Jakarta may all be interested in urban transformation, but they will not be able to participate if interfaces do not speak their language, both literally and figuratively.

Barriers may also arise from the visual language of digital platforms. Some users, particularly those with cognitive or sensory disabilities, may find interfaces that rely on abstract symbols, colour codes, or spatial conventions confusing. Visualization techniques must be inclusive in both appearance and usage (Osiobe 2024), offering low-bandwidth alternatives, voice narration, colourblind-safe palettes, and alt-text. More significantly, they must make it possible for users to perceive their communities, issues, and goals represented in the system—not just as data points, but as lived experiences deserving of careful consideration in design.

Therefore, representation is about being appreciated rather than merely being visible. By incorporating biases into their algorithms or statistics, interactive platforms all too frequently perpetuate systemic injustices. A generative design algorithm trained on datasets biased toward wealthy neighbourhoods, for instance, would value green rooftops and broad boulevards more than informal settlements or culturally distinctive spatial practices. Although these biases are frequently imperceptible to users, they have a significant impact because they influence which alternatives are created, which interventions are considered "optimal," and who gains from simulating the urban future.

Deliberate ethics of inclusion in data sourcing and modelling are necessary to address this. Datasets that are representative, de-identified, and ethically supplied must serve as the foundation for participatory platforms. The same rigor and weight should be given to community-generated data as to satellite imagery or Internet of Things sensor data, whether it be information on heat stress in informal markets, mobility issues for individuals with impairments, or spatial memory in historically marginalized neighbourhoods. This actively reinterprets what "intelligence" in urban intelligence means, in addition to diversifying the inputs into generative systems.

Dealing with privacy and monitoring is another aspect of designing the digital commons. Citizens must have faith that their input, whether it be locational, biometric, or behavioural, won't be abused to participate in smart systems. Strong data governance—consent procedures, data anonymization, usage transparency, and distinct lines separating civic participation from surveillance—must coexist with open participation. Trust in digital platforms is something that must be consistently gained, especially in settings with histories of marginalization.

As a result, the interface turns into a negotiation zone between rights and risks, visibility and vulnerability, and not just between the user and the system. In this situation, inclusive UX/UI design is about politics as much as aesthetics. It is about making sure that a visually impaired citizen can participate in a street redesign plan, that a child refugee can utilize a climate resilience dashboard, and that a neighbourhood in the informal perimeter is not left out just because it is not included in official databases.

Encouraging transparency is equally important. Transparent algorithms, open-source platforms, and interoperable data standards enable community organizations, researchers, and planners to comprehend and influence the workings of AI-driven decision-making. Instead of merely consuming official simulations, communities can create their own interpretations and narratives by adhering to open data principles. They transfer authority from the system's creators to its users.

Openness without equity, however, can still be discriminatory. Investments in co-design facilitation, digital literacy, and long-term participatory infrastructures are necessary to keep the digital commons from turning into another privileged domain. On the other hand, AI systems and digital twins need to be built with the ability to listen as well as take in information. This means that they may be challenged, modified, and refocused by group feedback.

Lastly, the objective is to gain access to transformation rather than merely tools. Creating processes that validate the validity of many perspectives on the city is a key component of designing for accessibility and representation. It entails putting the experiences of individuals who are frequently excluded from urban futures front and center and making sure that the city's intelligence is based on the knowledge of its citizens rather than just algorithms. This makes the digital commons more than just an interface; it becomes a civic arena, a place of democratic imagination, where co-authorship is allowed to design the future and inclusiveness is not merely a checkbox but a shared attitude.

8.3 Generative Co-design: AI as a Partner in Collective Imagination

A new chapter in participatory urbanism is emerging as it transitions into the digital age, one in which communities actively participate in creating their own futures rather than only being consulted after architectural concepts are developed. The rise of generative AI as a tool for collaborative imagination is at the center of this change. Generative AI is transforming technology from a passive tool to a creative collaborator by converting concepts into dynamic visualizations, evaluating many design iterations, and adjusting in response to user feedback.

Time, technological know-how, or the strictness of planning frameworks have frequently been the limiting factors in traditional participatory methods. Although they could express preferences or complaints, residents hardly ever saw how their suggestions were turned into final design results. That equation is altered by generative co-design. Communities can submit concepts for parks, public areas, transportation options, or housing types using user-friendly AI-powered interfaces, and they can view several iterations produced in real time. These systems present a range of options that change as a result of constant discussion rather than prescribing a particular result.

Generative co-design holds promise because it can combine many intelligences. Local knowledge, which is rich, embodied, and based on lived experience, is on one side. The other is computational intelligence, which is quick, broad, and capable of simultaneously modelling cost implications, accessibility metrics, climatic interactions, and spatial configurations. The interaction between the two is a dialogue rather than a transfer from human to machine. Residents contribute knowledge of social networks, aesthetic ideals, safety concerns, and community rhythms. AI enhances this by modelling how various designs function in various contexts, restrictions, and conditions.

A new type of agency is invited by this hybrid workflow. For instance, community members can sketch a plan for the co-design of a neighbourhood park, possibly favouring open play areas for kids, vegetable plots for local use, and shaded sitting for seniors. In order to maximize sun exposure, water runoff, tree covering, and maintenance costs, generative AI can then produce a variety of designs that adhere to those criteria. Until the design accurately reflects community want and systemic feasibility, participants can analyze trade-offs, modify parameters, and iterate.

Crucially, these tools make subjectivity explicit rather than eliminate it. Generative co-design helps close the gap between vision and pragmatism by allowing communities to test their own preferences against performance measures. It makes the frequently opaque optimization and design decision-making processes more transparent. Furthermore, it gives locals the confidence to pose more insightful queries, such as: How do our concepts impact accessibility? What occurs if we plant additional trees? How can we strike a balance between environmental restrictions and community needs?

This is especially effective in situations where underrepresented groups have historically been left out of spatial decision-making. Platforms for generative co-design can serve as levellers by offering user-friendly tools that get around technical gatekeeping and give people without formal design training the ability to create spaces. These systems can even replicate the effects of interventions in real time when combined with digital twins, enabling users to test how their ideas impact flood resilience, cooling potential, or traffic flow.

To facilitate this collaborative approach, generative interface design itself needs to be inclusive. Low-bandwidth compatibility, visual simplicity, voice-guided engagement, and language options are all crucial. These tools can be transformed from cutting-edge technologies into community assets through facilitated workshops, local design ambassadors, and iterative engagement cycles.

Additionally, generative co-design creates new opportunities for planning across generations. Together, children, young people, seniors, and newcomers can exchange ideas and investigate spatial futures. Visualizations produced by AI serve as a common platform, converting intangible discussions into concrete suggestions. By doing this, they transform planning into a multi-layered process of investigation, contemplation, and revision rather than a sequential, expert-led sequence.

However, the objective is to broaden the imagination rather than to take the position of planners or designers. Generative AI works best when it presents possibilities that might not have been considered otherwise—when it stimulates fresh ideas rather than passing judgment on preexisting ones. The machine thus turns into a partner in civic imagining. Finally, generative co-design reinterprets who is entitled to—and able to—influence urban environment. It transforms passive involvement into active authorship. By doing this, it brings to reality the democratic promise of planning, which states that cities are created not just for the people but also with them, using their combined imagination and inventiveness.

8.3.1 Embedding Local Knowledge in Generative Systems

The methods for incorporating Indigenous, cultural, and lived experience into AI models and urban digital twins are covered in this subsection. In order to guarantee that generative systems represent place-based knowledge rather than abstract optimization, it looks at participatory datasets, narrative mapping, and qualitative data integration. A crucial question that emerges when generative systems increasingly influence the visualization, simulation, and design of urban areas is whose knowledge informs these systems? AI-driven tools run the risk of reproducing abstraction, erasure, or homogeneity if they don't make a conscious effort to incorporate local, Indigenous, and culturally specific knowledge into their architecture. It is not appropriate to treat generative intelligence as value-neutral. Rather, it needs to be based on the voices, circumstances, and spatial memories of the communities it is meant to support.

Meaning, memory, and identity are all important aspects of urban design in addition to form and function (Cheshmehzangi 2023a, 2023b). Local stories, customs, daily routines, and intergenerational memory all preserve these intangible attributes. In example, indigenous knowledge systems frequently represent profound environmental understanding, spatial ethics, and custodianship values that go much beyond standard planning criteria. To support genuinely inclusive urbanism, generative systems need to be built with the ability to recognize and value these types of intelligence.

Data is the starting point here, but not in the traditional sense. The notion of data must be expanded by generative system designers to encompass qualitative mappings, oral histories, community narratives, and participatory datasets rather than just numerical data. These resources provide deep understanding of how people experience, perceive, and value space. Community-led mapping projects, for instance, can highlight unofficial meeting places, social corridors, or areas of felt safety—aspects essential to spatial justice that could never be shown on official land use maps.

Rethinking the inputs that influence machine learning is necessary to incorporate such information into generative systems. Participatory data-gathering techniques such as photovoice, sketch mapping, narrative workshops, and sensor-supported ethnography can be used to contribute into the training datasets that guide generative design, as opposed to depending exclusively on top-down information (such as zoning, census data, or climate models). The finer details of a place, such as how light feels beneath a tree, where unstructured play takes place after school, or which streets feel safe after sunset, are captured by these techniques.

Additionally, narrative mapping is essential. This method transforms a map into a living canvas of memory, meaning, and experience by superimposing stories onto geographical locations. Generative simulations can be guided by these stories once they have been digitalized and geotagged. The generative system can be educated to maintain, improve, or safeguard spatial qualities, for example, if a society consistently recognizes a space as sacred, dangerous, or socially significant. AI models can be encouraged to respect and promote community priorities by giving semantic weight to qualitative input.

Using vector embeddings from qualitative corpora is one new method in this field. Structured embeddings, which are mathematical representations that encapsulate links between words, themes, and attitudes, can be created from oral histories, interviews, or place-based narratives. These can serve as extra training layers in generative models, guaranteeing that design suggestions are culturally relevant in addition to being spatially rational.

Specifically, digital twins provide an effective platform for incorporating local expertise. These models don't have to be strictly administrative or technological. Rather, they can develop into "civic twins"—archives of contextual ethics, changing narratives, and collective memory. Communities become co-authors of their own spatial futures when they are given the opportunity to annotate and engage with digital twins by adding photographs, tales, or flags. Community annotations can sometimes even influence how AI analyzes social or environmental data, recalibrating the model to prioritize experienced realities over theoretical generalizations.

Particular consideration should be given to the integration of Indigenous knowledge systems. Relationality, accountability, and profound ecological awareness are frequently emphasized in these systems; these ideas provide vital counterpoints to extractive or technocratic conceptions of growth. Creating interfaces and workflows that allow Indigenous communities to directly influence what is encoded, how it is interpreted, and how it is applied is a more respectful approach than attempting to "translate" Indigenous knowledge into computational terms. This calls for agreements around data sovereignty, consent, and cultural integrity in addition to data pipelines.

Crucially, adding local information to generative systems improves the system's intelligence in addition to promoting fairness. Models that are culturally sensitive and contextually rich are better able to forecast usage trends, address community needs, and design resilient settings. AI systems acquire a more comprehensive view of a place when they are able to learn from both infrastructure and community wisdom patterns.

But humility is required in this integration. Not all information needs to be digitized or extracted. Algorithmic systems may need to be protected against delicate social dynamics, sacred information, or community trauma. The objective is to honour the existence and significance of knowledge in the design process rather than to translate it all into machine-readable form. To protect the integrity and dignity of local contributions, collaborative evaluation frameworks, ethics procedures, and participatory monitoring bodies are required.

Finally, creating AI tools that listen, learn, and react thoughtfully is all about reciprocity—integrating local knowledge into generative systems. It involves working together to co-create technologies that are rooted in culture as well as space awareness. By doing this, we move closer to creating cities where technology strengthens our ties to the past rather than erasing it.

8.4 Ethics, Power, and Procedural Justice in Participatory AI

Through a critical lens, this section asks who is in charge of the data, tools, and results in AI-assisted participatory urbanism. It challenges tokenism, consent, transparency, and digital paternalism. In order to guarantee that communities are not only consulted but also co-authors of their spatial futures, it also presents procedural justice frameworks for assessing participatory integrity. The alluring promise of "inclusion-by-design" needs to be critically examined as generative AI and digital twins become more popular in the field of participatory urbanism. Theoretically, technology tools can increase civic engagement, but they can also reinforce bias, concentrate power, and aestheticize participation without bringing about fundamental change. Therefore, the ethical landscape of participatory AI encompasses agency, ownership, and justice rather than just access or interface.

A basic question at the center of this investigation is who has authority over the instruments, information, and decision-making procedures. Although AI-mediated participatory platforms are routinely used under the guise of empowerment, their governance frameworks are typically still unknown. Developers write the code, technocratic teams edit the data, and institutional interests filter results. Communities, particularly those who are marginalized, are encouraged to "contribute" or "interact," but they are rarely given the opportunity to co-create on an equal basis. This disparity highlights a conflict between participation as a controlled spectacle and participation as a democratic right.

The first ethical fault line is transparency. Systems using generative AI that provide geographical solutions or policy objectives need to be transparent and auditable. Residents must be able to track the data used, assumptions made, and choices left out in order to see how a neighbourhood makeover based on AI-generated scenarios was created. Despite their sophistication, black-box systems undermine user confidence and disempower them, particularly when they are implemented in communities that are already subjected to systemic exclusion.

The next battlefield is consent. Although community members may be asked to contribute data, offer feedback, or "train" participatory systems, they are rarely told how their contributions will be used, who will benefit, or what their rights are in the event that they are misrepresented. A one-time checkbox is not sufficient for true participatory AI; continuous, informed consent is required. Additionally, it must provide safeguards and withdrawal procedures to stop cultural or community-specific knowledge from being appropriated for institutional or commercial benefit.

Additionally, participation technologies run the risk of becoming performative rituals rather than authentic engagements, a phenomenon known as tokenism. An AI model may take human choices for scenarios and a digital twin may be made available for public review, but the process is meaningless unless the input influences the final results in a significant way. When token involvement is enhanced by slick interfaces and data visualizations, it centralizes decision-making power while giving the appearance of empowerment. In places where promises of inclusion have previously failed, it can further worsen cynicism and disengagement.

An additional layer of difficulty is introduced by digital paternalism. AI models may be used to overcome community choices that are thought to be ineffective, illogical, or impractical when they are presented as "neutral" optimizers or "objective" planners. The power dynamics underlying technological rationality are concealed by such tales. Although communities are supposed to contribute, the machine—or the people who configure it—retains the final logic in this model. This reasoning must be resisted by participatory urbanism, which asserts that no matter how complex the algorithm, spatial justice cannot be delegated to it.

In order to overcome these moral conundrums, procedural justice frameworks—a perspective that considers not just results but also the legitimacy and fairness of the processes that generate them—must be used to hold participatory AI responsible. In AI-mediated planning, procedural justice is giving communities a say in defining issues, choosing tools, establishing agendas, and analyzing results. It calls for reflexive design teams, inclusive governance frameworks, and open conflict settlement and debate procedures.

Establishing community oversight boards, also known as "algorithmic councils," is one strategy that can be used to examine, question, and influence the creation of participatory tools. In order to guarantee that ethical considerations are incorporated into the design and implementation stages, these groups may consist of local activists, technologists, urban planners, inhabitants, and legal professionals. Prior to starting any AI modelling, another strategy is to institutionalize participatory design rules that prioritize community priorities. This flips the tool-first to community-first order.

Recognizing various types of information as legitimate and actionable is another aspect of procedural justice. Sensor data or statistical inference must be weighed equally with lived experience, cultural narratives, and social memory. One fact is a heatmap of foot traffic; another is a grandmother's recollection of the places where kids used to play. Instead of favoring one over the other, participatory AI has to create connections across various modes of knowing. This entails integrating narrative-based inputs, community validation phases, and qualitative feedback loops into generative workflows.

The ultimate objective is to prevent AI-assisted participation from turning into a digital stand-in for traditional hierarchies. A system is not necessarily equitable just because it is interactive or "open." Redistributing technical agency, changing institutional cultures, and designing with communities rather than for them are all necessary for true power-sharing. It entails approaching participation as an ongoing negotiation of urban futures rather than as a phase in the planning process.

Cities must be just as well as intelligent in a world that is becoming increasingly influenced by machine logic. With ethical governance and humble design, participatory AI presents an opportunity to reinvent democratic urbanism. Procedural justice must be the cornerstone of our digital interactions rather than an afterthought if that promise is to be fulfilled.

8.5 From Control to Co-creation: Designing Democratic Digital Twins for Just Cities

In the future, digital twins will be responsive, co-owned, and morally controlled democratic infrastructures, according to the part that ends. It synthesizes the chapter's findings into a set of tenets that serve as a framework for participatory AI in urbanism: heterogeneous epistemologies, radical openness, community data sovereignty, and ongoing feedback loops. Examples of cities where civic engagement is ingrained in digital urban systems rather than being an afterthought are provided at the end of the section.

As this chapter on community co-creation and participatory urbanism comes to an end, the question that remains is not just how generative AI and digital twins might be employed, but also how they can be shared and managed to support inclusive, democratic, and regenerative urban futures. Whether the technologies will strengthen democracy or digitize inequality depends on the institutions, beliefs, and practices that form them. The tools themselves are not intrinsically just.

In its most revolutionary form, the digital twin is a municipal infrastructure rather than merely a platform for spatial simulation. It must be planned as a shared space that is open, accountable, and co-owned, much like parks, libraries, and transportation systems. This calls for a significant change in institutional and technological culture. We must create digital twins as public knowledge commons—infrastructures that gather, visualize, and learn from urban life while integrating ethical checks, participatory controls, and local intelligences—instead of creating them as proprietary systems that fulfill certain planning purposes.

This chapter offers four guiding concepts for realizing such a future. Radical openness comes first. Open interfaces, open data, and open standards are essential for participatory digital twins. Closed systems are not conducive to civic engagement. Participation is performative if locals are unable to access the datasets that represent their neighbourhoods or track down the presumptions underlying an AI-generated scenario. Radical openness necessitates that digital twin architectures be transparent, both technically and cognitively, and made to be intelligible to individuals with varying degrees of digital literacy, cultural backgrounds, and modes of knowing.

The second is the sovereignty of community data. If communities lack control over the usage, storage, and monetization of their data, participation becomes meaningless (Bühler et al. 2023). Detailed environmental, behavioural, and spatial data—much of which is collected from or about communities without explicit consent—are frequently used in digital twins. Local governance must take precedence over data in democratic digital twins. This includes governance frameworks, community data trusts, and participatory permission procedures where locals assist in defining what information is considered sacred, sensitive, or shared. Rejecting extractive data techniques that mine community intelligence without providing value is another aspect of it.

Plural epistemologies come in third. Digital twins and generative AI frequently prioritize quantitative, computationally readable inputs (Datta 2024; Serreli 2025). However, there are qualitative nuances to urban living, such as identity, affect, memory, and belonging. Thus, multiple knowledge traditions—from Indigenous cartographies and oral histories to migrant experiences and adolescent imaginaries—must be accommodated and transformed by participatory digital platforms. Pluralism is a structural necessity for developing systems that are in tune with the whole range of urban activity, not just a token addition.

Fourth, loops of constant feedback. Participation is a continuous process rather than a one-time occurrence. As communities change, so too must democratic digital twins (Novelli et al. 2025). For communities to test treatments, evaluate results, and modify the twin's logic over time, iteration mechanisms must be integrated. Sensors and social media can fuel real-time feedback loops, but they also need to incorporate deliberative loops where locals congregate, think, and provide feedback for recalibration. In this way, digital twins ought to learn from communities and change together with them, rather than just modelling futures.

These values are not fictitious, even though they are aspirational. Cities are experimenting with civic tech ecosystems that reflect elements of this idea all over the world. The DECODE initiative in Barcelona uses blockchain-based, encrypted frameworks to give citizens authority over how their data is utilized for public reasons (Bano et al. 2019). Residents of Taipei participate in real-time policy and infrastructure decision-making using participatory platforms such as vTaiwan, which are frequently aided by AI-generated summaries and visuals (Tseng 2020). The PublicStack initiative in Amsterdam aims to create ethical (Kortlander et al. 2025), open, and collectively regulated digital infrastructures.

These examples demonstrate how the digital twin can become a site of radical urban imagination when it is viewed as a civic collaborator rather than a technocratic tool. Residents may be able to regain agency they were taught was out of their grasp, co-author designs they were never asked about and see futures they were never shown.

This chapter has claimed that improved data visualizations and more complex algorithms alone are not enough to pave the way for democratic digital twins. Trust, openness, and change are its paving stones, this cultural shift frames digital urbanism as a profoundly political, group endeavour.

When guided by civic principles, generative AI and urban digital twins can surpass their initial limitations in terms of efficiency and control. They can develop into co-authorship spaces, infrastructures of belonging, and instruments for spatial justice reparations. However, this future must be created, not taken for granted. It calls for inclusive design, deliberate governance, and the humility to listen as much as to lead. Let the city be wise if it wants to be smart. Let it be democratic if it is going to be digital. If it is to be generative, it should produce futures that we can all co-create and claim as our own, in addition to forms and projections.

References

Aragón P, Kaltenbrunner A, Calleja-López A, Pereira A, Monterde A, Barandiaran XE, Gómez V (2017) Deliberative platform design: the case study of the online discussions in Decidim Barcelona. In: Ciampaglia, G., Mashhadi, A., Yasseri, T. (eds) International conference on social informatics. Springer International, Cham, pp 277–287

Artopoulos G, Costa CS (2019) Data-driven processes in participatory urbanism: the "smartness" of historical cities. Archit. Cult. 7(3):473–491

Bano S, Bassi E, Ciurcina M, De Martin JC, Fenoglietto S, Santangelo A, Gutierres FS, Laniado D, Aragón P, Hoepman JH (2019) DECODE. https://decodeproject.eu/file/443/download.pdf (Accessed online on 22 August 2023).

Bühler MM, Calzada I, Cane I, Jelinek T, Kapoor A, Mannan M, Mehta S, Mookerje V, Nübel K, Pentland A, Scholz T (2023) Unlocking the power of digital commons: data cooperatives as a pathway for data sovereign, innovative and equitable digital communities. Digital 3(3):146–171

Cardullo P, Ribera-Fumaz R, González Gil P (2023) The Decidim 'soft infrastructure': democratic platforms and technological autonomy in Barcelona. Comput Cult (9), Available from: http://computationalculture.net/the-decidim-soft-infrastructure/

Chen X, Gao W, Chu Y, Song Y (2024) Enhancing interaction in virtual-real architectural environments: a comparative analysis of generative AI-driven reality approaches. Build. Environ. 266:112113

Cheshmehzangi A (2023a) Urban regeneration and building colours: mapping visual and perceptual dimensions of Dali's old towns. In: Cheshmehzangi A (2023a) Mapping urban regeneration: city life experiences in Yunnan, China. Springer Nature Singapore, Singapore, pp 105–137

Cheshmehzangi A (2023b) Regenerating the local characteristics: the impacts on city life experience and identity of Shangri-La's old town. In: Cheshmehzangi A (2023b)Mapping urban regeneration: city life experiences in Yunnan, China. Springer Nature Singapore, Singapore, pp 219–237

Cheshmehzangi A, Zou T, Su Z, Dawodu A, Ardakani SP, Sedrez M, Tang T (2024) Growing digital divide for expatriates population in China: a user perspective analysis during the COVID-19 pandemic. SAGE Open 14(4). https://doi.org/10.1177/21582440241274613

Datta S (2024) Digital twin, Didymos, meets digital cousin, Didymium. From paradox to paradigm or a paradoxical paradigm? https://www.preprints.org/frontend/manuscript/16d66d7e8804d88fb1d98d7af2821faf/download_pub (Accessed on 16 May 2025)

Gün A (2023) Urban design evolved: the impact of computational tools and data-driven approaches on urban design practices and civic participation. J. Contemp. Urban Aff. 7(1):242–260

Kortlander M, Sweep A-M, Ruarus I (2025) Democratizing green technology with the public stack. In: Moral design and green technology. Wageningen Academic, Wageningen, pp 27–47. https://brill.com/edcollchap-oa/book/9789004730779/BP000010.xml

Novelli C, Sánchez-Vaquerizo JA, Helbing D, Rotolo A, Floridi L (2025) A replica for our democracies? On using digital twins to enhance deliberative democracy. arXiv preprint arXiv: 2504.07138

Osiobe EU (2024) Enhancing data visualization accessibility: a case for equity and inclusion. Eng. Technol. Q Rev. 7(1):24–32

Rosener JB (2015) Making bureaucrats responsive: a study on the impact of citizen participation and staff recommendations on regulatory decision making. In Beckett J. and Koenig H.O. (eds.): Public administration and law. Routledge, New York, pp 136–146

Serreli L (2025) Building human digital twins through natural language processing: from conversations to knowledge. https://tesidottorato.depositolegale.it/handle/20.500.14242/208583 (Accessed on 21 October 2025).

Shahbaz Badr A (2023) Fostering spatial understanding through immersive technologies: the creation of interactive urban and forest virtual geoenvironments. https://ir.library.oregonstate.edu/concern/graduate_thesis_or_dissertations/w6634c301 (Accessed on 21 October 2025).

Tseng YS (2020) A comparative analysis of decide Madrid and Taiwan, two digital platforms for political participation. Doctoral dissertation, Durham University

Chapter 9
Policy, Regulation, and Ethical Governance of AI-Powered Urban Systems and Intelligence

9.1 The Policy Gap: Urban Innovation Ahead of Regulation

The increasing gap between technology development and regulatory readiness is described in this first part. It talks on how AI-powered urban systems have surpassed current legal frameworks, particularly regarding liability, consent, surveillance, and discrimination (Raghav et al., 2025). It presents the main problem: how can governments and cities manage systems that are infrastructural, dynamic, and opaque all at once?

Governance is unable to keep up with the rapid pace of urban innovation. A regulatory gap is growing as AI-powered systems and digital twins are incorporated more into municipal operations, planning, and management; in this gap, technological capability surpasses moral clarity, legal accountability, and democratic supervision. The current state of urban government is characterized by this tension: cities are evolving into experimental laboratories (Raven et al., 2019; Xie et al., 2023), yet the normative framework that governs these experiments remains precariously thin.

The application of AI in urban systems is the clearest example of this. AI-generated zoning recommendations, automated traffic controls, predictive policing algorithms, and real-time digital twins of entire metropolitan areas are just a few examples of the increasingly autonomous, sophisticated, and opaque instruments used to manage urban life (Xu et al., 2024). These systems are increasingly influencing decisions on behalf of human planners, frequently without adequate oversight or responsibility, rather than just supporting them. Rapid technological advancement is not the only issue; urban governance frameworks, which are based on legacy legal codes, procedural planning standards, and compartmentalized institutional processes, were not intended to govern systems that change, adapt, and function in mysterious ways.

This governance lag is made worse by three interrelated factors. The first is that AI systems are opaque. Many models are intrinsically non-interpretable, especially those constructed with generative or deep learning architectures. They base their decisions on patterns that are frequently impossible for human users to identify

A. Cheshmehzangi, *Generative AI-Powered Urban Digital Twins*, Urban Sustainability,
https://doi.org/10.1007/978-981-95-4766-1_9

or defend, whether they are related to policing resource allocation, flood scenario simulation, or mobility flow optimization. This creates what academics have dubbed "algorithmic opacity" (Hansen & Borch, 2021), making it challenging to both explain and challenge judgments. Causality and reasoning can be openly contested in conventional planning or infrastructure choices (Cheshmehzangi, 2025). Logic is frequently embedded in brain structures, probabilistic weights, and training datasets that are not accessible to the general public or policymakers in AI-enhanced systems.

Second, these AI systems are powered by non-neutral data. Real-time data is fed into AI systems and urban digital twins from a myriad of sources, including social media feeds, energy meters, mobile sensors, and surveillance cameras. However, this data is becoming commodified, gathered unevenly, and frequently prejudiced. Concerns about ownership, permission, and data rights have grown more pressing as cities form alliances with private digital companies to provide smart city services. Who is the owner of the data produced by public life? Can citizens in AI-optimized urban areas choose not to be tracked? Even as data-intensive systems are expanded citywide, most governments still have not fully addressed these fundamental problems.

Third, the distributed agency of AI-enabled urban systems is too complex for liability frameworks to manage. Who is accountable when a digital twin misleads an infrastructure investment decision or when an AI-powered flood forecasting system fails to sound an alarm? Is it the algorithm itself, the vendor who created it, or the city agency that employed the system? In a world where errors arise from non-linear interactions between data, models, infrastructure, and policy, traditional legal constructs—based on human purpose, contractual clarity, and post-facto accountability—find it difficult to assign culpability.

Technology transformation is not merely a passive consequence of this policy gap. The rate of innovation and the political economics around urban AI systems actively influence it. Vendors and solution providers frequently advocate for quick deployment and proprietary models, portraying AI and digital twins as ready-made "solutions" to complex urban problems. Under pressure to seem forward-thinking and creative, policymakers can adopt these techniques hastily without fully appreciating their limitations or long-term effects. A temporal and epistemic mismatch between the rate of technological embedding and the ability of democratic institutions to control, comprehend, and challenge these developments is the outcome, which is known as governance lag.

Furthermore, the public's trust in institutions and technology is eroding at the same time as this governance lag. Public distrust has been exacerbated by data breaches, algorithmic discrimination, and opaque decision-making, particularly among historically marginalized communities who frequently suffer the most from automated inequity or AI-enabled monitoring (Cheshmehzangi, 2025). Cities run the risk of increasing public mistrust rather than resolving urban issues when they are unable to establish clear ethical, legal, and procedural boundaries surrounding these technologies.

It is critical to understand that this is not a one-time catch-up situation. The difficulty is constant and ever-changing. AI systems are dynamic tools that change over time, retrain on fresh data, and adapt to shifting urban environments. As a result, regulatory strategies need to be reflexive, proactive, and iterative. The old regulatory paradigm, which presumes fixed technologies and linear implementation methods, must be significantly altered to achieve this. Rather, regulating AI-powered cities requires regulatory agility, or the capacity to modify standards and oversight procedures in tandem with the systems they are intended to regulate.

This problem also has a geopolitical component. Divergent methods to AI legislation are being developed by various nations; the EU's AI Act takes a rights-based and cautious approach (Mei & Sag, 2025), while other regions of the world adopt more laissez-faire or sectoral approaches. Cities that are in the forefront of the deployment of urban AI frequently lack the legal authority or jurisdiction to influence national policy, but they nonetheless suffer as a result. Because they are expected to behave responsibly using instruments that may not be completely understood or managed, urban leaders are placed in a hazardous situation.

Given this, the main concern of this chapter—and, in fact, of the urban future—is not just how to control artificial intelligence, but also how to control urban intelligence systems that are dynamic, opaque, and infrastructure-based all at once (Khan et al., 2012). This question necessitates reconsidering the fundamental structure of urban governance: who makes decisions, who is protected, and who participates. It necessitates new kinds of civic participation, interdisciplinary cooperation, and institutional capacity. Above all, it necessitates a normative reorientation—from speed to deliberation, from control to caring, and from innovation to rights.

The foundation for future in-depth investigations into institutional frameworks, ethical design, and the workings of democratic supervision is laid out in this section. However, the stakes are clearly obvious. The promise of AI in cities could be undermined by unforeseen consequences if prompt and strong governance is not in place (Sawhney, 2023). The disconnect between innovation and regulation is become a defining urban dilemma of our time, not just a hypothetical peril.

9.2 Governing the Algorithmic City: Legal and Institutional Frameworks

The need for robust institutional and legal structures to control AI's implementation has grown urgently as it becomes ingrained in modern cities' core systems. Regulatory structures that can handle both technical complexity and democratic accountability are necessary in the algorithmic city, where automated systems are mediating, speeding up, and obscuring decision-making. Several institutional reactions are now beginning to emerge, even if the quick spread of smart city technology and AI-powered urban services has frequently taken place in regulatory grey areas. However, these continue to be disjointed, administered unevenly, and inadequately tailored to the particularities of urban governance.

The Artificial Intelligence Act (AI Act) of the European Union, which establishes a risk-based classification system for AI applications, is one of the most important policy advancements to date (Grozdanovski & De Cooman, 2022). This framework divides AI systems into four risk categories: high-, limited-, minimal-, and unacceptable risk. Stricter standards, such as those for transparency, human oversight, data quality, and post-deployment monitoring, apply to high-risk systems, such as those employed in vital infrastructure, law enforcement, or hiring choices. Many urban applications, like algorithmic traffic control, facial recognition in public areas, and predictive policing, are classified as high-risk even though the AI Act is not specifically intended for urban areas.

Adopting such classification systems is a crucial first step for urban governance in defining the parameters of permissible AI use. Translating these theories into urban-specific circumstances, however, continues to be a challenge. Cities frequently lack the regulatory power to impose national or international norms, especially when using private vendors to purchase AI equipment. This poses important queries: Who is responsible for ensuring compliance? How can cities audit systems that they did not fully control and did not design? Furthermore, how can government agencies confirm the assertions made by proprietary systems whose inner workings are shielded by trade secrets?

Algorithmic audits have become a crucial instrument in urban AI governance to tackle these issues. These audits, which can range from external third-party evaluations to internal performance reviews, are designed to determine whether an AI system functions accurately, fairly, and within moral and legal bounds. Algorithmic audits can help cities in a number of ways, including screening vendors prior to procurement, assessing practical effects, guaranteeing adherence to public principles, and spotting unforeseen repercussions like prejudice or exclusion. However, audits run the risk of turning into performative checklists rather than meaningful forms of accountability in the absence of a standardized methodology or institutional support. Additionally, few municipalities have the resources or technical know-how to carry out thorough audits, so they must rely on outside consultants or academic collaborations.

As a result, there have been demands for the creation of specialized oversight organizations capable of bridging the ethical, legal, and technical facets of algorithmic governance. Such versions have previously been tested in a few towns. For example, AI registers—public portals where individuals can examine details on the algorithms used by municipal departments—have been introduced in Helsinki and Amsterdam. Barcelona has investigated a "city data commons" strategy to handle digital resources jointly (Calzati & van Loenen, 2025), while New York City has formed an Automated Decision Systems Task Force (Richardson, 2021). Although these programs provide encouraging models for instituting openness and public supervision, they are still the exception rather than the rule.

Importantly, new institutional cultures are needed for the algorithmic city to be governed effectively, which calls for more than just regulations. Organizations in the public sector need to change to become more flexible, multidisciplinary, and risk-responsive. Urban planners should be prepared to critically evaluate AI-driven findings; procurement authorities should comprehend algorithmic ethics; and legal teams should work in tandem with engineers. Although it will take time, establishing this institutional capability is essential to the validity and efficacy of AI regulation.

Shared governance techniques that acknowledge the multi-actor, multi-scalar nature of urban AI systems are necessary in addition to institutional transformation. Cities engage with national politics, international tech companies, transnational standards organizations, and regional governments; they do not function in a vacuum. Governance systems must therefore make it possible for various layers to coordinate. For instance, regional networks like Eurocities are pushing for shared AI governance principles across member cities, while worldwide standards organizations like IEEE and ISO are creating technical and ethical guidelines that can influence city-level practices (Estevez et al., 2021). Nevertheless, adoption is still unequal, and there is a chance that wealthy cities could develop more quickly than others, leading to a fragmented government environment.

Lastly, rather than just guaranteeing compliance, any institutional and legal response must prioritize public values—justice, accountability, fairness, and transparency. This necessitates reevaluating governance from the standpoints of civic legitimacy and procedural rights. What options do locals have if an algorithmic choice negatively impacts them? In what ways may communities influence the development of AI tools that affect their daily lives? Appeals, redress, and participatory design must be incorporated into governance frameworks as essential components of responsible urban AI systems, not as afterthoughts.

In conclusion, the gap between policy goal and regulatory enforcement is still quite large, even if cities are starting to experiment with new governance mechanisms, such as task forces, ethical charters, audits, and registries. Creating efficient institutional and legal frameworks for the algorithmic city is a democratic necessity, not just a technical one. In order to effectively manage the risks and transformative potential of urban artificial intelligence, cities must shift from reactive regulation to proactive, anticipatory governance.

9.2.1 *Tools for Accountability: Audits, Registries, and Impact Assessments*

The concrete procedures being used or proposed to control AI systems—such as algorithmic transparency registries, urban AI impact evaluations, redress protocols, and third-party audits (Raji et al., 2023)—are discussed in detail in this subsection. We will examine examples from the Canadian Directive on Automated Decision-Making (Scassa, 2021), the NYC Algorithmic Accountability Law (Baykurt, 2022), and the EU AI Act (Edwards, 2021). The need for accountability measures has grown essential and unavoidable as AI systems increasingly arbitrate judgments in the areas of housing, transportation, policing, welfare, and urban planning (Mansoor, 2026). The stakes are high: opaque algorithmic procedures have the potential to weaken public trust, increase prejudice, and decrease transparency. As a result, audits, registers, and impact assessments—a new generation of regulatory tools—have become essential tools for guaranteeing algorithmic accountability in urban settings.

Algorithmic Openness Among the most apparent instruments for demythologizing the inner workings of AI systems utilized by government agencies are registries. These registries, which were first established by cities such as Amsterdam and Helsinki, make available to the public the algorithms that are being used, their purposes, and the decision-making process. For example, Amsterdam's Algorithm Register offers comprehensive metadata on every algorithmic system that the municipality has implemented (Wieringa, 2025), including information on its goals, data sources, risk evaluations, and supervision frameworks. Registries hope to promote openness, public monitoring, and a common knowledge of how automated technologies impact everyday life by making such data publicly available. Standardizing what needs to be revealed and making sure that disclosures are understandable to audiences who are not experts, however, continue to be difficult tasks.

Responsible AI governance also includes Algorithmic Impact Assessments (AIAs). AIAs examine the dangers, negative effects, and moral ramifications of an AI system before it is put into use. They work similarly to environmental or social impact assessments. With the 2019 implementation of the Directive on Automated Decision-Making (DADM), the Canadian government has been leading the way in this strategy. Federal agencies are required by this regulation to evaluate algorithmic systems using an impact scale, with more thorough documentation, public notice, and review processes needed for higher-risk systems. Importantly, it mandates that before implementing high-impact tools, departments perform peer-reviewed Algorithmic Impact Assessments. Canada has done this by instituting a proactive, forward-thinking approach to AI governance, one that seeks to stop harm before it starts.

The AI Act of the European Union adopts a complementary, albeit more structured, strategy. It assigns corresponding responsibilities and classifies AI systems according to their level of risk. Conformance assessments, which may involve independent audits, technical documentation, and post-deployment monitoring, are required for high-risk systems. Systems used in traffic control, biometric surveillance, public service allocation, and critical infrastructure management may fall under this category for urban governments. The Act creates a legal foundation for audits and external scrutiny, which may provide municipal actors more negotiating power with vendors, even though it does not mandate open access to code or public algorithm registries.

A more thorough level of examination is provided by third-party algorithmic audits, especially where public actors lack internal knowledge. These audits can be procedural, looking at governance structures, data provenance, and human oversight, or technical, assessing code performance, fairness, and robustness. By creating a task force to investigate the city's use of automated decision systems (ADS), New York City's Algorithmic Accountability Law in 2018 set the stage for future audits of this kind (Shah, 2018). Despite logistical and political challenges, the task team identified the need for independent auditors, more transparent standards, and public involvement channels. One of the first legally binding audit regimes in the world was established by the city's more recent Local Law 144 in 2021 (Wright et al., 2024), which now requires independent bias audits for automated employment decision tools.

Particularly for high-stakes decisions, some countries are experimenting with redress methods and appeals systems in addition to these formal mechanisms. These systems guarantee that people who are affected by algorithmic decisions—like those who are refused housing, benefits, or mobility services—have an easy-to-follow procedure for challenging results. These are essential for procedural fairness, particularly in urban settings where underprivileged groups may be disproportionately impacted by judgments. A more responsive and rights-based AI governance structure can be produced by integrating redress mechanisms into digital platforms, whether through ombudsperson channels, contact points, or explanatory notifications.

However, there are some restrictions on these tools. There are questions regarding objectivity and accountability because many evaluations are carried out by the same organizations who are implementing the technology. Inconsistencies in scope and enforcement result from the lack of clear global standards for audits or registries. Furthermore, unless they are combined with legally binding penalties for noncompliance, procedural safeguards sometimes lack teeth. Nonetheless, audits, registries, and impact evaluations provide a potent trifecta for regulating AI in cities when used in tandem. They help transform complicated technical systems into publicly readable and contestable civic instruments; they produce records that may be used for future supervision and learning; and they add friction to systems that might otherwise be implemented with unrestrained speed. To prevent harm and gain public legitimacy and trust in the algorithmic infrastructures of tomorrow's urban life, it will be crucial to institutionalize these instruments as cities become increasingly dependent on algorithmic systems.

9.3 Privacy, Surveillance, and Data Sovereignty in the Urban Realm

The chapter now shifts to the contentious field of data ethics. It examines the threats to both individual and collective privacy posed by ubiquitous urban sensing and AI inference, particularly in the setting of smart cities. Data anonymization, privacy-promoting edge computing, surveillance capitalism, and Indigenous data sovereignty are among the subjects covered. The part advocates for frameworks rooted on urban justice and based on rights (Cheshmehzangi, 2022). The lines separating private data collecting from public infrastructure are blurring as cities grow more digitally connected. Mobile phones, rubbish bins, lampposts, traffic signals, and public transportation all have sensors built into them that continuously produce streams of data that serve as the basis for AI-enhanced urban systems. These technologies bring with them complicated issues regarding data ownership, consent, and surveillance, even as they offer efficiency, insight, and predictive power. The ethical landscape of privacy in urban AI is examined in this part, which calls for a move away from techno-solutionism and toward rights-based frameworks that prioritize data governance with an emphasis on urban justice.

The ubiquitous nature of urban sensing lies at the heart of the problem. The foundation of smart cities is the logic of visibility, which makes the movement of people, products, energy, and waste understandable to computer programs (Anthopoulos, 2017). However, as these sensing infrastructures develop, so does their capacity to follow, profile, and infer people. The days of science fiction are over for behavioural predictions, facial recognition, gait analysis, and emotional detection. Urban life is increasingly being monitored in ways that are opaque, unaccountable, and asymmetrically regulated in the name of security or optimization.

With the idea that eliminating personal identifiers might preserve analytical usefulness while protecting individual privacy, data anonymization has been suggested as a precaution. However, re-identification is frequently insignificant in practice. Identifications can be reconstructed with frightening ease when datasets are cross-referenced, such as transportation use with mobile location patterns. Therefore, anonymization is not a cure-all; it needs to be used in conjunction with architectural choices regarding the types of data that are gathered, who collects them, and why. Minimization, not extraction, must be the first step in the design of urban data systems.

Edge computing, where data is processed locally on the device or within the urban node instead of being sent to centralized servers, is one possible approach. This limits needless data retention, improves user control, and lessens vulnerability to intrusions. A smart lamppost with environmental sensors, for instance, can assess data on air quality on-site and merely send out aggregate findings. In a similar vein, edge AI in mobility systems can optimize routes without precisely tracking the positions of individual users. Cities can still profit from smart infrastructure while reducing surveillance threats by decentralizing computation.

However, the ethical discussion is not limited to individuals. Cities are now the sites of extractive economies due to the rise of surveillance capitalism, in which private platforms commodify and profit from behavioural data. Corporations frequently hold, process, and sell data created in public areas with little to no accountability to the communities from whom the data comes. A feedback cycle that perpetuates inequality and disempowerment frequently results when AI systems educated on this data are used to guide decisions on urban renewal, social services, or policing.

In light of the growing mapping and digitization of Indigenous communities' territory, history, and cultural knowledge, the idea of data sovereignty becomes crucial in this situation. The right of Indigenous peoples to control the gathering, ownership, and use of information about themselves and their lands is known as indigenous data sovereignty. information reframes data as a relational, contextual, and frequently sacred resource, challenging prevailing paradigms that view information as a neutral commodity. It takes significant changes in institutional culture, infrastructure design, and epistemology in addition to legislative changes to include these viewpoints into urban data governance.

In the end, the right to privacy in urban areas is fundamental to democratic life and goes beyond merely preventing injury. It influences how people engage in civic activities, use public areas, and voice their disapproval. A city that is constantly on guard is not neutral; rather, it is made to categorize, discipline, and forecast. We must go beyond merely adhering to data privacy regulations and pursue a rights-based framework based on urban justice if we are to create inclusive, reflective, and emancipatory cities. This entails working with impacted groups to co-develop privacy standards, including consent into digital system architecture, and adopting legal frameworks that acknowledge data rights as civic rights.

The problem of ensuring that cities continue to be places of freedom and plurality rather than algorithmic captivity is not only technological but also deeply political as the infrastructure of urban intelligence grows. Thus, privacy must be viewed as a civic virtue—a prerequisite for agency, dignity, and belonging in the algorithmic city—rather than as a design limitation.

9.4 Ethics by Design: Embedding Values into AI-Twin Systems

The ethical issues become more pressing as digital twins and AI systems are more integrated into infrastructure, daily life, and urban administration. The ability of these technologies to influence choices, shift power, and mould lived environments is just as powerful as their capacity to forecast or optimize. We must move from reactive ethical critiques to proactive, embedded ethics—ethics by design—if we want to guarantee that such systems advance justice, equity, and the public good.

Integrating normative principles—fairness, accountability, transparency, non-discrimination, and inclusivity—into the architecture of AI-powered urban systems from the beginning is the fundamental idea behind ethics by design. This method incorporates moral reasoning into the institutional and technical foundation of digital twin development, rather than viewing ethics as a last compliance check or an external audit. It acknowledges that values are active design characteristics that influence system behaviour, user engagement, and society results rather than only being management limitations.

Value-sensitive design (VSD) is one of the most important frameworks that directs this strategy (Betz & Fritsch, 2016; Borning & Muller, 2012; Davis & Nathan, 2013; Friedman et al., 2017; Sadek et al., 2024). VSD, which has its roots in human-computer interaction, provides a framework for methodically integrating human values into the design process (Eriksson et al., 2022). Identifying stakeholders and their various interests is the first step. Explicit value tensions (such as efficiency vs. inclusion) are then articulated and incorporated into technical requirements and prototypes. When it comes to AI-twin systems, VSD makes sure that urban technologies reflect the values of the general public (Cheshmehzangi et al., 2025) rather than just the optimization objectives of data providers or developers.

Human-in-the-loop (HITL) mechanism integration is a supplementary strategy (Chen et al., 2025; Emami et al., 2024; Kumar et al., 2024; Sreeram & Nof, 2021). These include ensuring that important decisions—especially those pertaining to rights, access, or public services—are meaningfully overseen by humans. This might entail requiring planners to examine and verify AI-generated zoning proposals in urban planning; in mobility systems, it might entail making sure algorithmic route recommendations can be overridden by transit authorities or even community input. HITL tactics support the idea that, in complex, value-laden situations, AI should support human judgment rather than take its place.

Yet, software is only one aspect of ethics by design. Additionally, it calls for institutional change. Development pipelines that incorporate interdisciplinary ethics boards can foster organized discussion of moral trade-offs. These boards can supervise the lifecycle of AI-twin projects—providing recommendations at critical design stages, evaluating data use protocols, and keeping an eye out for unforeseen consequences. They are made up of ethicists, urban planners, community representatives, technologists, and legal scholars. Ethical issues are raised from incidental to central by integrating ethical review into city technology projects' workflow.

However, there are many difficulties in integrating ethics into AI-twin systems. First, there is the danger of formalism, which is the reduction of moral obligations to checklists or impersonal, abstract ideas. Ethics by design must be contextualized within the unique cultural, physical, and historical conditions of each city in order to have any real value. In addition to being inadequate, a one-size-fits-all ethical standard has the potential to be detrimental since it could obscure regional sensitivities, worsen inequality, or uphold prevailing paradigms in the name of neutrality.

Second, there is the issue of power asymmetry. Who has the authority to specify the values that AI-twin systems are built with? Who gets to define "fairness" and "transparency"? Participatory responses are required for these political questions. Integrating ethics into the democratic process entails inviting the public to co-author the rules, regulations, and governance models of AI systems in addition to using and comprehending them. In the absence of such involvement, ethical design could turn into technocratic paternalism.

Finally, ethics by design must also account for long-term effects. AI-twin systems are dynamic instruments that change, grow, and influence the future. This necessitates an ethics of foresight: building systems to be accountable as they grow, change, and function in unexpected ways, in addition to meeting current standards. In this way, ethical design is a process of ongoing responsibility, introspection, and recalibration rather than a final product.

Integrating ethics is now essential to civic legitimacy in a time when cities are being computationally modelled, simulated, and governed at hitherto unheard-of levels. AI-powered digital twins can develop into more than just optimization tools by coordinating technological advancement with social ideals; they can also function as infrastructures for justice, caring, and introspection. But only if that is how we design them from the start.

9.4.1 Digital Sustainability and Long-Term Governance

This subsection, which focuses on the future, poses concerns about digital stewardship. How can cities guarantee the long-term sustainability, maintainability, interoperability, and social coherence of AI-twin infrastructures? In addition to proposing long-term governance models like digital commons, public–private digital covenants, and civic guardianship institutions, it presents the concept of digital public infrastructure.

The challenge of long-term digital sustainability surpasses initial deployment as cities adopt AI-powered digital twins as essential instruments of urban governance. The technical design and immediate uses of digital twins have received a lot of attention, but the long-term technical, social, and political viability of these systems has received less attention. This section makes the case that digital twins should be viewed as permanent public infrastructures rather than just tools, requiring civic responsibility, flexibility, and foresight to govern.

Digital sustainability questions whether a system can be maintained, interoperable, transparent, and socially useful over time, in addition to whether it can continue to operate. Too much reliance on proprietary software, poorly described code, data silos, or unsustainable finance methods have caused several smart city programs to fail. A sustainable digital twin, on the other hand, needs to be constructed as a dynamic platform that is open, extendable, and modular so that it may be modified to accommodate new social circumstances, governance requirements, and technological advancements without having to be completely redone or rendered obsolete.

Cities must approach AI-twin systems as digital public infrastructure in order to guarantee such sustainability. Digital infrastructures need to be maintained with the same level of institutional stewardship, long-term planning, and public funding as roads, bridges, or power grids. This covers funding allotments for ongoing cybersecurity, software upgrades, data maintenance, and user retraining. Beyond resources, though, it also entails building institutional memory, which makes sure that staff changes, contract changes, or policy modifications don't erase the understanding of how these systems operate.

The institutionalization of civic guardianship is one possible strategy. According to this idea, autonomous or semi-autonomous public organizations should be established to oversee AI-twin systems continuously. These organizations might function similarly to environmental regulators or public utilities, with duties to guarantee inclusivity, technical dependability, ethics, and openness. Their role would be civic in nature rather than just technical: to protect the public interest in a changing digital environment.

The concept of a digital commons has become popular as a governance model in addition to civic guardianship. Here, the digital twin is viewed as a shared resource that is co-produced and co-managed by a variety of stakeholders, including government organizations, academic institutions, private sector partners, and civil society, rather than as a corporate product or government-owned asset. Like natural commons (forests, fisheries) or knowledge commons (open-source software), digital commons require shared governance principles: access rights, stewardship obligations, and mechanisms for collective decision-making.

Digital covenants between the public and private sectors are one way to achieve this goal. These governance frameworks formalize long-term collaborations between private technology companies and government agencies. Covenants, as opposed to short-term vendor contracts, are designed to provide open access to essential system components, openness of algorithms, and reciprocal accountability. They are based on the reciprocity concept, which states that although the public maintains authority for long-term continuity, access rights, and ethical standards, the private sector gains from innovation incentives and income models. These covenants could include clauses requiring community participation in design choices, requiring the open-sourcing of essential components after a certain amount of time, or including contractual duties pertaining to data protection and digital rights.

Interoperability—the capacity of systems to function across platforms, time zones, and geographical boundaries—is also essential to digital sustainability. In addition to incorporating data from several sources, urban digital twins also need to adapt to new requirements. This entails preserving open data format compatibility, permitting modular system updates, and guaranteeing that parts created in one city can be modified or reused in another. Cities run the risk of technological lock-in and redundancy without interoperability, which is particularly troublesome (Markolf et al., 2018) in a world where technology is changing quickly (Cheshmehzangi, 2025), and social and climatic complexity is increasing.

The social alignment of AI-twin systems is perhaps the most important issue that long-term governance needs to address. Even if a system is technically sound, it cannot be sustained if it loses credibility, shuts out communities, or turns into a surveillance and control mechanism. As societies evolve, ongoing discussion, democratic governance, and recalibration are necessary to guarantee that digital twins represent public ideals. The objectives of AI systems may be contested, improved, or even repurposed by communities through embedded feedback channels, citizen panels, or recurring public evaluations.

Digital sustainability is ultimately a political and ethical necessity rather than only a technical issue. It calls on cities to assume accountability for the futures they are enacting. It calls for modesty in architecture, adaptability in design, and audacity in conceiving up novel forms of government. AI-powered digital twins have the potential to develop into long-lasting civic assets that become more intelligent, inclusive, and just over time if done properly. However, this won't occur automatically. Deliberate decisions, consistent funding, and a shared dedication to viewing digital systems as an integral part of the urban fabric—as deserving of preservation, revitalization, and public trust as any public park or bridge—will be necessary.

9.5 Governing for the Long Now: A Rights-Based, Resilient Digital Future

The chapter's concepts are synthesized into a forward-looking regulatory philosophy in the concluding section. It makes the case for flexible regulation that upholds rights and fosters creativity. To guide ethical urban intelligence through the uncertain decades ahead, it concludes by outlining the fundamentals of urban digital justice: openness, auditability, reparability, accountability, and public interest.

A significant governance dilemma arises as cities depend more on digital twins and AI-powered systems to handle complexity: how to control the present while protecting the future. The ethical, legal, and institutional issues raised by algorithmic urbanism have been examined in this chapter, ranging from sustainability and accountability to policy gaps and surveillance concerns. We distil these issues into a forward-looking regulatory philosophy based on urban justice (Allam et al., 2023), adaptive resilience, and digital rights in this concluding part.

The phrase "Long Now" describes a mindset that transcends business quarters, election cycles, and technological fads (Ialenti, 2020). It demands vision, accountability, and stewardship of the systems that will influence the future of humanity and the planet. Applying this to urban AI systems raises questions about whether they will continue to be equitable, safe, and inclusive for future generations in addition to whether they are effective now. This long-term focus is particularly important when it comes to digital twins, whose incorporation into infrastructure, governance, and planning produces long-lasting socio-technical assemblages with far-reaching effects.

A rights-based approach is the foundation of this future-ready government. The fundamental tenets of AI and the deployment of digital twins must be cities' enshrinement of digital rights: privacy, access, redress, and representation. This entails shifting from voluntary rules and ambiguous ethical declarations to binding legal frameworks that shield people from damage, marginalization, and exploitation. Digital systems must be built with privacy by default, making anonymity, permission, and data minimization prerequisites rather than optional extras. For individuals impacted to comprehend, contest, or appeal results, algorithmic decision-making must continue to be auditable and explicable. Cities must, above all, respect the equality principle, making sure that technologies don't reinforce or magnify already-existing disparities.

However, without institutional resilience—the ability of governing systems to adjust to complexity, unpredictability, and change—rights by themselves are inadequate. Risk profiles change, datasets deteriorate, and AI models change. Governance needs to change as they do. This necessitates adaptive regulation, which consists of rules and supervision systems that can be modified in reaction to emerging threats, insights, or social priorities. Iterative evaluations, dynamic standards, and regulatory sandboxes can all help make sure that cities are not constrained by inflexible frameworks that hinder innovation or neglect to address new risks.

Figure 9.1. Five key operational mandates for AI-Twin Development

We can identify the fundamental tenets of urban digital justice within this flexible, rights-based framework. Every stage of AI-twin development should be guided by these operational mandates, not only aspirational values (See Fig. 9.1):

- **Transparency**: Clear disclosure of what systems do, how they make decisions, and who is accountable.
- **Auditability**: Independent mechanisms to test, verify, and scrutinise algorithmic behaviour and outcomes.
- **Reparability**: Channels for individuals and communities to contest, correct, or reverse unjust digital decisions.
- **Accountability**: Legal and institutional structures that ensure both public and private actors are answerable for the impacts of their technologies.
- **Public Interest Orientation**: A commitment to designing and deploying systems that serve collective well-being, not just commercial or operational efficiency.

Rethinking how cities regulate not only technology but also their own functions is necessary to realize these ideals. Cities need to take on the role of digital stewards, actively establishing innovative ecosystems that put the common good ahead of corporate power. Building cross-sectoral alliances, investing in digital literacy, and establishing venues for significant public engagement in technological governance are all imperative. Since people most at risk from algorithmic injustices are frequently the least represented in AI design processes, it is crucial that they prioritize marginalized voices.

In the uncertain decades to come, a city's intelligence will be measured by how fairly it governs, how responsibly it adapts, and how bravely it defends the rights and dignity of its citizens, not by how many sensors it installs or how quickly its systems operate. Governing for the Long Now requires us to view AI as a design area, where civic engagement, policy foresight, and ethical creativity can—and must—shape the future of urban life, rather than as an inevitable development.

References

Allam Z, Cheshmehzangi A, Jones DS (2023) *Climate and social justice: The political economy of urban resilience and mercantilism*. Springer Nature

Anthopoulos LG (2017) *Understanding smart cities: A tool for smart government or an industrial trick?* vol 22. Springer International Publishing, p 293

Baykurt B (2022) Algorithmic accountability in US cities: Transparency, impact, and political economy. *Big Data & Society 9*(2). https://doi.org/10.1177/20539517221115426

Betz S, Fritsch A (2016) A comparison of value sensitive design and sustainability design. In: *Informatik 2016*. Gesellschaft für Informatik eV, pp 267–274

Borning A, Muller M (2012, May) Next steps for value sensitive design. In: *Proceedings of the SIGCHI conference on human factors in computing systems*, pp 1125–1134. Association for Computing Machinery, New York, NY, United States, https://doi.org/10.1145/2207676.220856

Calzati S, van Loenen B (2025) Beyond federated data: A data commoning proposition for the EU's citizen-centric digital strategy. *AI & SOCIETY 40*(2):945–957

Chen H, Li S, Fan J, Duan A, Yang C, Navarro-Alarcon D, Zheng P (2025) Human-in-the-loop robot learning for smart manufacturing: A human-centric perspective. *IEEE Transactions on Automation Science and Engineering*. https://ieeexplore.ieee.org/abstract/document/10836893/

Cheshmehzangi A (2022) ICT for acceptance of the rights of others in cities: Promoting social justice, inclusivity, and stability through the use of digital technologies. In: *ICT, cities, and reaching positive peace*. Springer Nature Singapore, pp 159–175

Cheshmehzangi A (2025) *Advanced city: For the future of cities and opposing smart cities*. Springer

Cheshmehzangi A, You N, Allam Z, He BJ (2025) *People-centered innovation: Local actions for sustainable cities and communities*. Springer Nature

Davis J, Nathan LP (2013) Value sensitive design: Applications, adaptations, and critiques. In: *Handbook of ethics, values, and technological design*. Springer, pp 1–26

Edwards L (2021) The EU AI act: A summary of its significance and scope. *Artificial Intelligence (the EU AI Act) 1*:25

Emami, Y., Almeida, L., Li, K., Ni, W., & Han, Z. (2024). *Human-in-the-loop machine learning for safe and ethical autonomous vehicles: Principles, challenges, and opportunities. arXiv preprint arXiv: 2408.12548.*

Eriksson E, Nilsson EM, Hansen AM, Bekker T (2022) Teaching for values in human–computer interaction. *Frontiers in Computer Science 4*:830736

Estevez E, Cenci K, Fillottrani P, Janowski T (2021) Review of international standards and policy guidelines for smart sustainable cities. In: Estevez E, Pardo TA, Scholl HJ (eds) *Smart cities and smart governance: Towards the 22nd century sustainable city*. Springer, pp 69–99

Friedman B, Hendry DG, Borning A (2017) A survey of value sensitive design methods. *Foundations and Trends® in Human–Computer Interaction 11*(2):63–125

Grozdanovski L, De Cooman J (2022) Forget the facts, aim for the rights! on the obsolescence of empirical knowledge in defining the risk/rights-based approach to AI regulation in the European Union. *Rutgers Computer & Tech. LJ 49*:207

Hansen KB, Borch C (2021) The absorption and multiplication of uncertainty in machine-learning-driven finance. *The British Journal of Sociology 72*(4):1015–1029

Ialenti V (2020) *Deep time reckoning: How future thinking can help Earth now*. Cambridge: MIT Press

Khan Z, Ludlow D, McClatchey R, Anjum A (2012) An architecture for integrated intelligence in urban management using cloud computing. *Journal of Cloud Computing: Advances, Systems and Applications 1*(1):1

Kumar S, Datta S, Singh V, Datta D, Singh SK, Sharma R (2024) Applications, challenges, and future directions of human-in-the-loop learning. *IEEE Access 12*:75735–75760

Mansoor SIU (2026) AI and the rule of law in urban security: Upholding police accountability in smart cities. In: *AI-driven policing and urban security in smart cities*. IGI Global Scientific Publishing, pp 55–80

Markolf SA, Chester MV, Eisenberg DA, Iwaniec DM, Davidson CI, Zimmerman R, Miller TR, Ruddell BL, Chang H (2018) Interdependent infrastructure as linked social, ecological, and technological systems (SETSs) to address lock-in and enhance resilience. *Earth's Future 6*(12):1638–1659

Mei, Y., & Sag, M. (2025). *The illusion of rights based AI regulation. arXiv preprint arXiv:2503.05784.*

Raghav A, Singh B, Raghav R, Edina KD (2025) AI and robotics in smart city governance: Ethical and legal pathways for sustainable urbanization. In: *Machine learning and robotics in urban planning and management*. IGI Global Scientific Publishing, pp 1–24

Raji ID, Chock SC, Buolamwini J (2023) Change from the outside: Towards credible third-party audits of AI systems. *Missing links in AI governance 5*

Raven R, Sengers F, Spaeth P, Xie L, Cheshmehzangi A, De Jong M (2019) Urban experimentation and institutional arrangements. *European Planning Studies 27*(2):258–281

Richardson R (2021) Defining and demystifying automated decision systems. *Maryland Law Review 81*:785

Sadek M, Calvo RA, Mougenot C (2024) Designing value-sensitive AI: A critical review and recommendations for socio-technical design processes. *AI and Ethics 4*(4):949–967

Sawhney N (2023) Contestations in urban mobility: Rights, risks, and responsibilities for Urban AI. *Ai & Society 38*(3):1083–1098

Scassa T (2021) Administrative law and the governance of automated decision making: A critical look at Canada's directive on automated decision making. *UBCL Review 54*:251

Shah H (2018) Algorithmic accountability. *Philosophical Transactions of the Royal Society A: Mathematical, Physical and Engineering Sciences 376*(2128):20170362

Sreeram M, Nof SY (2021) Human-in-the-loop: Role in cyber physical agricultural systems. *International Journal of Computers Communications & Control 16*(2)

Wieringa M (2025) Municipalities enacting algorithms: A typology of dutch municipal strategies for leveraging algorithmic systems. In: *Public governance and emerging technologies: Values, trust, and regulatory compliance*. Springer Nature Switzerland, pp 19–41

Wright L, Muenster RM, Vecchione B, Qu T, Cai P, Smith A, Comm 2450 Student Investigators, Metcalf, J. and Matias, J.N (2024, June) Null compliance: NYC local law 144 and the challenges of algorithm accountability. In: *Proceedings of the 2024 ACM conference on fairness, accountability, and transparency*, pp 1701–1713. Association for Computing Machinery, New York, NY, United States, https://doi.org/10.1145/3630106.3658998

Xie L, Cheshmehzangi A, Shao M, Zhang Y, Chan F (2023) Urban sustainability experiments in China: Plural approaches for transformation. In: *Handbook on China's urban environmental governance*. Edward Elgar Publishing, pp 169–185

Xu H, Omitaomu F, Sabri S, Zlatanova S, Li X, Song Y (2024) Leveraging generative AI for urban digital twins: A scoping review on the autonomous generation of urban data, scenarios, designs, and 3D city models for smart city advancement. *Urban Informatics 3*(1):29

Chapter 10
From Pilot to City-Scale: Implementation and Scaling Models for AI-Digital Twins Intelligence

10.1 AI-Digital Twins Intelligence: The Leap from Prototype to Platform

The crucial problem of transitioning from experimental pilots or innovation zones to the widespread urban deployment of AI-powered digital twins is highlighted in this introductory part of the chapter. In addition to outlining the enabling conditions—political will, cross-sector alignment, funding methods, and public trust—that are critical for scalability, it looks at why so many projects fail at the prototype stage. The section lays the groundwork for viewing scaling as an institutional transformation as opposed to just technical duplication.

An important turning point has been reached in the spread of AI-powered urban digital twins. Pilot projects—innovation districts outfitted with real-time data feeds, generative design modules, climate simulation engines, and citizen-facing visualisations (Thuermer et al. 2024)—have been tested by cities all over the world. The promise of digital twin intelligence is demonstrated by these testbeds, which include evidence-based governance, responsive services, more adaptive infrastructure, and participatory planning. However, many initiatives are still stuck in pilot purgatory, unable to go from small-scale tests to citywide systems, despite these apparent improvements. This section examines what it really takes to make that leap and why it is still so elusive.

At its core, scaling AI-digital twin systems is not a matter of simply replicating technical infrastructure across broader geographies. Instead, it is a significant act of urban transformation that includes redesigning data governance systems, rearranging institutional workflows, and integrating new operational, social, and ethical contracts into the urban fabric. By definition, a prototype is an isolated demonstration that is protected from bureaucratic inertia, limited to manageable geographic areas, and frequently supported by innovation funds. On the other hand, a platform needs to operate at scale, in a variety of environments, with long-term accountability and system-wide interoperability.

A. Cheshmehzangi, *Generative AI-Powered Urban Digital Twins*, Urban Sustainability,
https://doi.org/10.1007/978-981-95-4766-1_10

The fragmentation of data, governance, and ambition is one of the most frequent causes of pilots' failure to scale. Individual departments, start-ups, or research institutes operating independently frequently lead pilot programs. Agility and experimentation are made possible by this independence, but it also frequently results in technical silos, mismatched data standards, and a lack of common goals among organizations (Raven et al. 2019). Alignment between planning departments, IT teams, environmental agencies, transportation authorities, utilities, and civic stakeholders is necessary for scaling. This calls for more than just coordination; it calls for a single strategic directive for digital urbanism that is supported by executive leadership and incorporated into city policy.

The political aspect of scale is also significant. AI-digital twin systems at the city scale are not isolated entities. Political will—leaders who can effectively communicate a compelling vision, foster interdepartmental cooperation, and negotiate intricate stakeholder ecosystems—is essential to their success. Pilot results frequently stay in reports and dashboards without this leadership, never developing into operational platforms that influence governance choices. Public legitimacy must be combined with political will. Scaled digital twin systems must be trusted by the public to uphold democratic accountability, protect privacy, and serve the interests of all. This calls for open communication, inclusive co-design, and ongoing participation—not only during pilot stages but all the way through the system's lifecycle.

The sustainability of finances is another major obstacle to scale. Pilots frequently depend on research funding, philanthropic support, or short-term innovation grants. A distinct logic is required for scaling: procurement techniques that promote interoperability, modularity, and long-term maintainability; clear return-on-investment pathways; and consistent, multi-year finance. Cities must create funding sources that are commensurate with the criticality and lifetime of the systems they want to implement. Digital infrastructure bonds, performance-based contracting, and public-private partnerships are new instruments in this field, but many governments lack the competence and risk literacy necessary to implement them.

The transition from pilot to platform cannot be fuelled solely by technology. Maturity of the institution is crucial. This entails creating governance frameworks for cross-sectoral collaboration, fostering digital literacy across departments, and increasing internal ability to handle complex data ecosystems. Institutions must also change their operational paradigms, moving from static infrastructure management to dynamic, data-driven urban stewardship and from compartmentalized project delivery to systems thinking. Cultural shifts are just as necessary for this transition as technical know-how.

Lastly, scaling needs to be viewed as a reflexive and cyclical process. AI-digital twins are evolving, in contrast to previous infrastructure. Their users are diverse, their models are updated, and their capabilities grow (Li et al. 2025). Therefore, scaling is an ongoing cycle of iteration, adaptation, and recalibration rather than a one-time replication operation. A platform needs to be adaptable, flexible enough to accommodate new use cases, and resilient enough to endure pressure from the public, changing government goals, or an abundance of data. Thus, this chapter presents scaling as a complex issue that involves public ethics, technology, money, legislation, and institutional design. It makes the case that going from prototype to platform is about rethinking the system that makes it possible for such solutions to succeed rather than about extending an existing solution. The facilitators of scale will be covered in detail in the parts that follow, including governance models and institutional preparation, technological and interoperability issues, procurement and funding routes, and insights from cities that have made the transition successfully. When combined, they provide a road map for converting promising pilots into intelligent, resilient, and equitable urban infrastructures.

10.2 Institutional Readiness and Multi-Stakeholder Governance

It takes more than just technical skill to scale AI-powered digital twin systems from pilots to fully integrated urban infrastructure. It necessitates strong institutional preparedness as well as a cohesive governance environment that unites various parties around a common goal. To operationalize and maintain digital twin intelligence at scale, local communities, academic institutions, utilities, infrastructure agencies, data suppliers, technology vendors, and municipal governments all play vital roles (Cheshmehzangi and Pourroostaei Ardakani 2024). However, these positions frequently disintegrate in the absence of explicit directives, well-defined duties, and coordination mechanisms, which results in redundant work, competing objectives, and halted innovation.

The ability of a city to integrate digital twin practices into its organizational structures and workflows is referred to as institutional readiness. Innovation teams or specialized taskforces that perform outside of the main governmental tasks are frequently in charge of digital twin pilots. Despite being flexible and progressive, these teams' isolation prevents them from growing. Integrating digital twin technologies into city agencies' daily operations—transportation, housing, trash, environment, and emergency services—not as add-ons but as essential infrastructure is known as mainstreaming. Building institutional memory, educating current employees, and revamping legacy procedures that were never intended with real-time, predictive intelligence in mind are all necessary to achieve this.

The existence of a well-defined governance structure is one of the most important factors that facilitate institutional readiness. Data governance, infrastructure operations, AI modelling, and public interaction are just a few of the areas that digital twins touch, and each may be governed by a different set of laws or regulations. Projects run the danger of being contentious or lacking direction in the absence of a formalized governance structure. Cross-sectoral governance boards, inter-agency taskforces, or digital twin offices that serve as central coordinators are frequently established by successful city-scale deployments. These organizations establish performance metrics that are in line with more general urban objectives like equity, climate resilience, and liveability. They also define roles, mediate conflicts, and guarantee interoperability.

It is imperative that governance frameworks transcend internal bureaucracy. Multi-stakeholder governance is necessary for true scalability; in this approach, the digital twin ecosystem is co-shaped by public, private, academic, and community players. For instance, utilities and infrastructure companies create vital operational data and oversee extensive networks of physical assets, but they frequently function under different legal frameworks from local governments. Data-sharing agreements, incentive programs, and legal clarity regarding ownership and obligations are necessary to guarantee their active participation. Similarly, private sector technology providers need to be involved as long-term partners who share public interest principles, rather than just as suppliers. In place of proprietary lock-ins, procurement procedures must be changed to prioritize open architectures, modular systems, and cooperative service models.

Civic organizations and community groups also play a critical role in institutionalizing digital twin systems that are inclusive, equitable, and efficient. How communities participate in the planning, management, and supervision of these systems shapes public trust, social legitimacy, and user relevance. Cities need to transition from consultation to co-creation, which entails creating channels of participatory governance that let citizens, particularly those from marginalized communities, have a say in what data is gathered, how digital twins are utilized, and which scenarios are given priority. The institutional lifecycle should incorporate these participatory structures—not one-time events, but long-term collaborations that change as system capabilities and societal demands do.

One of the most enduring obstacles to expanding is institutional silos. Departments frequently use different planning cycles, performance metrics, and datasets. Cities must promote interoperability at the institutional level—shared taxonomies, common reference models, and unified data ontologies that enable information to flow smoothly across silos—if they want digital twins to function as integrated systems-of-systems. A cultural change is also necessary for this, moving away from territorialism and toward cooperation and proactive governance. By funding interdepartmental training, acknowledging cross-sectoral success indicators, and establishing safe places for experimentation and learning, leadership must actively foster this change.

Regulatory alignment is another pillar of institutional readiness. As digital twins integrate AI models for simulation, prediction, and optimization, they come into contact with changing regulatory frameworks pertaining to algorithmic fairness, data protection, and public accountability. By coordinating their digital twin initiatives with national and international legal frameworks—such as the EU AI Act (Teller 2021; Zoltick and Maisel 2023; Ren and Du 2024; Aloisi 2025;), municipal data commons laws (Fia 2024), or ISO smart city standards (Midor and Płaza 2020; Kristiningrum and Kusumo 2021)—cities may remain ahead of these changes. In addition to lowering legal risk, this shows prospective funders and partners that the institution is mature.

Lastly, strategic foresight is a key component of institutional preparation. Scaling digital twin systems is a continuous governance exercise rather than a technical goal. Institutions need to be able to handle complexity, foresee unforeseen outcomes, and adjust to emerging technologies and urban issues. This entails establishing cross-functional governance labs, resilience planning teams, and internal ethical review boards to maintain digital twins in line with changing risk profiles and public values.

In conclusion, cities that lack institutional readiness will not be able to scale digital twins. If the organizations that oversee them continue to be dispersed, risk averse, or estranged from the communities they serve, then the most sophisticated models and real-time sensors will be of little use. Multi-stakeholder governance and institutional preparedness are not incidental issues; they are the foundation for the development, expansion, and maintenance of urban intelligence.

10.2.1 Leadership Models and Capacity Building

Beyond interagency coordination and governance procedures, scaling AI-digital twin systems throughout urban settings necessitates visionary leadership and consistent institutional capacity investment. Distributed leadership models that can steer digital transformation through uncertainty, complexity, and institutional inertia are necessary for system-wide implementation, even though pilots might flourish under a small number of fervent supporters. In addition to outlining how cities may develop the internal capacity to not only embrace but also own and develop AI-twin infrastructure, this subsection examines several leadership approaches, including top-down, bottom-up, and networked governance.

The initiation of scaling agendas is aided by 'top-down leadership'. The best people to obtain funds, facilitate interdepartmental collaboration, and include digital twin projects into high-level strategic visions—like net-zero paths, smart city initiatives, or climate resilience plans—are frequently mayors, city managers, and executive-level decision-makers. These leaders send a powerful message to both external stakeholders and city administrations when they support AI-twin systems as essential urban infrastructure. However, technocratic imposition must be avoided by top-down leadership. Digital projects run the danger of encountering opposition, alienation, or flimsy compliance in the absence of inclusive consultation and stakeholder buy-in.

On the other hand, departments, communities, or civil society organizations that recognize the revolutionary potential of digital twins in their particular circumstances are the ones that exhibit 'bottom-up leadership'. For instance, a local mobility team may use AI-powered simulations to rethink bus routes, and community planners may visualize public space interventions using participatory digital twins. Though they usually lack the funding, political support, and cross-silo traction required for scale, these grassroots initiatives frequently produce priceless innovation, contextual nuance, and social legitimacy. Both types of leadership are fostered in successful cities, guaranteeing that civic co-creation and decentralized experimentation complement institutional vision.

The new paradigm of 'networked governance', a leadership approach that emphasizes cooperation across players, sectors, and scales, sits in the middle of these two extremes. In this case, leadership is dispersed throughout a governance ecosystem that consists of public administrators, private sector partners, academia, and the general public rather than being centralized in a single office. Formal coordination structures that guarantee strategy alignment, shared accountability, and knowledge exchange are necessary for this paradigm. Examples of these mechanisms include governance compacts, taskforces, and digital innovation boards. Because it represents the systemic character of digital twins, networked governance is especially well-suited for scaling them. For example, a platform that affects housing, energy, transportation, water, and other areas needs to be governed by a coalition that has a broad reach across these domains.

Regardless of the leadership approach, scalability is made possible by capacity building. Even with the demands of real-time AI integration, many municipal departments are still getting used to basic digitization. Investing in human infrastructure, such as retraining current employees, recruiting multidisciplinary talent, and promoting digital literacy across the board, is necessary to build capacity. IT teams need to learn how to handle modular, cloud-based systems; civil engineers need to comprehend data unpredictability; and urban planners need to learn how to analyze AI-generated models. To successfully navigate the intersections of data, design, ethics, and governance, cross-disciplinary fluency is now a fundamental necessity rather than a luxury.

Organizational cultures and procedures are also included in capacity building. Iterative, data-driven decision-making cycles must replace static, linear procedures in city departments. This frequently entails setting up "innovation sandboxes", or laboratory settings, where novel instruments and techniques can be tried out free from the limitations of established practices. In order to account for the modular, dynamic character of AI-twin systems, it is also necessary to update budgeting cycles, data-sharing protocols, and procurement regulations.

Furthermore, ethically sound and forward-thinking leadership is essential in the AI-digital twin era. Building capacity involves more than just honing technical abilities; it also involves developing institutional reflexivity, or the capacity to consider whether or not we are planning for equity. Are structural imbalances being exacerbated or lessened? Can the public understand and trust our systems? It is possible to make sure that scale does not compromise justice or trust by incorporating such reflective methods into governance seminars, ethics education, and leadership development programs.

Overall, a distributed, inclusive, and flexible leadership style is necessary for scaling digital twins, as is a methodical approach to capacity building that enables cities to operationalize intelligence rather than merely obtain it. Cities can reform their institutions and realize the potential of digitalization only by investing in people, culture, and coordination.

10.3 Technical Challenges in Scaling Urban Twins

The technological barriers to scaling digital twins are examined in this section, including platform extensibility, data interoperability, legacy system integration, and performance optimization across spatial scales. As systems grow, it also tackles the difficulties of preserving model accuracy, computational load, and AI retraining requirements. Cities face a number of intricate technical obstacles as they work to expand AI-powered digital twin systems from district-level trials to citywide platforms. These are structural problems that arise from the complexity of urban systems, the variety of stakeholders, and the requirements of long-term operational continuity; they are not just issues of expanding server capacity or adding new datasets. Scaling digital twins requires both architectural coherence and technological sophistication, from data interoperability and legacy system integration to model retraining and real-time responsiveness.

Data interoperability is one of the most enduring challenges in growing urban twins. City systems are infamously disjointed; social services, transportation, utilities, planning, and the environment frequently use separate data infrastructures based on schemas, formats, and access protocols that are incompatible. To facilitate integration, querying, and analytics, these diverse datasets must be harmonized into a single semantic structure when scaling a digital twin. The twin becomes fragile without this, unable to synthesize intelligence across geographical layers or sectors. Partial answers are provided by open data standards, ontologies like CityGML, and middleware designs based on APIs; however, sustained institutional alignment and data governance are necessary for genuine interoperability.

The problem of integrating legacy systems is closely related. Numerous city systems, such as utility networks, construction permit registries, and traffic control centers, are still operating on outdated software that was never intended to interact with modular, cloud-native digital twins. It takes careful institutional negotiating as well as technological reengineering to retrofit these systems for real-time data transmission. The promise of unified urban intelligence is undermined by the failure to integrate older systems, which not only creates data black holes but also strengthens silos. Hybrid architectures, which permit legacy systems to temporarily coexist while progressively switching to compatible platforms, are frequently essential to a successful scaling plan.

Platform extensibility is another major obstacle. Pilot digital twins are frequently created specifically for a given domain, such energy, mobility, or flood risk. In order to scale, these specialized systems must be transformed into adaptable platforms that can accommodate several use cases, stakeholders, and data streams. This necessitates switching from monolithic programs to modular, service-oriented platforms in terms of architecture. The capacity to gradually incorporate new datasets, tools, and AI models without compromising the integrity of the system is another aspect of extensibility. To handle technological debt as complexity increases, this calls for meticulous API design, data versioning, containerization techniques, and strong governance.

Performance optimization takes center stage at greater scales. AI-twin infrastructures must handle massive computational demands when simulating a whole city in real-time or nearly real-time, including its energy consumption, transportation flows, microclimates, and sociodemographic trends. Reactivity across various user types and applications requires effective load balancing, distributed computing, and edge-cloud orchestration. Downtime, jitter, and latency become significant operational hazards, especially in time-sensitive fields like flood monitoring, traffic control, and emergency response. In order to create systems that can adapt to urban complexity rather than become overwhelmed by it, a strong performance strategy must also account for future development and scalability.

Maintaining model relevance and accuracy as cities evolve over time presents another difficulty. AI models that drive digital twins are trained on certain historical data distributions, whether they are used to simulate air quality or forecast traffic patterns. In order to maintain prediction accuracy, these models need to be updated or retrained frequently as urban shape, behaviour, and environmental variables change. However, large-scale retraining adds complexity to version control, data pipeline dependencies, and computational costs. For urban twins to be adaptive rather than outdated, retraining procedures and lifecycles must be established, as well as active learning systems that integrate fresh data almost instantly.

The problem of temporal and spatial scaling is another. Not everything that works in a district will necessarily work in a metropolitan area. Models that can function at various granularities—from street-level interventions to citywide policy simulations—are necessary due to the heterogeneity of land use, infrastructure conditions, and sociopolitical dynamics. This entails planning for scalability—the capacity to selectively zoom in or out, manage complexity flexibly, and preserve coherence across resolution levels—rather than just spatial scale. Without this, urban twins run the risk of losing the local distinctiveness necessary for successful interventions or crumbling under their own weight.

Finally, technological stewardship presents a crucial but unseen difficulty. Digital twins require constant upkeep, security, and updating as they grow. This include controlling cybersecurity threats, making sure that changing standards are followed, and avoiding platform drift. In order to prevent an excessive dependence on third-party vendors or proprietary information, it also calls for continuous documenting, capacity building, and system auditability. A scaled twin is a living system that needs upkeep, care, and institutional memory to be an advantage rather than a liability. It is not a finished product.

To put it briefly, growing urban digital twins is a complex technical undertaking. In addition to engineering expertise, it calls for organizational dedication, long-term planning, and architectural adaptability. Cities run the danger of creating stunning pilots that never develop into functional systems if these issues are not addressed head-on. However, the technical transition from prototype to platform becomes not just possible but transformative with careful integration, iterative learning, and strong governance.

10.4 Financing, Partnerships, and Risk Management

It takes more than just technology to scale AI-powered digital twins from pilots to fully integrated citywide systems. Every successful urban-scale deployment is supported by institutional and financial frameworks that can align incentives across sectors, absorb risk, and sustain innovation. Cities must concurrently develop sustainable finance structures, establish long-lasting collaborations, and put strong risk mitigation plans into place as they investigate the transition from demonstration to infrastructure.

The issue of capital investment lies at the heart of the scaling dilemma. In addition to the initial deployment costs of hardware, data infrastructure, and cloud compute, developing and sustaining AI-driven digital twin infrastructure at the urban scale also involves long-term operating expenses such as cybersecurity, system updates, employee training, and stakeholder engagement. This results in a financial burden that is normally too great for local budgets to handle alone. In order to spread costs and share risks, cities are increasingly using blended finance models, which include private capital, public investment, multilateral funding, and performance-based systems.

One of the most practical avenues for this kind of cooperation is still public-private partnerships, or PPPs (Cheshmehzangi 2020; Chan et al. 2022). PPPs can facilitate the implementation of scalable urban technology without placing an undue financial strain on local governments by coordinating private sector innovation and efficiency with public sector oversight and purpose alignment (Cheshmehzangi et al. 2025). PPPs must be created with explicit governance rules, nevertheless, to make sure that business needs don't override data ownership, accountability, and public interest protections. Furthermore, because the life cycle of AI-twin systems might last for decades, they necessitate a careful balancing act between short-term deliverables and long-term value development.

The use of climate financing tools and green bonds is another new mechanism. Forward-thinking cities are increasingly using these to finance climate-aligned infrastructure, such as digital systems that increase flood resilience, lower emissions, or improve energy efficiency. These requirements are frequently met by AI-powered digital twins, particularly when they are connected to more comprehensive climate adaptation and mitigation plans. Cities must measure the environmental impact of their digital systems and incorporate sustainability indicators into project evaluation frameworks in order to access such funding sources.

As part of initiatives for smart infrastructure and urban resilience, international aid and multilateral development organizations like the World Bank, UN-Habitat, and the Asian Development Bank have also started to fund the deployment of digital twins in low- and middle-income nations. These channels provide cash awards, capacity-building support, and technical help, especially when projects are in line with the objectives for digital inclusion and the Sustainable Development Goals (SDGs). However, unless combined with robust local ownership and long-term sustainability planning, aid-based approaches run the risk of causing dependency and fragmentation.

Because AI and digital twin initiatives are dynamic and iterative, standard procurement methods are frequently not appropriate. Adoption of agile procurement models or strategies, such as outcome-based contracting and innovation collaborations, is enabling increased responsiveness and flexibility. Adaptive problem-solving is encouraged over strict specifications by these approaches, which allow communities to contract for capabilities rather than set answers. But they also demand that procurement teams understand new technologies and be able to evaluate qualitative performance metrics, which are abilities that need to be incorporated into institutional capacity-building initiatives.

Additionally, scaling adds another level of innovation risk. Artificial intelligence (AI) systems change quickly and can act unexpectedly in new situations, unlike physical infrastructure. As systems grow, cities must construct protections for testing, monitoring, and recalibration. The staged rollout paradigm, which gradually moves from sandbox settings to live districts and ultimately to city-scale operations, is one successful strategy. This stepwise approach lowers the chance of systemic failure by allowing technical and governance learning to be integrated into each subsequent phase.

Data breach insurance, performance guarantees, and resilience bonds are among the risk-sharing frameworks and insurance models that are starting to emerge in the smart infrastructure space. While preserving investor confidence, these financial tools assist cities in mitigating operational and reputational risks. Furthermore, preserving public trust requires third-party audits, real-time monitoring systems, and transparent impact indicators, especially when AI systems interact with delicate areas like housing, mobility, or surveillance.

Lastly, partnership or cooperation ecosystems need to be developed not only between governments and digital companies but also between community organizations, utilities, academics, and civil society. Cities can share responsibilities, co-produce knowledge, and guarantee that solutions are not only technically sound but also socially sound thanks to these multi-actor ecosystems. Co-governance boards, collaborative research frameworks, and strategic memorandums of understanding (MoUs) can all serve to formalize these partnerships and shield initiatives from market or political fluctuations.

In sum, scaling AI-powered digital twins is a very institutional and financial undertaking. Even the most promising pilots run the risk of stagnating in the absence of strong funding, cross-sector collaborations, and uncertainty management procedures. Cities must adopt the ideas of shared governance, sustainable investment, and long-term risk stewardship in order to scale with purpose and transcend the logic of innovation procurement. Only then can digital urban intelligence develop into a long-lasting municipal infrastructure, rather than just a theoretical promise.

10.4.1 Procurement Innovation and Agile Implementation

The innovative agile procurement and delivery approaches highlighted in this subsection include challenge-based competitions, performance-based tenders, and modular contracts. It talks about how iterative deployment and ongoing improvement during scale-up can be facilitated by flexible contracting. The constraints of traditional procurement processes have become glaringly apparent as cities struggle to scale AI-powered digital twin systems. Because urban AI technologies are adaptive, data-intensive, and constantly changing, traditional approaches—rigid, specification-driven tenders and long-term contracts with little flexibility—are not appropriate. A new breed of procurement methods that place an emphasis on agility, iteration, and cross-sector collaboration is emerging in an effort to close the gap between technological dynamism and public sector accountability.

The shift to agile procurement is at the center of this change. Agile procurement is based on the concepts of responsiveness, modularity, and continual feedback, which are taken from the software development industry. Agile techniques enable cities to contract for results and capabilities rather than pre-defined solutions, as opposed to trying to define the entire scope of a project up front. This change allows for experimentation, learning, and course correction—all of which are essential in intricate urban systems where policy objectives and technical capabilities are changing simultaneously.

The modular contract is among the most effective strategies in this regard. Large-scale projects are divided into manageable, distinct parts through modular procurement, such as data ingestion, interface design, model training, citizen involvement, etc., which can be offered independently or in succession. This facilitates parallel innovation streams, and the incorporation of lessons learnt at each milestone, in addition to allowing governments to onboard specialized suppliers for each step. Importantly, modularity promotes market competition and reduces vendor lock-in by supporting exit options and vendor swapping without endangering the system's integrity.

Performance-based contracting is another cutting-edge strategy in which payments are based on key performance indicators (KPIs) as opposed to set deliverables. This could include goals for model accuracy, data latency, system uptime, or user engagement levels in the context of AI-digital twins. Performance-based approaches enable vendors to optimize for real-world impact rather than just fulfilling contractual checklists by tying incentives to actual system outcomes. But in order to properly monitor performance, cities must create strong evaluation frameworks and internal technical know-how, underscoring the necessity of capacity building in addition to procurement reform.

Challenge-based procurement, also known as open competitions or innovation challenges, is becoming increasingly popular among national and local governments. These models encourage a wide range of stakeholders, including startups, academic teams, and well-established businesses, to suggest solutions to well-defined urban issues, like "how can we simulate real-time flood risk using heterogeneous sensor data?" Challenge-based methods encourage a spirit of co-creation and provide access to unorthodox ideas. Additionally, they open doors for fresh actors to get involved in public projects that are usually controlled by big incumbents, such as civic tech organizations and local entrepreneurs.

Crucially, there is no mutual exclusion between these procurement methods. They are increasingly being combined by cities into hybrid procurement channels that are suited to institutional maturity and project needs. A municipality might, for instance, start with a challenge competition to gather ideas, construct prototypes using modular contracting, and then switch to a performance-based model for rollout throughout the entire city. The multi-phase nature of digital twin scaling and the requirement that procurement be a continuous process rather than a one-time event are reflected in such adaptable, tiered approaches.

The rise of 'pre-commercial areas' and 'procurement sandboxes' supports these new procurement approaches. These are safe spaces where governments can test out novel contracting methods and technology without being constrained by conventional regulatory requirements. Before making a long-term commitment, sandboxes enable quick development, iterative testing, and cross-agency collaboration. Additionally, they offer a platform for institutional learning, assisting cities in adapting procurement practices to the reality of technology.

However, agile procurement is not without its challenges. It may be challenging to conform to current audit criteria and put stress on legislative frameworks intended for consistency and predictability. Public institutions with risk-averse mindsets may gravitate toward tried-and-true procurement methods, even when they are clearly unsuitable for innovative projects. Building procurement officers' ability is crucial to addressing this; this includes teaching them new contracting techniques, impact assessment, collaborative governance, and emerging technology.

Transparency and equity also remain vital. It is possible for agile and challenge-based procurement to unintentionally favor well-resourced companies who can participate in competitions or iterative procedures. To guarantee that small businesses, organizations, and marginalized communities may also participate and gain from these models, cities must incorporate explicit inclusion protections into their design. These safeguards should include stipends, pre-bid workshops, and phased onboarding.

Finally, procurement serves as a lever for urban change. Cities' technology contracts influence not just what is constructed but also how it develops, who is involved, and what values are incorporated. Cities can unleash the promise of AI-powered digital twins—not as permanent infrastructure, but as dynamic civic platforms—by adopting agile, outcome-oriented, and modular procurement approaches. Procurement stops being a bottleneck and turns into a catalyst for resilient, inclusive, and intelligent urban futures when it is transformed into a place for co-creation and learning.

10.5 Lessons from the Field: Scaling with Equity and Purpose

It takes urban reimagining to scale AI-powered digital twins from pilot areas to full cities; it is not a straightforward technical reproduction process (Cheshmehzangi 2025). One thing is abundantly evident from the early adopters' successes and failures: implementation needs to be extremely sensitive to place, people, and purpose. Not because they sought growth at any costs, but rather because they scaled with purpose, cities like Singapore, Helsinki, Amsterdam, and Melbourne have developed into innovation hotspots. Their stories demonstrate that responsible growth of digital twins depends not only on sophisticated infrastructure but also on institutional bravery, public confidence, and a keen awareness of equity.

The development of digital twins in Singapore has coincided with the country's long-standing integrated planning history. Planning simulations, community involvement, and disaster preparedness have all benefited from the Virtual Singapore project, which uses an interactive 3D model integrated with real-time data. However, its capacity to harmonize across ministries, data custodians, and utility providers through strong interoperability protocols and a whole-of-government architecture might be its most significant accomplishment. The lesson is that size necessitates extensive horizontal and vertical cooperation across industries and bureaucracy in addition to data.

Helsinki offers a different trajectory. Instead of implementing a single platform, the Finnish capital has welcomed innovation and modularity. Helsinki's model is flexible, civic-minded, and iterative, ranging from AI-powered mobility management to interactive digital twins in urban renewal. Transparency has been crucial in this case; open data policies, algorithm registers, and citizen dashboards have made sure that the instruments of urban intelligence are accessible to the general public rather than hidden behind institutional barriers. This fosters trust as well as creativity, demonstrating that responsible scaling entails scaling communication and transparency on par with systems.

Amsterdam's strategy has brought attention to how important values are. The city, being in the forefront of digital rights and urban tech ethics, has made sure that its growth in digital twin technologies follows strict normative guidelines. The city maintains that data must serve the public interest rather than just operational efficiencies through programs like the Amsterdam Algorithm Register and the TADA Manifesto (Mollema et al. 2022; Bottenbley 2023; De Kreek et al. 2023). Scaling is never neutral, as this method serves as a reminder. Every stage of growth, including deciding what information to gather, what to model, and what to optimize, is based on presumptions about the city's current state and future development. Cities may only protect justice in their digital futures by explicitly stating these ideals.

In Melbourne, the focus has been on incorporating digital twin capabilities into precinct-scale architecture and climate resilience (Gardner 2024). Simulation techniques have been used to estimate energy demand, shadow affects, flooding concerns, and transport flows across a range of planning scenarios for projects like the reconstruction of Fisherman's Bend (Tara et al. 2018). Crucially, Melbourne's scaling plan involves collaborations with private-sector innovators, utilities, and universities, proving that inclusive ecosystems—rather than lone vendors—create scalable intelligence (Maddox et al. 2023). The city is concentrating on adaptive governance and long-term public benefit as it moves from district pilots to metropolitan systems.

These varied case studies show that there is no race to uniformity when it comes to scaling. Context is important. Cultures of governance are important. History of the social contract is important. When success stories are copied and pasted from one urban area to another, the subtleties that initially make them work are frequently lost. Instead, responsible scaling involves balancing technical aspirations with public engagement and institutional maturity. It's important to understand that a digital twin in one city might be a command center, while in another it might be a participatory common. Both are legitimate as long as they are based on ethical foresight and local needs.

Four guiding concepts for scaling digital twins with equity and purpose can be distilled from these instances (Fig. 10.1). Modularity comes first. Layers of systems must be constructed with the ability to expand, change, and adapt. This guarantees that scaling doesn't necessitate complete redesign at every stage, but rather adaptable infrastructure that can react to new information, collaborators, or requirements. Transparency comes in second. Visibility of data sources, algorithms, performance indicators, and governance frameworks must all be included in scaling. By making the unseen infrastructure of intelligence both understandable and accountable, cities can foster the trust of their citizens.

Co-creation comes in third. Involving local businesses, community organizations, and citizens in the scaling process helps cities create more resilient, socially

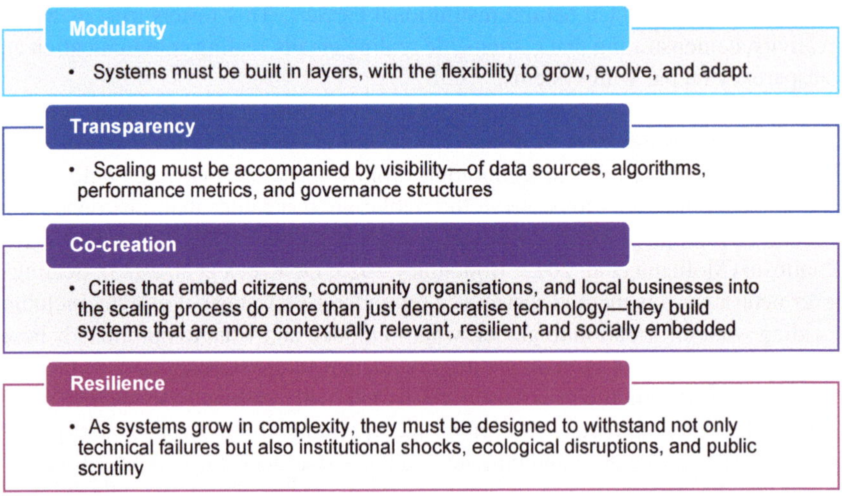

Fig. 10.1. We can distil four guiding principles for scaling digital twins with equity and purpose

embedded, and contextually relevant systems in addition to democratizing technology. Scaling should always increase the range of inclusion rather than centralize decision-making. And lastly, resilience. Systems must be built to survive institutional shocks, ecological disruptions, public scrutiny, and technology failures as they become more complex (Allam and Cheshmehzangi 2024). An infrastructure that embraces uncertainty, learns continuously, and is managed as a long-term civic asset rather than a temporary experiment is said to be resilient.

In conclusion, expanding AI-powered digital twins is about building the foundation for decades of intelligent, equitable, and flexible urban administration, not about finishing a race. Cities may institutionalize smart, equitable, and long-lasting digital twin systems by establishing expansion based on the concepts of modularity, transparency, co-creation, and resilience. Not only what we construct, but also how and for whom we decide to scale, will determine the future of AI-augmented (Swathi et al. 2025) urbanism.

References

Allam Z, Cheshmehzangi A (2024) Technological innovation and sustainable transitions. In: Allam Z, Cheshmehzangi A (2024) Sustainable futures and green new deals. Springer Nature Switzerland, Cham, pp 55–79

Aloisi A (2025) Integrating the EU twin (green and digital) transition? Synergies, tensions and pathways for the future of work. https://www.bollettinoadapt.it/wp-content/uploads/2025/02/JRC140964_01.pdf (Accessed online on 21 October 2025).

Bottenbley A (2023) The algorithm agenda: a discourse analysis of the Dutch algorithm register. Master's thesis, Utrecht University.

Chan FKS, Li L, Cheshmehzangi A, Thadani DR, Ives CD (2022) The transformation of the green infrastructure intervention under the case of Sponge city program: positions, challenges, and prospects in China. In: Cheshmehzangi A (ed) Green infrastructure in Chinese cities. Springer, Singapore, pp 97–122

Cheshmehzangi A (2020) Towards urban energy management: a brief review of China's recent transition in urban energy demand. Low Carbon Econ. 11(01):1

Cheshmehzangi A (2025) Urban planning for the contemporary age: navigating complexities and shaping urban futures. Encyclopedia 5(1):19

Cheshmehzangi A, Pourroostaei Ardakani S (2024) Navigating the future with the nexus between digital twin computing and urban intelligence. In: Pourroostaei Ardakani S and Cheshmehzangi A, (eds.) (2024) Digital twin computing for urban intelligence, Singapore, Springer Nature Singapore, pp 245–256.

Cheshmehzangi A, You N, Allam Z, He BJ (2025) Eco-rehabilitation of the city park "Chaikovoye lake" in Kazan, Russia. In: Cheshmehzangi A, You N, Allam Z, He BJ (2025) People-centered innovation: local actions for sustainable cities and communities. Springer Nature Singapore, Singapore, pp 135–148

De Kreek M, Alfrink K, de Waal M, Kortuem G, Turel T, Visser B, Samson L (2023) When 'doing ethics' meets public procurement of smart city technology–an Amsterdam case study. In: The international association for societies of design research conference (IASDR) 2023: life-changing design, Design Research Society, October 2023

Fia T (2024) Governance of urban data commons as a matter of value redistribution in the smart city. Sens public (SP1639)

Gardner N (2024) Scaling the smart city: the design and ethics of urban technology. Elsevier, Amsterdam

Kristiningrum E, Kusumo H (2021) Indicators of smart city using SNI ISO 37122: 2019. IOP Conf. Ser.: Mater. Sci. Eng. 1096(1):012013

Li T, Long Q, Chai H, Zhang S, Jiang F, Liu H, Huang W, Jin D, Li Y (2025) Generative AI empowered network digital twins: architecture, technologies, and applications. ACM Comput. Surv. 57(6):1–43

Maddox A, Waters-Lynch J, Parasol M (2023) Harnessing digital twins for fostering city-scale entrepreneurial ecosystems: extending a case study of Melbourne. In: 2023 IEEE engineering informatics. Conference held in Melbourne, Australia, IEEE, pp 1–9. https://doi.org/10.1109/IEEECONF58110.2023.10520526

Midor K, Płaza G (2020) Moving to smart cities through the standard indicators ISO 37120. Multidiscip. Asp. Prod. Eng. 3(1):617–630

Mollema T, Wijffels J, Beijerbacht M, Dom L, Joziasse J (2022) Citizens, surveillance and sensing responsibly. Utrecht University, Digital Ethics (FRRMV16017), Utrecht. https://responsiblesensinglab.org/storage/files/cb8e366f-2e10-4bc2-b6d7-be3a391a0f1e/DRH%2D%2D-PubVersion_Group3_CrowdManagement-DataEthicalConsultation.pdf

Raven R, Sengers F, Spaeth P, Xie L, Cheshmehzangi A, De Jong M (2019) Urban experimentation and institutional arrangements. Eur. Plan. Stud. 27(2):258–281

Ren Q, Du J (2024) Harmonizing innovation and regulation: the EU artificial intelligence act in the international trade context. Comput. Law Secur. Rev. 54:106028

Swathi A, Raghavendra C, Karthick K, Balakrishnan P, Ponnusamy S, Revathi R (2025) Smart city oriented engagement platforms utilizing collaborative artificial intelligence systems internet of things and augmented reality for urban transformation. In: Kannadhasan S, Sivakumar P, Saravanan T, Kumar SS (eds) International conference on sustainability innovation in computing and engineering (ICSICE 2024). Atlantis, Amsterdam, pp 1030–1043

Tara A, Ninsalam Y, Anderson C (2018) Interrogating urban renewal scenarios using skyline analysis in Fishermans Bend, Melbourne. J. Digit. Landsc. Archit. 3:2–11

Teller M (2021) Legal aspects related to digital twin. Philos. Trans. R. Soc. A 379(2207):20210023

Thuermer G, Walker J, Simperl E, Carr L (2024) When data meets citizens: an investigation of citizen engagement in data-driven innovation programmes. Data Policy 6:e12

Zoltick MM, Maisel JB (2023) Societal impacts: legal, regulatory and ethical considerations for the digital twin. In: Crespi N, Drobot AT, Minerva R (eds) The digital twin. Springer International Publishing, Cham, pp 1167–1200

Chapter 11
Rethinking Regenerative Urbanism and Design Through AI, Digital Twins, and the Ethics of Care

11.1 From Smart to Regenerative: A New Paradigm of Urban Intelligence

The main argument of the book is summarized in this first part of the concluding chapter, which traces the conceptual transition from efficiency-driven "smart cities" to cities as living, learning, and healing systems. It considers the evolution of digital twins and artificial intelligence from operational tools to design logics for regenerative urbanism.

The language of "smart cities" has dominated urban discourse in these recent two decades, implying an era of efficiency, automation, and optimization (Cheshmehzangi 2022). However, what occurs when efficiency is no longer sufficient—when the very mechanisms we have simplified contribute to social disintegration, ecological deterioration, and the decline of civic life? We are on the cusp of a crucial paradigm shift—from smartness to regeneration—as we face the mounting constraints of resource depletion, inequality, and climate change. This is not merely a technological pivot (Cheshmehzangi 2025). It is a significant reinterpretation of urban intelligence, emphasizing care rather than control; healing, adaptability, and evolution rather than just predicted accuracy. Where smart cities stop, regenerative urbanism starts. It poses the question: How can cities develop into living systems that are sensitive to the deeper rhythms of culture, ecology, and collective memory in addition to data? How might digital twins and artificial intelligence (AI), which have traditionally been thought of as tools for management and observation, be rethought as tools for renewal?

When directed by regenerative values, generative AI and urban digital twins are no longer just efficiency tools (Pourroostaei Ardakani and Cheshmehzangi 2024). They turn into transformational tools, promoting biodiversity, facilitating resource cycles, and promoting the well-being of both humans and non-human species for generations to come. The city is now a co-evolving organism that is grounded in place but fed by information, rather than a machine that needs to be optimized.

A. Cheshmehzangi, *Generative AI-Powered Urban Digital Twins*, Urban Sustainability,
https://doi.org/10.1007/978-981-95-4766-1_11

A radical reconsideration of our technological usage is encouraged by this regenerative lens. For example, the urban digital twin is frequently used to track utilities, replicate logistics, or mirror infrastructure. However, what if it reflected a park's soil health? The tree canopy's capacity to cool? the neighbourhood's intergenerational well-being? What if artificial intelligence (AI) could map the emotional geographies that influence urban belonging or track the gradual violence of spatial inequality in addition to traffic forecasting? Asking new questions and empowering alternative modes of knowing are the first steps toward regeneration.

Data is a catalyst rather than the ultimate aim in this new paradigm. AI is a connective tissue rather than the brain. Cities are now seen as open ecologies of response and relationship rather than closed circuits of consumption and control. Feedback is the foundation of regenerative intelligence—not simply quick feedback loops for infrastructure, but also lengthy, introspective loops that allow for learning, disagreement, and iteration. Cities that learn alongside their residents, not just about them, are the focus.

An epistemic change from top-down technocratic expertise to plural, embodied, and situated knowledges is essential to the transition to regenerative urban intelligence. A regenerative city is one that pays attention to environmental cues that have been disregarded for a long time, Indigenous wisdom, and frontline communities. It accepts civic imagination as an independent intellect. Here, generative AI aids in community foresight, narrative co-creation, and iterative re-design rather than taking center stage in urban design.

This is also a shift in temporality. The immediate—the predictive dashboard, the real-time optimization, the frictionless instant—is given priority in smart cities. In contrast, cities that are regenerative embrace deep time. They can sense the lingering effects of damage and the desire for healing. They model what is feasible, desirable, and just in addition to what is likely. Thus, AI systems built under this paradigm need to go beyond performance indicators and explore the domains of planetary reciprocity, interspecies solidarity, and long-term stewardship.

We are beginning to see glimpses of this future. AI is being utilized in Singapore to plan nature-based cooling lanes that restore urban biodiversity in addition to monitoring energy use. Circular digital twins in Amsterdam simulate material flows that support the city's ecology and economics (Askar et al. 2024). Digital platforms are being co-designed in Indigenous-led planning across parts of Canada and Australia to include seasonal cycles, ancestral routes, and cultural landscapes into spatial decision-making (Woodward et al. 2020; Butler et al. 2023; Moola et al. 2024). These aren't only clever apps. They are regenerative manifestations that are ethically informed, contextually grounded, and receptive to new ideas. To embrace this paradigm is to acknowledge that intelligence without empathy is insufficient, and efficiency without equity is hollow. In addition to optimizing itself, a regenerative city learns how to take care of its most vulnerable citizens, fix what has gone wrong, and develop in ways that improve the quality of life. The citation "Askar, 2024" has been changed to "Askar et al. 2024" to match the author name/date in the reference list. Please check if the change is fine in this occurrence and modify the subsequent occurrences, if necessary.all ok and thanks.

As we enter this final chapter, we close not with answers but with renewed questions. Rather than designing around life, what does it mean to design with it? Can AI stop being an arbitrator of optimization and start acting as a custodian of shared futures? What kind of cities are owed to future generations as well as to each other? The transition from smart to regenerative is an extension of intelligence, not a rejection of it. It invites us to reimagine AI as a civic, ecological, and cultural force. It calls us not just to build systems that are smarter, but to craft cities that are wiser—attuned to the richness of their ecologies, accountable to the dignity of their inhabitants, and capable of cultivating futures that sustain the possibility of life itself.

11.1.1 Learning from Living Systems: Biomimicry and Urban Ecology

By examining how AI may assist cities in simulating natural systems—looping flows, fostering diversity, and building resilience through feedback-rich environments—this subsection takes inspiration from ecological intelligence. We must radically shift our understanding of intelligence if we are to move from smart to regenerative cities. This change calls on us to look to nature as a mentor, teacher, and role model in addition to technology growth. The most durable models of flexibility, resilience, and harmony with complexity can be found in ecological systems. Cities must imitate the logic of life itself if they are to survive.

This is the promise of biomimicry, not as metaphor, but as method. Biomimicry reminds us of the genius of nature in a world that is becoming increasingly characterized by artificial settings and constructed systems (Nasir and Arif Kamal 2022). Without a single algorithm, forests store carbon and control water flows. Coral reefs use natural resources to create intricate, self-repairing structures. Similar to a fungal internet, mycelial networks exchange information, disperse nutrients, and adjust to stress (Sirimorok 2024). In terms of computation, these systems are not "smart". They are relational, regenerative, and extremely context-aware, which makes them intelligent.

By allowing energy, water, materials, and information to flow through nested loops of use, reuse, and renewal, biomimicry encourages us to view the urban fabric as an ecosystem unto itself. We learn from urban ecology that cities are a part of nature, both influencing and being influenced by its cycles. Cities can create with nature, not against it, if generative AI is tuned to this ecological paradigm.

In previously unthinkable ways, generative systems can assist biomimetic planning when combined with ecological data and life-based concepts. Imagine a computer twin of a metropolis that guides the installation of native plants and green roofs by mapping heat sinks and pollinator routes in addition to simulating traffic flows. Imagine artificial intelligence (AI) algorithms that learn from mangrove root networks to provide urban buffers against storm surges, or models that analyze wetland hydrology to recommend stormwater retention systems (Abera 2025). These aren't just hypothetical. The emergence of early prototypes of these tools marks the beginning of ecological computation.

Importantly, regenerative cities become centered around looping flows, which are a characteristic of living systems. Waste is always food in nature. Materials never stop cycling. Decomposition serves as a prelude to fresh growth and returns nutrients to the soil (Zhan 2024). In contrast, cities are essentially linear: extract, consume, and discard. Cities may shut their loops by using generative AI and digital twins to find areas where materials leak, energy is squandered, and organic processes can take the place of mechanical ones.

AI-enhanced circularity models, for instance, can monitor food waste from homes and restaurants, model local composting possibilities, and provide information to urban farming systems that close the food-soil-food cycle. Building stock may be transformed into a dynamic, circular resource by using AI to track waste flows from construction and deconstruction, identify reusable materials in real time, and provide insights into material passports and adaptive reuse plans. The city turns into a living metabolism rather than a sink.

Resilience through diversity is another important lesson to be learned from living systems. Natural ecosystems flourish due to decentralization, variability, and redundancy. On the other hand, monocultures break down under pressure. Cities run the risk of becoming brittle—prone to shocks and unable to recover—if they are only planned with efficiency in mind. However, urban systems acquire the ability to adapt, absorb, and renew when they are biomimetically constructed, with diversity incorporated into housing types, energy sources, mobility options, and green infrastructure.

Here, generative AI becomes a co-explorer of design diversity. AI can produce thousands of variations rather than just one "optimal" solution, testing different streetscapes, housing types, and ecological corridors under a range of future conditions. It enables communities and planners to investigate not just what is effective right now but also what will remain effective in the face of uncertain demographic, economic, and climatic futures. Thus, AI aligns with the adaptive complexity of life by amplifying several alternatives rather than acting as a narrowing factor.

Feedback-rich environments play an equally important function in this ecological intelligence. Feedback is how nature changes. Adaptive responses arise from ongoing sensing, learning, and recalibration, whether through genetic mutation or forest succession. Similar processes must be incorporated into the design of regenerative cities: cities that pay attention, pick up knowledge, and change in reaction to data and personal experience.

This feedback orientation can be operationalized through digital twins. They offer a living interface for tracking the city's health by continuously ingesting data from urban sensors, such as those measuring air quality, heat, movement, noise, and biodiversity. When systems deviate from their objectives, emissions increase, or drought stress levels increase, AI algorithms can identify these events and initiate alarms or even self-corrective measures. Perhaps more significantly, though, these systems can also record positive feedback, such as when walkability improves social cohesion, urban greening initiatives lower depression rates, or Indigenous knowledge incorporated into land planning enhances ecosystem function. In this situation, feedback transforms from a control mechanism to a moral compass.

Finally, studying biological systems necessitates a humility that technology cannot provide. A cloud server is not necessary for the forest to be intelligent. Real-time analytics are not necessary for the river to determine its path. Place, time, and profound co-evolution are the origins of these innate intelligences. Generative AI needs to be ingrained in this ethic in order to promote regenerative urbanization. Slowness, ambiguity, multiplicity, and local knowledge must all be respected. AI therefore replicates nature, learns from it, and eventually helps to create space for it in a regenerative city rather than replacing it. Our goal is to build partnerships that enable cities to become thriving environments for life in all its forms, not to control complexity through computation.

11.2 The City as a Platform for Collective Agency

With an emphasis on civic empowerment, this part demonstrates how digital twins and generative AI may democratize urban design, elevate marginalized voices, and incorporate local knowledge into systemic planning. It reinterprets urbanism as a continuous, collaborative act of co-creation in which ecological, social, and cultural repair are all part of regeneration. Our notion of design must be broadened from that of professionals and specialists to that of a communal civic act if we are to move toward truly regenerative cities. Cities are collective manifestations of histories, values, and ambitions; they are more than merely constructed surroundings. We now have strong tools to make that collective agency visible, palpable, and actionable in the era of generative AI and urban digital twins.

Historically, urbanism has frequently been top-down, the result of elite imagination, market logic, or state ambition. When they do occur, even participatory processes are frequently performative, late in the design cycle, and restricted to a small number of options. A new paradigm, however, is needed for regenerative urbanism: urban design as co-creation, in which communities influence not just the results of development but also the very frameworks that are used to envision futures.

When used responsibly, generative AI can facilitate this change. AI has the potential to democratize urban imagination by converting complicated data into easily understood visual formats and enabling citizens to model, contrast, and iterate many possibilities. Understanding how a new park could lessen local heat stress or how green roofs could enhance neighborhood health outcomes doesn't require a degree in planning. AI becomes a translator of complexity through user-friendly interfaces—voice-driven models, community dashboards, and augmented reality overlays—giving the general public access to design tools.

However, collective agency encompasses both inclusion and accessibility. Voices that have long been marginalized—those of Indigenous peoples, low-income inhabitants, migrants, seniors, youth, and populations that have previously been left out of planning tables—must be taken into consideration when urban regeneration takes place. Digital twins that solely depict energy flows or infrastructure and do not account for cultural geographies are not regenerative; instead, they replicate damage. With the use of narrative mapping, participatory data, and qualitative insights that go beyond abstract optimization, generative AI presents a chance to incorporate lived experience into urban intelligence.

For instance, in addition to hydrological models and sensor data, a digital twin of a neighborhood that experiences flooding can also contain community memories of land-use change, oral histories of displacement, and tales of cultural resilience. More morally sound interventions are informed by these layers when they have been digitized and respected. In a similar vein, communities might use generative AI tools to suggest their own housing typologies, public space enhancements, or mobility improvements, led not only by algorithmic logic but also by local needs and cultural coherence.

Digital twins' true power is in amplifying several futures rather than in predicting control. Urban areas are diverse. What is effective in one neighbourhood might not be in another. This diversity is honoured by regenerative design. It encourages multi-scale thinking, in which lived experiences and hyperlocal insights work together to drive policy. The foundation of the regenerative effort is this distributed intelligence—between people and machines, between organizations and communities.

Furthermore, communal agency needs to encompass stewardship as well as design. Regeneration is a continuous interaction between people and their surroundings rather than a one-time occurrence. AI can help communities evaluate ecological health, social well-being, or design effect over time through continuous feedback loops. It enables urbanism to become relational, reflexive, and adaptive—elements that are fundamentally ecological.

Importantly, these changes rely on governance as much as technology. Collective agency is crucially enabled by open data, civic education, inclusive procurement, and rights-based digital frameworks (Plantinga et al. 2023). We need to make sure AI systems benefit society as a whole, not just the market. Instead of becoming places for surveillance capitalism, cities should be venues for civic creation. Digital twins must not be black-boxed assets under the control of third parties, but rather co-owned and co-curated. Urban knowledge is fostered rather than exploited in a regenerative city. Power is shared rather than centralized. Additionally, design is co-authored—across generations, cultures, and species—rather than imposed. The city transforms into a living process rather than a final result, a stage when ecological restoration and public imagination collide.

11.3 Designing Futures, Not Just Managing Systems

This part shifts the focus of AI from optimization to creativity. To answer the question, "What should a city become?" it investigates speculative design, scenario generation, and multiple future-building techniques that use AI. It promotes thoughtful, inclusive foresight and challenges deterministic ideas. All too frequently, the promise of AI in urbanism has been presented in terms of control: simplifying infrastructure, cutting emissions, and improving traffic flows. These efficiencies are useful, but they fall short of AI's full potential, which is to envision what may be rather than to control what is.

Regenerative cities need creative insight in addition to functional mechanisms. They call for a change in perspective from determinism to possibility—from forecasting a single future to fostering multiple futures. This enlarged function is made possible by generative AI's ability to create scenarios and vary designs. It enables us to come up with several options, each of which reflects a unique set of values, trade-offs, and goals, in addition to the most effective one.

This is the field of speculative design, which approaches urban planning as a query rather than a solution. If elder knowledge were given priority, how might a city look? What shapes might arise from Indigenous cosmologies of land care or from a child's view of play? Artificial intelligence (AI)-powered simulations can assist in visualizing such provocations—not to make decisions for us, but to encourage discussion and consideration.

Crucially, this work challenges the idea that futures are predetermined locations. Many of the current ideas for smart cities are technocratic and linear; they are framed by master plans for infrastructure, economic growth, or efficiency metrics. They do not allow for dissent, question, or dreaming. In contrast, regenerative futures value co-authorship, introspection, and ambiguity. Instead of being forced into compliance, they create room for communities to navigate their futures together.

Building institutional muscles for moral foresight, narrative construction, and intergenerational accountability is a necessary part of designing futures. It entails teaching cities to have thoughtful dreams. In this situation, AI stops being a predictor and starts acting as a collaborator in research, producing ideas that challenge our preconceptions and encourage us. In the end, regenerative urbanism poses the question, "What matters?" rather than, "What works?" It restores design's place as a moral and cultural activity that is informed by justice, empathy, and beauty. Furthermore, it urges us to use AI as a tool of hope rather than as a neutral optimizer, enabling cities to become better places for people to live rather than just better machines.

11.3.1 Generative Foresight: Ethics, Time, and Long-Term Urbanism

For cities to become regenerative, they need to reframe their relationship with time. Currently, urban planning is often limited by election cycles, fiscal years, and project deadlines—temporalities that obscure the long-term consequences of decisions made today. Generative foresight challenges this short-termism and demands a shift toward deep time thinking: planning that takes into account the rights, needs, and dignity of future generations as well as non-human life. This subsection examines temporal justice, the ethics of future generations, and how AI-driven planning must integrate multi-generational stewardship, interspecies coexistence, and climate responsibility into the DNA of urban futures.

Urban digital twins driven by AI provide a new tool for this recalibration. These technologies can expose trajectories that are otherwise unseen to modern politicians by simulating long-term scenarios, such as resource depletion curves, sea-level rise over decades, and urban heat consequences into the next century. However, foresight is more than just technical. It's moral. It is necessary to address important issues in order to use these simulations effectively: What sort of ancestors do we wish to be? Whose futures do we protect? Who are we neglecting?

Temporal fairness, or the belief that future city dwellers, both human and non-human, should have a habitable environment, is at the core of generative foresight. There is substance to this justice. It calls for workable solutions, such as frameworks for climate budgeting, intergenerational councils, and legally recognized environmental guardianship. Additionally, it requires that AI systems used in urban governance embody this duty by enhancing our moral imagination, allowing both citizens and planners to see more broadly, care more deeply, and make more informed decisions, rather than by automating long-term decisions.

Importantly, foresight needs to go beyond the human. Cities must be planned for the coexistence of all species, including pollinators, wetlands, soil ecosystems, and migratory birds (Adrianzen Abanto 2025). Prototyping cities where the natural and the constructed coexist can be aided by generative models that are based on ecological data and biodiversity objectives. These simulations show how actions affect species and environments that we may never see but whose survival is intertwined with our own.

Rethinking who owns the future is another aspect of integrating foresight into AI-urban systems. All too frequently, elite visions—developers, technocrats, and remote consultants—capture speculative planning. To democratize the future, regenerative foresight calls for include adolescents, elders, Indigenous communities, and marginalized groups in the process of determining the city's temporal arc. AI can help with this by converting intricate projections into narratives that involve participation, allowing a variety of audiences to envision and assess long-term results.

Finally, generative foresight is more than just forecasting. The habit of taking care of futures we cannot yet envision and creatures we may never meet is what it is all about. When this ethic is ingrained in urban systems, it can assist cities in moving past reaction, resilience, and even sustainability in the direction of a long-lasting, inclusive, and profoundly regenerative way of life.

11.4 Principles for Regenerative Urban Intelligence

The book's observations are condensed into guiding principles for intelligent, regenerative, and design-driven cities in the conclusion part. These include radical inclusion, distributed intelligence, civic imagination, ecological reciprocity, and ethical

Fig. 11.1. Five interconnected concepts or key message take-outs from the book, served as five principles forming the foundation of a new kind of urban intelligence—an intelligence that is not obsessed with prediction, but alive with possibility; not built for extraction, but for healing

autonomy. The section ends with a call to action: rethink cities as ecosystems to be nourished, alive with potential and driven by compassion, rather than as machines to be controlled. As this book comes to an end, we go back to its main question: What if cities were regenerative as well as intelligent? What if the ability to repair, include, empower, and endure—rather than efficiency, control, or speed—was what truly characterized urban intelligence?

This final vision is based on five interconnected concepts, which are compass points rather than blueprints (See Fig. 11.1). Together, they map out a course for a time when living will be supported by digital tools and cities will be cultivated as ecosystems rather than machines.

First, ecological reciprocity must be the foundation of regenerative urban intelligence. Cities are interwoven with nature, not separate from it. The systems we create pulse with heat and energy, the roads we pave redirect water, and the walls we construct breathe air. We now have the ability to replicate these flows, restore equilibrium, and design with nature rather than against it thanks to generative AI and urban digital twins. Reciprocity, however, requires more than just modeling. In order to promote biodiversity, temper the climate, and restore the soil, it calls on cities to give back. This is more than just an engineering problem. Designing with the humility that cities, like forests and rivers, are a part of a living planet is an ethical requirement.

Second, civic imagination as a catalyst for urban change needs to be reclaimed. All too frequently, the terminology used to describe smart cities reduces the future to efficiency and probability. However, the first step in regeneration is to ask new questions, such as what is feasible rather than merely what is likely. What matters, not just what works? Communities can envision plural, just, and bold futures with the aid of AI-assisted co-creation, speculative design, and participatory foresight.

Urbanism needs to become a collective story that is written by citizens' aspirations rather than just algorithms.

Additionally, urban intelligence must be dispersed rather than centralized. Data centers and command rooms are not the only places where a regenerative city's wisdom can be found; it can also be found in the lived knowledge of neighbourhoods, Indigenous customs, community adaptive behaviours, and the natural rhythms. Digital twins and AI must be built to work with and learn from these various intelligences. This necessitates the blending of technical and cultural systems, where each street becomes a sensor and each citizen a designer of their surroundings, and where code interacts with tradition rather than suppressing it.

Radical inclusivity is another requirement for a regenerative city. Unchecked technology has the potential to reinforce current disparities by excluding people without access to digital tools or concealing bias behind opaque algorithms. However, with careful design, urban AI can also be a force for justice. This entails making certain that systems are representational, transparent, and easily available. It entails creating interfaces that cater to all age groups and skill levels as well as platforms that prioritize underrepresented voices. Inclusion is the very prerequisite for legitimacy in a city that aspires to revitalize; it is not a check list.

Lastly, ethical autonomy must serve as the compass for regenerative urban intelligence. The temptation to delegate judgment to machines increases with the complexity of digital twins and AI models. However, the future cannot be handed over. It needs to be discussed. Instead of being added as an afterthought, ethics must be ingrained in the design of our systems. This calls for new kinds of oversight, such as interdisciplinary ethics boards, human-in-the-loop designs, and government agencies that look after digital infrastructure. It calls for us to build systems with fairness, dignity, reparability, and care in mind, in addition to performance.

These five ideas collectively constitute the basis of a new type of urban intelligence, one that is alive with possibilities rather than preoccupied with forecasts, and that is designed for healing rather than extraction. They encourage us to adopt a care mindset in place of techno-solutionism. a way of thinking that views cities as complicated, flawed, resilient living systems and holds that intelligence is not what makes a city effective but rather what enables it to coexist peacefully with its inhabitants and the environment.

This book is an introduction rather than a conclusion. To construct cities that breathe, evolve, and dream, planners, designers, technologists, and communities are urged to go beyond dashboards and data streams (Ondiviela 2021). We've got the equipment. We know. The will to act—clearly, bravely, and compassionately—is what we need now. Moreover, this book is not a guide. It is a start, or better to be regarded as, a call to action for communities, technologists, planners, and designers to rethink the city as an ecosystem to be nourished rather than a machine to be controlled. It's a call to construct with caution, bravery, and the belief that cities, like all living systems, can become more than merely smarter. The equipment is available. We have the option. Let's create cities that are more alive as well as more intelligent. Cities' future is more than just intelligent. It is regenerative by design—driven by compassion, anchored in justice, and alive with remembrance.

Abera (2025). Adrianzen Abanto (2025). Askar et al. (2024). Butler et al. (2025). Cheshmehzangi (2022). Plantinga et al. (2023). Sirimorok (2024).

References

Abera L (2025) The growing role of artificial intelligence in tomorrow's urban hydrological infrastructure. Institute for Homeland Security. Washington D.C., US. https://shsu-ir.tdl.org/items/f2eadd8c-5419-4a88-a256-17cb87d411eb (Accessed online on 21 October 2025).

Adrianzen Abanto VV (2025) Embracing coexistence: urban design strategies for creating wildlife-friendly cities. https://openresearch.ocadu.ca/id/eprint/4688/ (Accessed on 04 October 2025)

Askar R, Karaca F, Salles A, Lukyanenko A, Cervantes Puma GC, Tavares V, Khaidarova A, Nadaždi A, Pineda-Martos R, Díaz-Cabrera JM, Honic M (2024) Driving the built environment twin transition: synergising circular economy and digital tools. In: Bragança L. Griffiths P. Askar R. Salles A. Ungureanu, V. Tsikaloudaki, K. Bajare D. Zsembinszki G. Cvetkovska M. (eds.) (2024) Circular economy design and management in the built environment: a critical review of the state of the art. Springer Nature Switzerland, Cham, pp 459–505

Butler K, Kember H, McGrath S, Biurra-Hoy I, Brooker C, Kelly R (2023) Partnering with first nations communities in city and regional planning: an international review. https://openresearch.newcastle.edu.au/articles/report/Partnering_with_First_Nations_communities_in_city_an (Accessed on 04 April 2024).

Cheshmehzangi A (2022) The application of ICT and smart technologies in cities and communities: an overview. In: Cheshmehzangi A (2022) ICT, cities, and reaching positive peace. Singapore: Springer, pp 1–16

Cheshmehzangi A (2025) Advanced city: for the future of cities and opposing smart cities. Springer, Singapore

Moola F, Jolly H, Borah J, Roth R (2024) The potential for Indigenous-led conservation in urbanized landscapes in Canada. Front Hum Dyn 6:1340379

Nasir O, Arif Kamal M (2022) Inspiration from nature: biomimicry as a paradigm for architectural and environmental design. Am J Civil Eng Archit 10(3):126–136

Ondiviela J (2021) Beyond smart cities. Springer International Publishing, Cham

Plantinga P, Dlamini N, Pienaar G, Nkosi M, Davids YD, Okem A, Dlamini S (2023) The governance of eParticipation: towards a rights-based approach. In: 2023 IST-Africa Conference (IST-Africa). IEEE, Conference held in Tshwane, South Africa, pp 1–16. DOI: 10.23919/IST-Africa60249.2023.10187782

Pourroostaei Ardakani S, Cheshmehzangi A (eds) (2024) Digital twin computing for urban Intelligence. Springer, Singapore

Sirimorok N (2024) Plant data networks in smart farming. https://kyutech.repo.nii.ac.jp/records/2000924 (Accessed on 02 Sep 2025).

Woodward, E., Hill, R., Harkness, P., & Archer, R. (2020). Our knowledge our way in caring for country: indigenous-led approaches to strengthening and sharing our knowledge for land and sea management. Best practice guidelines from Australian experiences

Zhan C (2024) Microbial decomposition and soil health: mechanisms and ecological implications. Mol Soil Biol 15(2):59–70

MIX
Papier aus verantwortungsvollen Quellen
Paper from responsible sources
FSC® C105338

FSC
www.fsc.org

If you have any concerns about our products,
you can contact us on
ProductSafety@springernature.com

In case Publisher is established outside the EU,
the EU authorized representative is:
Springer Nature Customer Service Center GmbH
Europaplatz 3, 69115 Heidelberg, Germany

Printed by Libri Plureos GmbH
in Hamburg, Germany